History Beyond the Text

Historians are increasingly looking beyond the traditional, and turning to visual, oral, aural, and virtual sources to inform their work. The challenges these sources pose require new skills of interpretation and require historians to consider alternative theoretical and practical approaches.

In order to help historians successfully move beyond traditional text, Barber and Peniston-Bird bring together chapters from historical specialists in the fields of fine art, photography, film, oral history, architecture, virtual sources, music, cartoons, landscape and material culture to explain why, when and how these less traditional sources can be used. Each chapter introduces the reader to the source, suggests the methodological and theoretical questions historians should keep in mind when using it, and provides case studies to illustrate best practice in analysis and interpretation. Pulling these disparate sources together, the introduction discusses the nature of historical sources and those factors which are unique to, and shared by, the sources covered throughout the book.

Taking examples from around the globe, this collection of essays aims to inspire practitioners of history to expand their horizons, and incorporate a wide variety of primary sources in their work.

Sarah Barber is Senior Lecturer in the History Department at Lancaster University. Her publications include *Regicide and Republicanism: Politics and Ethics in the English Revolution* (1998) and *A Revolutionary Rogue: Henry Marten and the English Republic* (2000).

Corinna M. Peniston-Bird is Senior Lecturer in the History Department at Lancaster University. Her publications include *A Soldier and a Woman: Women in the Military* (co-edited with G. J. DeGroot, 2000) and *Contesting Home Defence: Men, Women and the Home Guard in the Second World War* (with Penny Summerfield, 2007).

Routledge guides to using historical sources

Routledge guides to using historical sources is a series of books designed to introduce students to different sources and illustrate how they are used by historians. Each volume explores one type of primary source from a broad spectrum and, using specific examples from around the globe, examines their historical context and the different approaches that can be used to interpret these sources.

Reading Primary Sources
Miriam Dobson and Benjamin Ziemann

History Beyond the Text
Sarah Barber and Corinna M. Peniston-Bird

History and Material Culture
Karen Harvey

History Beyond the Text

A student's guide to approaching
alternative sources

**Edited by Sarah Barber
and Corinna M. Peniston-Bird**

LONDON AND NEW YORK

First published 2009
by Routledge
2 Park Square, Milton Park, Abingdon, Oxon OX14 4RN

Simultaneously published in the USA and Canada
by Routledge
270 Madison Ave, New York, NY 10016

Routledge is an imprint of the Taylor & Francis Group, an informa business

Typeset in Times New Roman by
Keystroke, 28 High Street, Tettenhall, Wolverhampton
Printed and bound in Great Britain by
CPI Anthony Rowe, Chippenham, Wiltshire

British Library Cataloguing in Publication Data
A catalogue record for this book is available from the British Library

Library of Congress Cataloging in Publication Data
History beyond the text: a student's guide to approaching alternative
sources/edited by Sarah Barber and Corinna Peniston-Bird.
        p. cm. – (Routledge guides to using historical sources)
    Includes bibliographical references.
    1. History–Sources.   2. History–Research.   I. Barber, Sarah.
    II. Peniston-Bird, C. M.
    D5.H556 2008
    907.2–dc22   2008023473

ISBN10: 0–415–42961–7 (hbk)
ISBN10: 0–415–42962–5 (pbk)

ISBN13: 978–0–415–42961 0 (hbk)
ISBN13: 978–0–415–42962–7 (pbk)

To Lee and Karl in this generation,
and Amelie in the next

Contents

Illustrations

Contributors

Barber, Sarah Co-editor of this volume and co-tutor of the Lancaster University Masters' course, 'History beyond the Text', is the author of *Regicide and Republicanism: Politics and Ethics in the English Revolution* (1998) and *A Revolutionary Rogue: Henry Marten and the English Republic* (2000), and co-editor of *Conquest and Union*; currently working on a monograph on *English Folk*, incorporating many of the fields of study outlined in this volume.

Blenkinsop, Lisa Lisa Blenkinsop completed her Ph.D. at Lancaster University in 2007 on 'Writing Histories: Narratives of Integration and Poles in Great Britain since the Second World War', out of which her current publications are emerging. She is currently an International Officer at the University of East Anglia.

Hood, Adrienne D. Adrienne Hood received her Ph.D. in early American history from the University of California in San Diego in 1988. In 1984 she began working as a curator in the Textile Department at the Royal Ontario Museum in Toronto. In 1994, she moved to the University of Toronto, where she teaches early American history and Material Culture. She publishes in all areas of her interest: textile history, material culture, and museums. Her book, *The Weaver's Craft: Cloth, Commerce and Industry*, was published in 2003, and she is presently working on a book about Canadian hand weaving.

Long, Christopher Christopher Long is an associate professor in the School of Architecture at the University of Texas at Austin. His interests centre on modern architectural history, with a particular emphasis on Central Europe between 1890 and 1940. Trained in history rather than architecture, his approach borrows from cultural and intellectual history, as well as political and economic history. He is the author of *Josef Frank: Life and Work* (University of Chicago Press, 2002) and *Paul T. Frankl and Modern American Design* (Yale University Press, 2007).

Palmeri, Frank Frank Palmeri is the author of *Satire in Narrative* (1990) and *Satire, History, Novel: Narrative Forms, 1665–1815* (2004), and the editor of *Humans and Other Animals in Eighteenth-Century British Culture* (2006). He has published essays on Giandomenico Tiepolo, Gibbon and paintings of ruins, and George Cruikshank and *Punch*.

Peniston-Bird, Corinna M. A senior lecturer in the History Department at Lancaster University, Corinna M. Peniston-Bird is the co-convenor with Sarah Barber of the course that triggered this edited collection. She combines a deep interest in the pedagogy of history and a fascination with twentieth-century European History, and has recently completed a monograph based on oral histories with Penny Summerfield entitled *Contesting Home Defence: Men, Women and the Home Guard in the Second World War* (Manchester University Press, 2007), as well as multiple related journal articles.

Peretti, Burton W. Professor and Chair of the Department of History at Western Connecticut State University, Dr Peretti is the author of *Lift Every Voice: The History of African American Music* (2008), *Nightclub City: Politics and Amusement in Manhattan* (2007), *Jazz in American Culture* (1997), and *The Creation of Jazz: Music, Race, and Culture in Urban America* (1992).

Richards, Jeffrey Jeffrey Richards is Professor of Cultural History at Lancaster University. He is general editor of the *Cinema and Society* (Taurus) and *Studies in Popular Culture* (Manchester University Press) series. Among his books are *Films and British National Identity* (1997) and *Hollywood's Ancient Worlds* (2008).

Sayer, Derek Derek Sayer is Professor of Cultural History at Lancaster University. His books include *The Great Arch* (with Philip Corrigan, Blackwell, 1985), *Capitalism and Modernity* (Routledge, 1991), and *The Coasts of Bohemia: A Czech History* (Princeton University Press, 1998). His long-standing interest in visual cultures is currently being explored in his forthcoming book *All the Beauties of the World: Prague, Surrealism, Modernity* (Princeton University Press).

Williamson, Tom Tom Williamson is Reader in Landscape History at the University of East Anglia and has written widely on landscape archaeology, agricultural history and the history of designed landscapes. His recent books include *The Archaeology of the Landscape Park* (1998); *The Origins of Hertfordshire* (2000); *The Transformation of Rural England: Farming and the Landscape 1700–1870* (2002); *Shaping Medieval Landscapes* (2003); and *Chatsworth; a Landscape History* (with John Barnett; 2005).

Acknowledgements

We are indebted to the people and archives listed below for permission to reproduce photographs or original illustrative material. Every effort has been made to trace copyright-holders. Any omissions brought to our attention will be remedied in future editions.

Figure 2.1 Juan Sánchez Cotán, *Still Life with Quince, Cabbage, Melon and Cucumber*, c.1600, signed lower centre: Ju⁰ Sãchez Cotan F., oil on canvas, 69.2   85.1 cms, San Diego Museum of Art, Gift of Anne R. and Amy Putnam. Reproduced with permission of the San Diego Museum of Art.

Figure 3.1 James Gillray, 'New Morality' (1798), Paul Mellon Collection, B1981.25.1001, reproduced with permission from the Yale Center for British Art (YCBA).

Figure 3.2 William O'Keefe, 'Ducking a Pickpocket' (1797), Paul Mellon Collection, B1981.25.1521, reproduced with permission from the Yale Center for British Art (YCBA).

Figure 3.3 HB [John Doyle], 'A Venerable Spider & a Buzzing Fly' (1832), Paul Mellon Collection, B1981.25.1626, reproduced with permission from the Yale Center for British Art (YCBA).

Figure 3.4 Matt Morgan, 'The Doomed City!' (1869), in *The Tomahawk* © British Library Board. All rights reserved. PP 572b.

Figure 3.5 Walter Crane, 'Mrs. Grundy Frightened at her own Shadow' (1886), in *Cartoons for the Cause*. Image from Marxists Internet Archive (www.marxists.org).

Figure 4.1 Roger Fenton, 'The Valley of the Shadow of Death', Salt print, 1855. Library of Congress, Prints and Photographs Division, Washington DC.

Figure 9.1 The distribution of ridge and furrow in the south-east Midlands, plotted from the 1946 RAF aerial photographs Source: For Buckinghamshire, Oxfordshire, Warwickshire, and Bedfordshire: Harrison, M.J., Mead, W.R. and Pannett, D.J. (1965), 'A Midland Ridge and Furrow Map', *Geographical Journal* 131, 366–9. For Northamptonshire: Royal Commission on Historical Monuments (England).

Figure 9.2 Houghton Park, Norfolk, as depicted in Colen Campbell, *Vitruvius Britannicus*, 1725.

1 Introduction

*Sarah Barber and
Corinna M. Peniston-Bird*

Spurred on by the sources themselves, and encouraged by subject centres, funding bodies, institutions and pedagogic frameworks, historians are increasingly turning to visual, oral, aural, virtual and kinaesthetic sources. These sources issue challenges to the historian, to the discipline of history and to its practice; yet, in the experience of the editors of this collection of essays, there is still too rarely a clear explanation of why, when or how they can be used. Every year we are faced by groups of Masters' level students open to discover how to incorporate such sources into their own work, but more comfortable with the well-worn notions of empirical evidence, the primacy of the document, and the reification of prose. Over the years we have felt our way through the darkness alongside our students, searching, often somewhat in vain, for insightful readings on approaching less traditional sources of particular value to students of the discipline of history. Seven years after first offering this Masters' level course, we decided to bring together chapters from historical specialists in the fields of fine art, photography, film, oral history, architecture, virtual sources, music, cartoons, landscape and material culture. Each author was asked to explore the theoretical and practical aspects of using the particular primary source while providing one case study or more to illustrate that process. In this introduction we address some of the issues of commonality and distinctiveness exhibited by the sources discussed in these chapters.

Document and documentary

Often discussion of less traditional sources employs language which is not only familiar to historians of documents, but is also taken from it. Hence, one often hears the phrase to 'read' a film or photograph; musicologists argue that the symbols used to represent musical sound annotate in the way of a text.[1] The term 'document' has a history which charts a turn-around in meaning and application. Its root, *docere*, meaning to teach, determined its early usage to mean 'a lesson, an admonition, a warning'.[2] The implication within scholastic pedagogy was that a documentary was far from value-free, but carried a deliberate and calculated message. It was directive of the manner in which one should read. Particularly with the growth of the discipline of history, the document became the core tool of historical interpretation and defined the responsibility of historical practitioners.

Hence, Arthur Marwick, in his exploration of a discipline of which he felt himself at the core but increasingly alienated from its other practitioners, stressed the division of primary and secondary sources involving precision and facts, and decried the notion that history could 'signify some *a priori*, unsubstantiated conception' in which historians exist to give meaning to history.[3] In his taxonomy of primary sources, Marwick placed above all others 'documents of record'. Such a source is one which 'by its very existence records that some event took place . . . it embodies the event itself', for example acts of parliament, peace treaties, charters and so on, and thus contains 'fact' or 'event', not 'ideology' or 'opinion'; these should be distinguished from 'records' – Marwick cites court transcripts or those of the Inquisition – which are subject to the accuracy of the scribe and the fallibility of the human agents involved in their telling or recall.[4] This distinction, however, can be masked by the elevation of prose so that, say, the parallels between the minutes of a meeting and a cartoon – both interpretations following certain genre-specific conventions – have not been obvious to our students.

Within the twentieth century, the term 'documentary' came to acquire connotations of dispassion, objectivity and factual accuracy which the original usage did not suggest. In a study of writing, painting and photography, John Corner has argued that 'documentary expression relates to the physicality of the object world', giving documentary a 'distinctive phenomenological character, rooted in obdurate particularity'.[5] In the 1920s, John Grierson coined the term 'documentary film' – as opposed to 'narrative fiction' and '*avant-garde*' – to describe 'the creative treatment of actuality', having witnessed a filmic anthropology of the people of Samoa, produced by Robert Flaherty, and *Nanook of the North* (who entered popular culture). He bemoaned that a similar record was not made of the lives of industrial, urban Britons.[6] Grierson's documentary film *Drifters* was, however, an account of Shetland herring fishermen, and its description emphasised the difference between documentary and artifice: '"Drifters" is about the sea and about fishermen, and there is not a Piccadilly actor in the piece. The men do their own acting, and the sea does its.'[7]

In 1934, Paul Otlet extended the definition of document to objects themselves, provided human beings are informed by the observation of them: the following year, Walter Schuermeyer's definition was 'any material basis for extending our knowledge which is available for study or comparison'.[8] This was extended by Suzanne Briet in the 1950s, for whom a document was 'any physical or symbolic sign, preserved or recorded, intended to represent, to reconstruct, or to demonstrate a physical or conceptual phenomenon'.[9] Frits Donker Duyvis's anti-materialist attempt to include a spiritual dimension within documentation as 'expressed thought' – which he adopted from Rudolf Steiner's Anthroposophy – could be said to pre-figure the twenty-first century in which virtual communication can render materiality redundant.[10] The growth of the study of semiotics – the object as sign – resulted in signifying objects' inclusion within the category of document, since before they fulfil any other function, signs have 'first furnished us with information', and for Barthes, objects 'function as a vehicle of meaning' which might be deconstructed to the point of the 'death of the author'.[11] A colleague thus queried our title, arguing that the sources we investigate are not 'beyond the text', but are themselves 'text'. In our experience, however, the ways in which this could be true require a journey of discovery for students well versed in the primacy of the written word. Lurking behind their implicit value hierarchy is an assumption of a clear distinction between fact and fiction, document and interpretation: the sources discussed here, however, often remind us that that distinction is not so easy to draw, in any source of any genre. Furthermore, the parallels between prose and alternative sources should not mask differences between them, and the methodologies these require, as these chapters illuminate.

Subjectivity and intersubjectivity

Having strayed from his traditionalist definition, let us return to the comforting security of Marwick. In articulating a definition of the primary document of record as one that 'by its very existence records that some event took place' and thus 'embodies the event itself', he was, in fact, overlaying traditional history in the archives onto the rather more modish concept of intersubjectivity, which can be found particularly within philosophy, psychology, anthropology, performance theory and linguistics. All human communication posits a tri-partite relationship: the person communicating, the manner or means of the communication, and the receiver or audience. Thus, within speech we have the speaker, speech act (utterance), and hearer; in our sources this could translate to, for example, the painter, the painting, and the viewer; or interviewer, tape/transcript, interviewee, and so on. Intersubjectivity suggests the relationship between the three elements, alerting us to potential mutualities.[12] But the discussion so far has focused on objectivity, not subjectivity. It is the level of subjectivity in both the creation and the understanding of such sources as art, film, music, oral testimony, or chat rooms, which supposedly sets them apart. Marwick's definition of the document of record posits an unproblematic relationship between the intention of the author of the document, and its subsequent interpretation by the historian. Elements of human bias, fallible memory, or hidden agendas are subsumed by the accurate and dispassionate recording of events, such that Marwick could be as sure as he could be that his historical document was stripped of elements of human subjectivity, to produce the idealised objective historical fact.

Marwick's respect for the document of record stems from this ability to seem to reduce it to objectivity, but the historian must still continue to ask questions of even the most objective-looking document, and in any event, should human communication, past or present, be subject to such reductionism? Is historical investigation of subjectivities not of equal interest? As part of their craft, historians excel at placing any information within a context: such a context involves subjective judgements of the creator, the object and its receivers. All media are extensions of human expression and a historian might wish to be alert to the implicit elements of human expression, the unanticipated consequences of innovation and technologies, unwitting testimony, or political (a term used here in its widest application) intent. Every change in scale, pace or pattern which an invention or innovation brings to human affairs changes the message of humanity because it brings a change in inter-personal dynamics. Thus, the significance of a news broadcast lies not only in the events described, but also in the reasons behind the timing of its airing and concurrent changes in public perception of, say, immigration, or in the creation of a climate of fear. As Mark Federman argues, 'we can know the nature and characteristics of anything we conceive or create by virtue of the changes – often unnoticed and non-obvious changes – that they effect', and we have a definition of Marshall McLuhan's famous 'Equation', in effect itself a statement on the intersubjective trinity: 'the medium is the message'.[13]

Subjective elements constantly affect the relationship between creator, creation and receiver. Some of these are born of our humanity: how as a historian, can we ever detach emotion from less subjective forms of human expression and should we try? An art-work may invoke the sublime, or may provoke pity; a cartoon relies on the audience recognising ridicule, disdain, or burlesque; a piece of music is seldom composed without an intention of stirring some emotion in its hearer. A medium which relies on performance – story-telling, drama, oral testimony, music and song, correspondence in cyberspace – introduces elements which are unique and ephemeral. The historian has also to recognise that the introduction of new technologies – film, the internet, sound recordings – changes the nature of the thing itself by capturing and freezing it.[14]

Each type of source has its own history which overlaps and influences those of other sources. The *camera obscura*, for example, provided a technology deployed by artists to capture an image and to 'distort' a scene beyond what could be taken in by the naked eye, but the process of capturing and fixing that image by discovering photo-sensitive papers and compounds, rather than re-creating it using the artist's own painterly skill, led to a series of experimenters – Professor J. Schulze (1727), Thomas Wedgwood (1800), Nicéphore Niépce (1816), Henry Fox Talbot (1834), Louis Daguerre (1837), Richard Leach Maddox (1871) – who transformed the camera and thus the photograph. Other pioneers altered the role of the photograph. In the space of fifty years, key roles for the photographer were established. In mid-century Paris, Felix Toumachon and Adolphe Disderi sparked an explosion of interest in studio portrait photography; a decade later, Mathew Brady and his team processed 7,000 negatives documenting the American Civil War; the United States Congress sent William Jackson, Tim O'Sullivan and others to document the opening up of the West; George Eastman's Dry Plate Company led to the first half-tone photograph appearing in a daily newspaper, the *New York Graphic*; and in 1890, the publication of Jacob Riis's collection of photographs from the New York tenements, *How the Other Half Lives*, announced photography as a medium of social history and reform.[15] Together these ousted the painting as the visual medium of record, and blurred the boundaries between fine art and photography. As photographic techniques were employed in art – for example Man Ray's 'rayographs' (from 1921) – artists were freed to explore the abstract and the surreal, and photographers began their own debate about the relationship between documentary and creativity, for example through the creation of the f.64 group (Ansel Adams, Imogen Cunningham, Willard

Van Dyke, Edward Weston and others), dedicated to 'straight photographic thought and reproduction'.[16] All these changes affected the relationship between the photographer and the viewer, opening up the issue as to whether the object might be the camera, the photograph or the subject of the photograph. Finally, from the inception of the 'box brownie' camera in 1900, a series of commercial decisions and technological changes transformed photography into a medium with mass affordability, and separated technological knowledge from the taking and producing of photographs. With the arrival of digital imaging – which could be said to take the process full circle, in that the image has become mutable and, digitally represented, is no longer necessarily 'fixed' – photography took another step as a democratic medium and the relationship between photographer, image and viewer has changed once again.[17]

It is not the case, therefore, that analysis of these sources can be reduced to a simple and direct inter-relationship between author, object and receiver, such that it parallels that between writer/document-of-record/historian. There is often no single author, or the work cannot be traced to an identifiable author. A painting may be the work of a number of hands, as a workshop production, or the carving in a church the work of 'humble' artisans. A website often functions on the basis of such extensive democratisation that the author is untraceable, or a person being interviewed may wish to adopt a pseudonym. Consider the transformation that has taken place in the presentation of feature films in the past sixty years. In the 1940s, when actors, writers, directors and crew were owned by the company, the person credited with the creation of a film was the producer. Increasing recognition given to the multiplicity of roles in the creation of moving pictures now means that the credits roll for many minutes after the narrative has concluded.

Creator, created, and audience

Approaches to source analysis have chosen to focus on different elements of the tri-partite relationship between creator, created and audience. The narrative which most frequently determines historical analysis is that of authorial intent, although postmodern literary criticism holds that trying to determine authorial intent is futile.[18] In Film and, subsequently, Media Studies, we find a school of analysis focusing on the *auteur*. Auteur theory was coined in the work of French film critic and theorist André Bazin (1918–58), who, having begun to write about film in 1943, was one of the co-founders, in 1951, of the influential film magazine *Cahiers du Cinéma*. Bazin's original views were based on a person-centred, humanist ontology which constructed a theory of film based around 'objective reality' and 'true continuity' rather than experimental effects and editing, in which the director became invisible and scenes representational, such that the interpretation of a scene was the responsibility of the viewer. Ironically, this led to his belief that the film should represent the director's 'personalist' vision, which gave birth to auteur theory in a piece in *Cahiers* by François Truffaut who in 1954 referred to 'les politiques des auteurs': the conscious decision to look at a film and to decide on its remit and value.[19] The originators of auteur theory – almost exclusively film directors themselves – also assessed actors' input, and the legion influences which determine the film's overall shape.[20]

A work may be a commission, and thus reflect the interests of the commissioner as much as the creator. What audience does the creator have in mind when a work is created, or is there a specific audience in mind? How has the gaze changed over time? A portrait was usually painted at the behest of the sitter, to grace private rooms in which in the gaze was strictly regulated by the subject. Once that painting has been detached from its original purpose and becomes the property of a gallery, the gaze is democratised, made dispassionate sometimes to the point of anonymity, and is constantly in motion past the painting. A building remains relatively fixed, but it contains both a public and a private architecture. The gaze of a potentially universally available website is atomistically private; a film viewed within a cinema is the subject of highly directed gaze, whilst the same images projected via television broadcast or DVD is not.[21] Whilst the painting, cartoon, photograph, film, building, or interview can be frozen at the point of creation, its reception by successive audiences, across time, cannot, such that as historians we can also follow the critical cultural reception of a work and its changes. A landscape or a website is subject to change, whereas the visual representation of the landscape within a map, or the date of access to or date of last review of a website, can be fixed, the object itself is subject to change.

The historian is encouraged to distinguish between the multiplicity of creative inputs, object creations and audiences which are represented by the intersubjective trinities which attach to each of the types of source represented in this volume. With a traditional document, we are more seldom asked to trace these. Either an individual author is known and his/her personal slant in creating the text known to the historian, or the very anonymity of the individual creating the historical record invests the resulting historical text with documentary objectivity. For example, the historian is able to read the primary printed text of United States' government debates, *The Congressional Record*, which noted that on Thursday 4 December 1873, 'Mr. Sumner' presented a petition, in support of his civil rights bill, and recited its words to the Senators: '[w]e meet the greatest barrier when we present our children at the public schools and are rejected. All this, and more, we are compelled to endure because we are colored'.[22] Alternatively, we could be presented with an accounts ledger from a mid-nineteenth-century factory – a documentary record of incomings and outgoings.

The account of the Senate debate makes the assumption that the transcriber made an accurate transcription, that he or she caught every word and printed every word. It makes no comment about the reception of Sumner's reading of the petition, and the historian seeking to use Sumner's speeches is unlikely to use the full text. Factory accounts ledgers were arranged in standardised format, but without background context about how this format came about – double-entry book-keeping, for example – or any attempt to question whether the figures might be accurate. How many insurance or compensation claims are accurate[23] and how many wages slips altered? The historian must be aware of the extent to which this record is determined by the employer or agent.[24] Information contained within even the most straightforwardly textual historical document is, by the nature of the information being captured and the partial survival of information over time, ephemeral. One consequence of engagement with the concept of intersubjectivity is the encouragement it gives to historians to be aware of their own narrative voice, possible implicature and the degree to which they may be identifying with elements of the trinity of intersubjectivities.

In some of the sources discussed here, oral history and virtual communications in particular, the impact of the mode of communication and the medium on intersubjectivity is a particular focus of analysis: Mark Dery commented on emails, for example,

> electronic messages must be interpreted without the aid of non-verbal cues or what socio-linguist Peter Farb terms 'paralanguage' – expressive vocal phenomena such as pitch, intensity, stress, tempo, and volume . . . [as a correspondent suggested] 'I think the attempt to signal authorial intent with little smileys is interesting but futile'.[25]

The collection of oral testimony, and more particularly its transcription, introduces the problem of re-presenting the data at the most basic level: does the sound copy of the interview accurately convey the intent behind an utterance and does the transcriber include marginal notes of this within its textual form? The three transcriptions of the statement,

- I had no idea what I was doing;
- [laughs] I had no idea what I was doing;
- [crosses arms] I had no idea what I was doing [coughs];

include a variety of possible authorial intent markers, alert us to the presence of the interviewer in assigning meaning of both aural and physical cues, and highlight some of the issues of translating from one medium to another.[26]

The historian's concern with time, chronology and the placement of objects, ideas and individuals within an identifiable past introduces yet another layer of interpretation. The ways in which the products of an artist,[27] architect,[28] cartoonist, musician,[29] interviewee, or landscape designer function may be a consequence of authorial intent, but may also be interpreted as a witting or unwitting consequence of contextual influences on the creators, reflecting the historical period in which they were framed. The term which is most often appropriated to describe a medium's relationship to the period in which it was created is the German *Zeitgeist*, meaning, in literal translation, 'time-spirit'.[30] *Zeitgeist* has been appropriated into several languages, and is most commonly translated as 'the spirit of the age'. Although it possesses earlier origins, it is most associated with the dialectical philosophy of history promulgated by Georg Hegel (1770–1831). Hegel was a key figure in what might be termed the 'speculative philosophy of history', and held that each nation-state has its own mind or spirit (*Volksgeist*), which conjoined to produce a spirit of the world (*Weltgeist*). For Hegel, human thought culminated in its creative output, art, for example, not being solely a means to express or evoke feelings, but a kind of thought and a means to apprehend reality.

Such progressivism, however, cuts across another concept beloved of historians, that in which the transmission of ideas remains constant, or continuously borrows from previous expression. A historian (sociologist, anthropologist or folklorist), for example, might express this as 'tradition'.[31] Artists might be considered to be working within genre traditions, or cartoonists within a tradition of satire, and thus the historian who wishes to use such work is faced with the prospect of distinguishing that which is personal to the creator and is innovatory from that which borrows from a past.

Tracing expression across time also introduces the manner in which interpretation is determined by the audience and audience reaction is determined by their own cultural concerns and contexts. Take a moment to imagine a street scene in the nineteenth-century American Mid-West. Dwell on its individual components. Now consider: does the scene include a wide, single main street, stretching back like an exercise in drawing perspective, its most prominent buildings a saloon with louvered swinging doors? Is there a horse tied up on a post outside, assailed by swirling dust and tumbleweed? This view bears little relation to that represented in living history museums, such as Bodie, California, Old Cowtown, Wichita, Kansas, or the Pioneer Living History Village, Phoenix, Arizona. Instead, individuals from a period after the birth of film are influenced by their consumption of film, and within that, a genre of film itself – the (Spaghetti) Western.[32] The twelfth-century history of Midlands England may never be viewed in the same way after the varieties of mythical re-workings of the story of Robin Hood and, in the late eighteenth century, the highest form of painting was the representation of historical scenes, but through the prism of first the Enlightenment and then the Romantics' love-affair with the classical past.[33] When a contemporary is interviewed, tying the interviewer, interviewee and interview in coincidental time, oral historians must consider how the recollections of the interviewee – his or her memory – are affected by the passage of time which has elapsed between the history being related and the point of relation. All these are examples of the 'cultural circuit', whereby a continuous inter-relationship between memories of events and cultural representations of events, and thus between past and present, is set up, which the historian seeks to disentangle while aware of the impossibility of ever doing so. The cultural circuit can be identified in all eras, but the impact of some of the technologies discussed here – film being one obvious example – cannot be overstated.

Truth, veracity and authenticity

Historians often praise their own sense of scholarship. We like to think of ourselves as purveyors of a discipline which not only seeks after truth but also provides as much verification and corroboration of statements as possible. We often talk of triangulation – that a piece of information should be corroborated in two other ways

– as a means to check and cross-check a point we wish to make. If we work on the basis that the non-traditional sources outlined in this collection should be treated in the same way as, or at least in similar ways to, traditional documentary sources, then it behoves us as historians to reference and cite works by providing as much detail for the reader as is extant, to enable them to locate, if possible, the source for themselves and verify or question the statements the historian has made about it or about using it. Corroboration can come from other sources within the genre – thus one type of source can be compared and contrasted with its own type, and with the genre's archetype.[34] Corroboration can be introduced across non-traditional genres; thus, attached to any particular statement could be references from within music, oral testimony drawn from a musician, and examples of art-work or folkloric oral testimony claimed as inspiration for the musician. Finally, corroboration can come from more traditional textual sources. If this is the case, historians have to resolve for themselves whether any type of evidence is privileged, not assuming the written, manuscript or printed source to have primacy and the non-traditional source to be illustrative.

Are all sources equal, or are some more equal than others, because their information is more verifiable? The historian's obsession with the written source lies in its unchanging physicality: the source is unchanging across time and can be returned to time after time, unlike, for example, the spoken word which exists only in the moment of speaking, or the landscape which is in constant flux.[35] It is easy to argue that a verifiable, unchanging source provides the historian with more accurate information about the past. It is the case with some of the sources studied here – in the case of oral testimony being captured on tape and then transcribed,[36] a film-screenplay, musical notation and orchestration,[37] or the capture of a landscape and terrain on a map or plan[38] – that the visual, oral or aural source is translated into text. As such, does the written, fixed source become more verifiable – have greater veracity – at a point at which its increasing distance from its original lessens its authenticity?

The more layers of reading we have to sift in order to extract accurate information about the past, the more we question the authenticity of the source. Can the interpretation of a painting which may be read in several ways, which contains hidden meanings, or which is replete with metaphor, imagery and allegory, be seen as capturing the authentic voice of the artist? If a film is commissioned, or the finance is provided by a partial source, or provides a vehicle for a star performance from a particular actor, what is its meaning? If a cartoon is received in the spirit of the creator by a pre-determined receptive audience, do the majority of people who are unreceptive to its message doubt the authenticity of the viewpoint it projects? There is a danger here of a confusion between history, as a narrative of 'what actually happened in the past', and the construction of the historian's craft. John Adams in 1789 – '[m]y experience has very much diminished my faith in the veracity of History' – and again in 1814 – '[w]hat are we to think of history when, in less than forty years, such diversities appear in the memories of living persons, who were witnesses?' – was referring to the historian's craft in the former instance, but more to the truth of history in the latter. [39]

History, then, is one form of a system of human knowledge that seeks the Truth, and the 'critical' branch of the philosophy of history is concerned, amongst other things, with the possibility of achieving objectivity in historical description and the roles and responsibilities of historical agents. [40] This branches away from the 'common-sense' theory of truth, which posits that a statement is true if it corresponds to the facts (correspondence theory of truth). Idealists hold that the external world is created by the mind, and thus Truth can only refer to the whole experience because knowledge is part of a single coherent system. Thus, what people would common-sensibly refer to as 'true' and 'false' should properly be referred to as 'partially true' and 'partially false' (coherence theory of truth).[41] Wittgenstein attempted a path between the correspondence and coherence theories of truth, in which the relationship between truth and reality was likened to that between a painting and that which it represents: basic statements are those containing the atoms (as it were) of knowledge and experience which directly correspond to reality; other, more complex statements are derived from these, the truth of which is dependent on their coherence with the basic statements.[42] This process may be likened to that of the historian who seeks to sift out the statements of fact from those of interpretative implication and context. Essentially, these definitions of truth derive from a logic-based Anglo-American philosophy. From within continental philosophical schools in the later twentieth century, these definitions of truth were assailed. Postmodernism (Lyotard, Rorty[43]) argues that there is no truth, only a plethora of interpretations, and no objective reality, only a plurality of perspectives. Post-structuralism (Derrida, Foucault, Barthes, Kristeva, Saussure[44]) was a philosophical approach which rejected structuralism – that is, the idea that a signifier can be identified, independent of its interpreter – and repudiated the reader as having interpretative mastery over the text, rather seeing author and reader themselves as texts and open to deconstruction.

The authors included in this collection suggest that practitioners of history remain committed to a notion of truth, in which some interpretation is more justifiable than others: a process supported by the application of a methodology to their source materials. Each chapter seeks out a methodology appropriate for the source: these methodologies vary from the relatively well established (in oral history, for example) to more exploratory methodologies devised by the author and borrowing from a variety of approaches (music, for example). Readers who wish to explore other historical approaches to these sources are encouraged to use the endnotes for recommended further reading. What the historian specifically brings to these methodologies is an awareness of the significance of two factors: context and time. What the authors here demonstrate is that on the one hand, unsurprisingly, methodologies for alternative sources have much in common with the methodology for more traditional ones, for example, with the attention to authorship and audience, analysis of specific content and context, hypotheses on the historical significance of the source. However, first and foremost they must also respond to the unique nature of the source under investigation, specifically its visual, aural, or physical character. The referencing conventions for each of these sources (as exhibited in the endnotes of each chapter) provide a telling indication of this distinctiveness (the importance of scale in art; the significance of the presence of both interview partners, and the date of the interview in oral histories, for example; or the significance of the date of access for web pages liable to change or disappear, etc.). The chapters also all suggest and reflect the challenge of translating these sources into prose, a process which risks flattening the distinction between these sources and textual ones. We hope this volume will inspire practitioners of history to explore a wide variety of sources, and to emulate and further develop the appropriate methodologies outlined here in doing so.

Notes

1 Wen-hsin Yeh, 'Reading photographs: visual culture and everyday life in Republican China', *European Journal of East Asian Studies* 6.1, 2007, pp. 1–3; Julia Thomas, *Reading Images*, London: Palgrave Macmillan, 2000; James Monaco, *How to Read a Film: The Art Technology Language History and Theory of Film and Media*, Oxford: Oxford University Press, 1981; K. Stone, *Musical Notation in the Twentieth Century*, New York: W.W. Norton, 1980.

2 J.A. Simpson and E.S.C. Weiner (eds), *The Oxford English Dictionary* (2nd edn, 20 vols), Oxford: Clarendon Press, 1989, iv, p. 916.

3 Arthur Marwick, *The New Nature of History: Knowledge, Evidence, Language*, Houndmills: Palgrave, 2001, pp. 26–7, 29, 152ff.

4 Ibid., pp. 164–6.

5 John Corner, 'Documentary expression and the physicality of the referent: observations on writing, painting and photography', *Studies in Documentary Film* 1.1, 2007, p. 5.

6 'The Moviegoer' (pen name of John Grierson), *New York Sun*, 8 February 1926; Jack C. Ellis, *The Documentary Idea: A Critical History of English-Language Documentary Film and Video*, Englewood Cliffs, NJ: Prentice Hall College Division, 1989; Jack C. Ellis and Betsy A. McLane, *A New History of Documentary Film*, New York and London: Continuum, 2005; *Nanook of the North: A Story of Life and Love in the Actual Arctic* (Director/Photographer/Editor: Robert J. Flaherty), b+w, 35mm, 1921, Revillon Frere; *Moana* (Director/Writer/Producer Robert J. Flaherty), b+w, 1926, released by Paramount Pictures.

7 *Drifters* (Director John Grierson, Cinematographer Basil Emmott), b+w, 1929, financed by the Empire Marketing Board; Ian Aitken, *Film and Reform: John Grierson and the Documentary Film Movement*, London: Routledge, 1990.

8 Paul Otlet, *Traité de Documentation*, Brussels, 1934, p. 217; Walter Schuermeyer, 'Aufgaben und Methoden der Dokumentation', *Zentralblatt für Bibliothekswesen* 52, 1935, pp. 533–43, 537; Trudi Bellardo Hahn and Michael Buckland (eds), *Historical Studies in Information Science*, Medford, NJ: American Society for Information Science and Technology, Silver Spring, MD, 1998; Michael K. Buckland, 'What is a document?', *Journal of the American Society of Information Science* 48.9, 1997, pp. 804–9.

9 Suzanne Briet, *Qu'est-ce que la Documentation?*, Paris: EDIT, 1951, p. 7.

10 Frits Donker Duyvis, *Nomalisatie op het Gebied der Documentarie*, The Hague: Nider, 1942; N.A.J. Verhoeve, 'F. Donker Duyvis and standardization', in *idem*, *F. Donker Duyvis: His Life and Work*, The Hague: Netherlands Institute for Documentation & Filing, 1964, pp. 39–50, translation of quotation on p. 48.

11 M. Dufrenne, *The Phenomenology of Aesthetic Experience*, Evanston, IL: Northwestern University Press, 1973, p. 114; Roland Barthes, *Roland Barthes*, London: Macmillan, 1988; Barthes, *Camera Lucida: Reflections on Photography*, New York: Hill and Wang, 1981; Barthes, *Criticism and Truth*, London: The Athlone Press, 1987; *Elements of Semiology*, New York: Hill and Wang, 1968; Barthes, *Image, Music, Text*, New York: Hill and Wang, 1977; Barthes, *Mythologies*, New York: Hill and Wang, 1972.

12   In the case of some of the elements of the trinity, the relationship is one way, and not two way. The difference lies in the degree to which the central element of the trinity possesses agency in itself; in the production of a play where the trinity consists of author/production/audience, for example, as opposed to the trinity of author/script/reader.

13   Mark Federman, 'What is the meaning of "the medium is the message"', retrieved 18 December 2007 from http://individual.utoronto.ca/markfederman/article_mediumisthe message.htm (23 July 2004); Marshall McLuhan, *Understanding Media: The Extensions of Man*, New York: McGraw Hill, 1964.

14   Alan Stockdale, 'Tools for digital audio recording in qualitative research', *Social Research Update* 38, 2002, http://www.soc.surrey.ac.uk/sru/SRU38.html, accessed 10 November 2005.

15   The *New York Graphic* (also known as the *New York Evening Graphic*) was published between 1924 and 1932 by Bernarr Macfadden; Jacob A. Riis, *How the Other Half Lives: Studies Among the Tenements of New York*, London: Penguin Classics, 1997.

16   Brooks Johnson (ed.), *Photography Speaks: 66 Photographers on Their Art*, New York: Aperture, 1989; Charles Swedlund, *Photography, a Handbook of History, Materials, and Processes* (2nd edn), New York: Holt, Rinehart and Winston, 1981; Paul Spencer Sternberger, *Between Amateur and Aesthete: The Legitimization of Photography as Art in America, 1880–1900*, Albuquerque, NM: University of New Mexico Press, 2001; Keith J. Laidler, *To Light Such a Candle: Chapters in the History of Science and Technology*, Oxford: Oxford University Press, 1998; Helmut Gernsheim, *Masterpieces of Victorian Photography*, London: Phaidon, 1951.

17   Jonathan Jones, interview with David Hockney, 'Disposable cameras', *Guardian, G2*, 4 March 2004, pp. 12–13.

18   Lawrence Stone, 'History and Post-modernism', *Past and Present* 135.1, 1992, pp. 189–94; Marc W. Steinberg, 'Fence sitting for a better view: finding a middle ground between materialism and the linguistic turn in the epistemology of History', *Qualitative Inquiry* 3.1, 1997, pp. 26–52.

19   Jim Hillier (ed.), *Cahiers du Cinéma; The 1950s: Neo-Realism, Hollywood, New Wave*, Cambridge, MA: Harvard Film Studies, Harvard University Press, 1985; Jim Hillier (ed.), *Cahiers du Cinéma: 1960–1968: New Wave, New Cinema, Reevaluating Hollywood*, Cambridge, MA: Harvard Film Studies, Harvard University Press, 1992.

20   André Bazin, 'The life and death of superimposition' (1946), reproduced and translated in *Film-Philosophy* 6.1 2002, URL: http://www.film-philosophy.com/vol6–2002/n1bazin, accessed 29 December 2007; André Bazin, 'Will CinemaScope save the film industry?' (1953), reproduced and translated in *Film-Philosophy* 6.2 2002, URL: http://www.film-philosophy.com/vol6–2002/n2bazin, accessed 29 December 2007; Burt Cardullo, 'Andre Bazin on Rene Clement and literary adaptation: two original reviews', *Literature Film Quarterly* (2002) and 'Andre Bazin on Claude Autant-Lara and literary adaptation: four original reviews', *Literature Film Quarterly* (2002).

21   In a seminal article, feminist film criticism argued that film offered the male gaze that objectified women: see Laura Mulvey, 'Visual pleasure and narrative cinema' (1975), reproduced in Bill Nichols (ed.), *Movies and Methods: An Anthology*, vol. ii, Berkeley and London: University of California Press, 1985, pp. 303–14; Jacques Lacan, *The Four Fundamental Concepts of Psycho-Analysis* (trans. Alan Sheridan, ed. Jacques-Alain Miller), New York: Norton, 1977; John Berger, *Ways of Seeing*, London: Pelican, 1972.

22   *Congressional Record*, 4 December, 1873, p. 50.

23   For example, once the English state had regained some semblance of control in Ireland, following the 1641 rebellion and subsequent civil war, it invited those who had lost land, crops, livestock or had personal injury or death at the hands of the 1641 rebels to make 'depositions' of their losses and claim reparation. The dreadful tales of horror recorded provided the main material for historical accounts of the rebellion as a series of genocidal atrocities – Sir John Temple, *The Irish Rebellion*, 1646 – while the

depositions seem to record, with statistical objectivity, the level of wartime damage, but how many people, from the safety of their exile or with an eye to maximising their compensation exaggerated both the level of violence against them and their material loss? Nicholas Canny, 'Historians, moral judgement and national communities: the Irish dilemma', *European Review* 14, 2006, pp. 401–10.

24 To give an example from mixed genres represented in this collection, Mr Cecil Moore related to Sarah Barber an anecdote about a woman sacked from the grain hauliers near Burston, Norfolk, at which he worked in the 1930s, because she was altering her wages slips, changing the figure seven to a nine, or three to an eight; H. Thomas Johnson, 'Early cost accounting for internal management control: Lyman Mills in the 1850s', *The Business History Review* 46.4, 1972, pp. 466–74.

25 Mark Dery, *Flame Wars: The Discourse of Cyberculture*, Durham, NC, and London: Duke University Press, 1994, quoting an anonymous correspondent in a private email to the author, 17 April 1993.

26 Robyn Carston, *Thoughts and Utterances: The Pragmatics of Explicit Communication*, Oxford: Blackwell Publishers, 2002.

27 David Summers, 'E.H. Gombrich and the tradition of Hegel', in Paul Smith and Carolyn Wilde (eds), *A Companion to Art Theory*, Oxford: Blackwell Publishing, 2002, pp. 139–49.

28 Folke Nyberg, 'From Baukunst to Bauhaus', *Journal of Architectural Education* (*JAE*) 45.3, 1992, pp. 130–7, for a discussion of Nikolaus Pevsner's reading of Hegel's *Zeitgeist*; Richard Betts, 'Historical determinism, or historical precedent be damned', *JAE* 34.1, 1980, pp. 3–6.

29 Steven Helmling, 'During Auschwitz: Adorno, Hegel, and the "unhappy consciousness" of critique', *Postmodern Culture* 15.2, 2005.

30 Friedrich Kreppel, 'Das Problem Zeitgeist', *Zeitschrift für Religions und Geistesgeschichte* 20.2, 1968, pp. 97–112.

31 Edward Albert Shils, *Tradition*, Chicago: University of Chicago Press, 2001, pp. 274–5; A.E. Denham, 'Review article: The moving mirrors of music: Roger Scruton resonates with tradition', *Music and Letters* 80, 1999, pp. 411–32.

32 Dydia DeLyser, 'Authenticity on the ground: engaging the past in a California ghost town', *Annals of the Association of American Geographers* 89.4, 1999, pp. 602–32; Peter Cowie, *John Ford and the American West*, New York: Harry Abrams Inc., 2004; Henry Nash Smith, *Virgin Land: The American West as Symbol and Myth*, Cambridge, MA: Harvard University Press, 1950.

33 A.U. Abrams, *The Valiant Hero: Benjamin West and Grand-style History Painting*, Washington, DC: Smithsonian Institution Press, 1985; Edgar Wind, 'The Revolution of History Painting', *Journal of the Warburg Institute* 2.2, 1938, pp. 116–27; Thomas S. Grey, 'Tableaux vivants: landscape, history painting, and the visual imagination in Mendelssohn's orchestral music', *19th-Century Music* 21.1, 1997, pp. 38–76.

34 Archetypes of portraiture are compared across fine art and cartoon in the essay by Fintan Cullen on the Irish Rebellion of 1798: Fintan Cullen, 'Radicals and reactionaries: portraits of the 1790s in Ireland', in Jim Smyth (ed.), *Revolution, Counter-revolution and Union: Ireland in the 1790s*, Cambridge: Cambridge University Press, 2000, pp. 161–94.

35 William Chase Greene, 'The spoken and the written word', *Harvard Studies in Classical Philology* 60, 1951, pp. 23–59: Socrates was famously more suspicious of the written than the spoken word, because writing things down committed mis- and partially remembered details to fixed form.

36 Dennis Tedlock, *The Spoken Word and the Work of Interpretation*, Philadelphia: University of Pennsylvania Press, 1983; Robin Humphrey, Robert Miller and E.A. Zdravomyslova (eds), *Biographical Research in Eastern Europe: Altered Lives and Broken Biographies*, Aldershot: Ashgate Publishing, 2003.

37 Richard A. Peterson, *Creating Country Music: Fabricating Authenticity*, Chicago, IL,

and London: University of Chicago Press, 1997; H. Stith Bennett, 'Notation and identity in contemporary popular music', *Popular Music* 3, 1983, pp. 215–34; Charles J. Stivale, *Disenchanting Les Bons Temps: Identity and Authenticity in Cajun Music and Dance*, Durham, NC, and London: Duke University Press, 2003.

38 Eric Kaufmann and Oliver Zimmer, 'In search of the authentic nation: landscape and national identity in Canada and Switzerland', *Nations and Nationalism* 4.4, 1998, pp. 483–510; P. Cloke and P. and O. Jones, 'Dwelling, place, and landscape: an orchard in Somerset', *Environment and Planning* 33.4, 2001, pp. 649–66.

39 Michael G. Kammen, *Selvages and Biases: The Fabric of History in American Culture*, Ithaca, NY, and London: Cornell University Press, 1989: quotes are drawn from p. 86.

40 For the development of the critical philosophy of history, see Wilhelm Dilthey (1833–1911), Benedetto Croce (1866–1952) and R[obin] G[eorge] Collingwood (1889–1943), *The Idea of History* (Oxford: Clarendon Press, 1946).

41 Hence the varieties of teleological approaches to history.

42 Ludwig Wittgenstein (1889–1951), *Tractatus Logico-Philosophicus* (1921, English translation 1922), concerned with language as a representing medium, a means of conveying how things are: see translation by David Francis Pears and Brian McGuinness, London: Routledge, 2001.

43 François Lyotard (1924–98), *The Postmodern Condition* (first pub. 1924), Manchester: Manchester University Press, 1984; Richard Rorty, *Contingency, Irony and Solidarity*, Cambridge: Cambridge University Press, 1989.

44 Jacques Derrida (1930–2004), 'Structure, sign, and play in the discourse of the human sciences' (1966), in Jacques Derrida, *Writing and Difference* (trans. Alan Bass), London: Routledge, pp. 278–94; Roland Barthes (1915–80), 'Death of the author' (first published in *Aspen*, 1967) and subsequently in *Image-Music-Text* (1977); Ferdinand de Saussure, *Writings in General Linguistics*, Oxford: Oxford University Press, 2006; Michel Foucault (1926–84), 'Les mots et les choses' (1966), taking as its starting point Velázquez's painting *Las Meninas* as a discussion of layers of meaning, which develops the claim that all historical periods possess underlying conditions of truth which determine the episteme's scientific discourse, which shift dramatically over time in what Piaget would liken to Kuhn's theory of the paradigm shift, and 'L'archéologie du savoir' developing a theory of speech acts; Julia Kristeva (1941–), *Nations without Nationalism*, New York: Columbia University Press, 1993.

2 Fine Art: the creative image

Sarah Barber

Everyone has an opinion about art. At one end of the scale is the quotidian – 'I know what I like and I like what I know' – and at the other, Aristotle, for whom art (in its widest sense) meant imitation (mimesis) and understanding, by taking the form of something into the mind and allowing it to shape one's thinking (literally, information): '[a]ll art is concerned with coming into being . . . with contriving and considering how something may come into being which is capable of either being or not being'.[1] The latter refers to the huge spectrum of artistic representation, which philosophy has come to recognise as aesthetics; the former is usually concerned with the 'visual arts', and, more specifically, tends to focus on the directly representational. This chapter will, for the purposes of clarity and space, restrict itself to fine art, within that to painting, and within that smaller category, to representative art, although we will touch on movements such as abstraction by way of exposition. The aim is to guide the historian through the process, starting with the theoretical and concluding with examples of works of art and the ways in which historians might read them.

The person who says 'I know what I like' is exercising aesthetic judgement, although such discrimination usually involves making the initial judgement about the non-art subject of the art, such as a sunset or a tree, and often reflects how faithfully the work of art captures a sense of its subject. Aesthetics itself reflects the two poles of the spectrum of appreciation. Deriving from the Greek, *aisthanomai*, meaning perception and the application of the senses, the term dates back only to the mid-eighteenth century, when the German philosopher Alexander Gottlieb Baumgarten, responding to the rapidly increasing autonomy and consequent status of the artist freed from the constraints of patronage, introduced elements of ethical and metaphysical judgement and attempted a distinction between 'good' and 'bad' art. Thus, with the introduction of such slippery concepts as beauty, feeling and judgement, the discipline was divided into the philosophy of aesthetic experience, which could apply to the appreciation of anything, a construct of humanity or nature; and the philosophy of art, the nature of representation.

The question of evaluation and judgement, therefore, is intimately bound up with object and subjectivity, emotion and rationality. Does one need to view art with a particular frame of mind which can focus, disinterestedly, on the intrinsic nature of an object? Such was the theory of aesthetics developed by Immanuel

Kant, who observed that beauty (or its absence) was the concept of pleasure or displeasure provoked by an object, entirely devoid of any clouding circumstances under which the object might be seen – that is 'the thing itself'. Kant maintained that aesthetic judgement was entirely subjective (unlike theoretical, cognitive judgement, or practical, moral judgement), but that since human subjectivity rests in the same common ground, it commands universal assent, and can rejoin the otherwise separable worlds of the theoretical and practical, or nature and freedom.[2] This aesthetic, however, privileges the gaze of the observer over the object, whilst making a claim that the gaze and the judgement will be the same for all, reflective of our common humanity. In the twentieth century, feminist aesthetics (though not on its own) has challenged this hierarchy, seeing in the active gaze which holds the power of evaluation and the consequent passivity of the object, a reflection of patriarchy.[3] Also in the eighteenth century, British empiricist philosophers posited a universal conceptualisation of beauty grounded in the sensation or experience we have when we view an object. These philosophers – such as John Locke and, particularly in this context, Francis Hutcheson – could hold that beauty was in the eye of the beholder, and that 'absolute beauty' – objects that are beautiful in themselves – can be distinguished from comparative or relative beauty in which an object – say, a work of art – is beautiful insofar as it faithfully represents a beautiful subject.[4] There existed objects and representations of intrinsic beauty, and, as such, the manner in which works of art were conceived and executed – their composition – was important. William Hogarth, for example, popularised, but by no means invented, the 'line of beauty', a serpentine S curve, embodying life and movement and stimulating the viewer, in contrast with straight lines which signified stasis, paralysis and inanimate objects.[5]

Art is therefore a sub-category within representation. The mind represents the world to us through our senses, but the philosophical debate continues about the degree to which that representation is reality. We see the sky as blue, but this is not the reality – Kant's 'thing in itself': this is our representation of the sky. Does art, therefore, add a further layer of obfuscation by attempting to represent, as faithfully as possible, a scene presented to the artist? It could be argued that art is an attempt by the artist to represent reality, by overcoming and correcting misperception, to create a more real image of 'how things really are', perhaps by capturing passion, emotion, danger or melancholy in a scene which would not have been present if the same were represented solely by words. We tend to use the word 'essence'. The 'I know what I like' response took a battering in the twentieth century, as a divide opened up over representation, between the artist's conceptualisation of essence and the viewer's potentially philistine approach to realism. Embedded within the modernist movement was the concept of 'modern art', concerned with essential qualities, such as colour or flatness, thereby reducing the primacy of the subject-matter. Postmodernism reversed the process, starting with the created – constructed – model: 'facts no longer have a specific trajectory, they are born at the intersection of models . . . this precession, this short-circuit, this confusion of the fact with its model . . . is what allows each time for all possible interpretations, even the most contradictory'.[6] Thus, historians are faced with two questions. First, do they need to concern themselves with the work's aesthetic? Does it matter whether it is a good or bad piece of art and whether or not its representation is beautiful, or, as Hutcheson would have it, displays taste? Second, if all and any interpretation of a piece of art is equally valid, does it have anything to tell the historian at all?

The creation of art – like all the sources in this collection – is an act of human expression, and thus it should not surprise us that parallels can be formed with the philosophy of language: is 'reading' – finding meaning in – what a philosopher would term a 'speech act' similar to 'reading' a work of art? The central guiding figure behind this approach was Oxford Professor of Moral Philosophy J.L. Austin, who articulated it in a lecture to Harvard University in 1955 and published it seven years later as *How to do Things with Words*.[7] Austin divided a speech act into 'constative' (what it constates) utterances which report a state of affairs measured against its correspondence with facts, either true or false, and the 'performative' aspect of an utterance which says more about the person using the language, in which the thoughts, feelings and attitudes of the utterer are important. The relationship between the utterer, the utterance and the interpreter, always involving these three elements, is 'intersubjectivity'. Taken up by anthropologists and sociologists, it can explain the construction of society and culture. It is used by performance theorists, in which the central element of human expression could be a performance – speech, ritual, performance of artistic work, item of material culture, whilst philosophers continue to work within this framework, to find means to articulate the elements of human expression which are hidden, disguised or implied. We need a means to distinguish between literal and non-literal meaning in our reading of works of art, to determine how far the work is strictly repre-sentational – factually accurate – and how far it implies information about the world.[8] Historians seeking to construct their own interpretation from images, therefore, need always to bear in mind the relationship between artist, work of art and viewer, which is both triangular and lineal.

Art images illustrate history books more often than most of the other genres featured in this volume, but what function do they serve? Do they corroborate and thus cede primacy to the text; do they break up otherwise dense and potentially intimidating text? Another colloquial interpretation might be that the greater the number of images in a work, the less scholarly it becomes, with the entirely textual, heavily annotated, high-brow monograph at one end of the scholarship scale, and the coffee-table or picture book at the other. But at the same time as there has been a tendency to prioritise text and therefore downplay the authority of the work which carries images, art as a source in itself has also provided the subject of reflection for historians. In the first instance, this is because certain historical periods and places witnessed an explosion in the visual arts which enables historians to claim that the age can be expressed through its paintings. Art is deemed to capture the *Zeitgeist* more fully, more accurately, or more comprehensibly.

This is an essentially Eurocentric approach. In 1860, Swiss historian Jacob Burckhardt influenced Western history-writing for two generations by suggesting that the Renaissance represented a period, revealed in particular through its art, in which there was a paradigm shift in the quality, sophistication and modernity of thought and expression: the (re)birth of individualism and its creative genius.[9] Medievalists, faced with the view that their period represented darkness and ignorance, countered that either the Renaissance owed much to earlier times which Burckhardt left unacknowledged, or that a distinctive Renaissance period could not be compartmentalised; rather there were several parallel and overlapping re-births over a much longer timeframe. But, it could be argued, because of the emphasis which art played in defining the concept of Renaissance for historians such as Burckhardt and Burke, the term maintains its purchase for scholars of history.[10] Meanwhile, historians of the seventeenth century have suggested that the baroque art of the courts of particularly Spain and France represented the puissance, grandeur and pomp of empire, monarchy and aristocracy, which mirrored auto-cratic politics. Coterminous with the baroque extremes of the *ancien régime* were other regions of Europe which announced their 'golden age' through artistic expression, in particular the United Provinces of the Netherlands. For Simon Schama, the Dutch art of this period portrayed the confusion which had been produced by a society and polity rooted in the elites' abstemious Calvinism who found that Providence signalled their godliness by conveying vast material wealth: the embarrassment of riches.[11] The art could represent the affluence of Dutch society, or it could provide images of moral example of the godly response to such providential riches. On the other hand, Adrien van Deursen used the art to argue that the owning of pictures in the Netherlands was a luxury which had travelled much further down the social scale than elsewhere in Europe, and that its subject-matter often replicated the domestic, small-scale lives of a bourgeois society.[12] Julie Berger Hochstrasser has begun to use the art of the Dutch Republic to study the relationship between the representations of objects – clothing, foodstuffs, collectables for example – which featured in the paintings and the global trade which supplied them.[13] For other historians, an interest in the subject of art has been evoked by its relevance to a particular field of historical enquiry, such as Ludmilla Jordanova's history of science and medicine, or Marcia Pointon's placement of the visual within wider cultural history.[14]

In the case of them all, studying works of art emerged from, or engendered, an interest in wider questions which redefined the nature of cultural history in the later twentieth century, along with a wider discussion of the nature of the historical discipline itself. Pointon's work, for example, is part of a wider concern with the human body, in which certain genres of art, such as the nude or the portrait, are particularly apposite.[15] Portraiture could report (constate) what a historical individual looked like, but more interestingly – and not least because the rela-tionship between painted portraits and physical resemblance is not clear and cannot, historically, be verified – portraits imply something about the era which generated them, the attitude of the artist towards the sitter, and the role of the sitter in their society. Something of these issues will be discussed below in relationship to the work of Joseph Wright of Derby. Jordanova discusses the historian's craft, and the role of other disciplines within it, particularly, in the context of art, the publication of *Art and History: Images and their Meaning* and the work of Michael Baxandall and Svetlana Alpers in altering the focus of 'cultural history' away from Art, 'which implies aesthetic value judgements', and towards 'visual culture', which studies 'whatever a given culture throws up'.[16] Peter Burke has gone on to make larger studies of the nature of the gaze, particularly that of the historian, as part of his wider interest in the degree to which history should employ and engage with other disciplinary theories, particularly anthropology and sociology.[17]

These studies equate the importance of art as a historical source with a question of meaning through context. Jordanova calls on historians to contextualise their visual sources, such that art is not privileged as a source with special status, offering a window on, or reflection of, past worlds, because the view that art reflects life is not one which historians claim of their written sources.[18] Burke argues that images are extensions of the contexts in which they were produced and should therefore be viewed as a means to elucidate social constructions and the economics of images, as, for example, paintings were market commodities in themselves. Rather than see the world in the image, Alpers has gone on to extend the contextualisation to the artist and the means of production: being studio-based reflected 'the relation of the artist to reality . . . seen or represented in the frame of the workplace'.[19] Critics of this approach have questioned whether, in fact, the constant recourse to context and supplementary evidence in order to 'read' a painting in fact makes the case for text-based, documentary history.[20] Thus, reading a piece of art requires us to decipher the intention of the artist, the possibility of a whole range of meanings, either implicational or overt, but period-specific and lost to modern audiences ('hidden symbolism'), or, in the absence of any textual confirmations, it may be impossible to read the meaning of a painting, or possible to read any number of meanings into the same image.[21]

The problem for the historian is that in the case of the visual image, it is not possible to isolate the triangular intersubjectivity of artist, art-work and viewer/gaze from the wealth of context surrounding all three elements. Even the degree to which the relationship can be read as a direct one is a historical variable; so, for example, art-works from a period before Burckhardt's individual geniuses were the often anonymous products of a workshop of craftspeople, under the auspices of a patron. Or, to give an example from the other end of the trinity, the gaze is not always the same: three people simultaneously viewing a work may read into it three different narratives; or a privately commissioned portrait was designed for the gaze of the sitter and his or her immediate circle, but, once it is dispersed into a wider commercial or cultural market, with the break-up of the family connection, that portrait may hang in a public gallery or in the private collection of a person with no personal connection to the sitter.

Amongst the questions which contextually interfere with the direct relationship a historian may have with the intersubjective trinity are: whether the artist is known; how much is known about the life and work of an artist or his or her oeuvre; the artist's gender; the cultural milieu; whether the work was a commission to order; who commissioned the work and why; when the painting was made and how 'realistic' is the scene it claims to represent; whether studio-based or *plein-air*; whether from life, photograph, sketches or imagination; and other questions pertinent to particular enquiries. When it comes to the work of art, the historian may need to be aware of its compositional techniques; whether the work is allegorical or contains symbolism; in what medium the painting was created and on what surface; whether it is typical of the work of a known artist or of contemporaneous works; the scale on which the painting was produced; its provenance and where it can be viewed by the historian's readership. As to the gaze, how far can viewers detach their own cultural and personal concerns from a reading of a piece; does it matter whether the viewer regards it as 'good' or 'bad' art, and should they take their aesthetic opinion into account; does the creativity and skill of the artist lend their vision precedence over the opinion of the viewer; in what environment is the image viewed; and, when one sees the image in a book or on the internet, in much reduced scale and possibly in monochrome, how is one's reading affected? There are prosaic questions which affect the writing of the history, such as who owns the copyright of the image, whether the holder is prepared to allow its reproduction, how much will that cost, who will pay the copyright and reproduction costs and will a publisher be prepared to compromise the cost of producing and marketing the finished piece by including relatively expensive images? All these variable factors, through which the direct relationship between painter, art-work and researcher is filtered, are believed to distort art as a potential source for historians, for 'what we can learn from paintings can actually conflict with what we learn from other (and more factually reliable sources)'.[22]

Like any other source, the information the historian provides for the reader should be as full, scholarly and enabling as possible, irrespective of type. The aim of the references will be two-fold: first to demonstrate the nature of the evidence the historian has used, and thus to add authority to his or her argument; and second, to enable the reader to verify that source and confirm or challenge its interpretation. Thus, for example, if known, one needs to provide the 'author' of an art-work, the title given it by the painter, or the title by which it is commonly known, the date on or around which it was painted, the medium and manner in which it was painted – oil on board, watercolour on paper – the scale of the work, some short details on provenance, including the current location where the image can be accessed, and, if the image is being reproduced, the details required to be included by the holders of the reproduction copyright. Historians seldom give all such detail, but each element is important if we are to understand the intersubjectivity of source, and the filters of context.

As a child discovering a love of history, I scoured the commonly available books of 'kings and queens', the format of which usually accompanied a short biography with a matching image.[23] When the two giants of English Reformation history, Elton and Scarisbrick, debated Henry VIII, they drew attention to his portraiture and the imposing image which would glare down at courtiers and ambassadors from palace walls.[24] The plate 'after Holbein' in my schoolbook measured 15×10.5cm, and thus it was many years later, on a visit to the National Portrait Gallery, that I was able to experience the awe with which Tudor courtiers might have greeted the huge originals: the Holbein cartoon for the mural which adorned Hampton Court Palace is nearly 250 times the size of the book-reproduced image.[25]

In similar vein, it is important for the purpose of the painting itself that the scale of the content be part of the impact and message it conveys. Pablo Picasso was asked to produce an image for the Spanish Pavilion at the 1937 World Fair at the Paris Exposition. The only public display of this type made by Spain's Republican government, Picasso's response to the Francoist bombing of a Basque village was a canvas depicting death and dismemberment which measured nearly eight metres in length by three and a half metres in height.[26] Another type of image in which scale is important in assessing interpretation is panorama: the term 'panoramic painting' was coined by Scottish painter Robert Barker in 1791, to describe a concept in longer usage, of extended views of scenes in which the eye pans across the image from one side to the other; in Barker's case, by revolving the image around a cylinder. Panorama Mesdag in The Hague is a purpose-built gallery to house the nineteenth-century panorama of Hendrik Willem Mesdag, depicting the town and environs of Scheveningen, which enables the viewer to 'get the feeling of life as it was in 1881'.[27]

In order to evaluate the historicist content of a piece of art we require a method which takes into account both the direct intersubjective relationship of producer, work and audience, and the variable factors, such as commissioner, artistic medium, genre, composition and so on. Some values will be historical and others aesthetic, though both might and most often will affect one's historical judgement of a piece. I am going to propose a two-part system of analysis. The first part I shall call 'depictive', which takes (as closely as possible) at face value the direct intersubjectivity of painter, art-work and viewer; and its depictive content will be illustrative of a number of categories of historical thinking, such as social history or intellectual history. The other I term 'implicational', taking variable factors into account and illuminating content less immediate than that offered by depiction. The difference between using art-works as historical sources and history composed entirely from documentary evidence is that it is possible to imagine a piece of manuscript evidence which is treated as entirely and exclusively depictive/ descriptive, taken at face value. That is not to say that a historian should not employ the same scepticism towards documentary evidence: a diary entry, for example, might be tainted by self-delusion or deliberately aimed at posterity; a printed piece might be published anonymously, with consequent implications; or one might wish to discuss the implications of a piece published in gothic type. With (particularly) manuscript sources, however, the historian has a tendency to employ the inter-subjective trinity only, whereas there is a belief that art-works will always be more obtuse in their meanings.

I propose to discuss my examples within a context which is almost devoid of illustration. This is both to illuminate the practicalities of reproducing images within published work, and to explore more abstract questions of the relationship between words and pictures. A historian for whom the sole or primary source material was documentary – manuscript and/or print – would not expect or be expected to reproduce all the text on which (s)he based the interpretation. The historian might include short quotations from primary sources, but most of the time, readers have to take the historian's interpretation of the source on trust, and follow up the reference if they wish to view the source for themselves or posit an alternative reading. Even if the historian was editing a manuscript or book for publication, the interpretation and description of its context would be separated from the edition itself. Why, then, do we expect the publication of history in which works of art form all or part of the primary evidence to reproduce the image for the reader, rather than to ask readers to content themselves with the historian's description of what the work conveys and his or her interpretation of it? If a reader is given full reference notes, directed to the location of the original art-work, and possibly to a high-quality reproduction in, say, an exhibition catalogue, should that not suffice, and furthermore, in 'translating' the visual into words, address the issue of the primacy of text over image?[28] The ability to see an image within a publication may be an immediate means whereby the reader can assess the historian's interpretation, but could also be a means to obscure: a painting in which colour is important to interpretation is rendered in black and white; one in which scale is vital is rendered far too small; one in which detail is what is being discussed is rendered in such a way that the detail is not visible or is foregrounded. If a work depends on a systematic use of images, what criteria are applied in deciding which images are included within the history and which should be left out?

There is only space to provide brief examples here and from a relatively limited span of fine art. All fall squarely within the Western European tradition. There is clearly a great deal more that could be said about all the artists, their works and historical analysis of painting: the final section is designed to be indicative of questions which a historian could ask of art-works. The first work I intend to discuss is known as *The Haarlem Lock, Amsterdam*, and was painted by Meindert Hobbema.[29] We know the name of the artist because he signed the work, but we do not know the year in which the work was painted, and thus we can date the painting to within the life of Hobbema – 1638 to 1709 – and attempt a closer dating of this particular painting from contextual details, such as other works by Hobbema, or his contemporaries, its style within the artist's developing oeuvre, or details of fashion within figures in the scene, for example. The work now hangs in the National Gallery, London, and art experts have narrowed down the date of the painting to somewhere around 1663 to 1665, even though the work depicts buildings which were demolished in improvement work during 1661–2, and none of the buildings in the painting still stand in contemporary Amsterdam. The work is 'titled' according to what it depicts (represents) and we do not know of any title accorded it by the artist or, indeed, Hobbema's contemporaries.

Depictively, this image portrays the intersection of the *Haarlemmersluis* and the *Brouwersgracht*, within the *trekvaart* of seventeenth-century Amsterdam.[30] There are no figures within this scene, but even in their absence, the scene is busy – the numbers of ships' masts visible – and depicts a place of activity and dynamism – the tower being a recent embellishment of the city's late-medieval fortifications. The other prominent building is the Herring Packers' Tower (*Haaringpakkerstoren*), evidence of the importance of the Baltic fishing industry to Amsterdam's reputation as a hub of international trading: though its sources were usually more exotic, fish from the northern waters formed a key element in the goods itemised in Dutch still-life genre paintings.[31] At this point, implicational factors start to come into play, because, it could be argued, the authority with which such statements can be made is dependent on the corroboration of other sources. Indeed, since none of the buildings represented in Hobbema's painting are still standing, a traditionalist historian could make the case that the seemingly obvious depictive elements of this image are, in fact, implicational.

Some of the implicational content could be gathered by comparing a source-type with its fellows: with works by the same painter or by another in a similar style or genre. The focus on scene rather than figures is typical; it occurs also in the fashionable Dutch church interior paintings, in which figures are few and incidental and the absence of figures makes it difficult to make a case for these images as evidence of social history.[32] The image is atypical of Hobbema's work: as an Amsterdam townscape it does not reflect the majority of his (earlier) work, focused on the wooded landscapes of the east.[33] Documentary context marks this out as one of Hobbema's last paintings. Shortly after his marriage in 1668 to the kitchen maid of an Amsterdam burgomaster, he moved back to the city, where, despite the seeming lowliness of his marriage, he became a tax-farmer in the wine trade (*octroi*), lived on the Haarlemmerdijk, depicted in the background-left of this painting, and ceased to paint much. A number of further implicational judgements follow. The increasing realism with which Dutch land- and townscapes were rendered in the seventeenth century was part of increasing pride within the newly independent United Provinces of the Netherlands; as, it could be implied, was the bustle and affluence of Hobbema's scene, even without factoring in his change of status from patronage-led, poorly recompensed painter to comfortable worthy of Amsterdam, the most urbanised and mercantile city within a state which increasingly relied on these characteristics for its identity.[34] This image is thus part of a wider historical debate about state formation and national identity.

The representation of inanimate objects – 'still life' – is represented by the Spaniard Juan Sánchez Cotán, who was painting in the opening years of the seventeenth century. The image chosen, again attributed with a purely descriptive title – *Still Life with Quince, Cabbage, Melon and Cucumber* – possesses such strength of composition, coloration and naturalism that it forms the frontispiece to exhibition catalogues and to the search facility of the website of the San Diego Museum of Art, the current holder of this work (Figure 2.1).[35] The still life is illustrated in this book, but one of the restrictions on contributors to this collection is that the publication is only viable within the limitations of copyright, printing and publishing costs if illustrations are in black and white. This makes a considerable difference to the aesthetics of this piece. In stark contrast to the still lives which were produced in greater number in Hobbema's Netherlands, those of southern Europe frequently relied on the darkness of the background to push forward the colour and tone of the items depicted. In the case of Cotán, the background is flat black, and whilst the colour with which the shelf and the food items are rendered is derived from a limited and comparatively muted palette, it is vital to the realism with which the fruit and vegetables are painted and the contrast of colour against background that we are able to see the painting in colour.

Figure 2.1 Juan Sánchez Cotán, *Still Life with Quince, Cabbage, Melon and
Cucumber*, *c.* 1600, signed lower centre Ju° Sãchez Cotan F., oil on canvas,
69.2 × 85.1cm, San Diego Museum of Art, gift of Anne R. and Amy Putnam.
Reproduced with permission of the San Diego Museum of Art.

As with Hobbema, the painter's identity is given fact, part of the work's descriptive characteristics, both possessing verifiable signatures. It appears to be an
entirely naturalistic – almost 'photographic' – representation of five different whole
or pieces of fruit and vegetables, in a strongly articulated frame, which is depicted
as if it were a window. Juan Sánchez Cotán painted several similar pieces and
inspired a small school of followers working within this style.[36] We can add a series
of further descriptive, depictive statements. Two of the items – a quince in the top
left and a cabbage to its right – are painted as if they are hanging on a string, the
cabbage falling lower than the quince. To the right, as if sitting on a shelf, is the
melon – first the main part of the fruit, three-quarters cut so as to reveal the seeds
– next to a slice from the same fruit, and finally the cucumber to the bottom-right.

As alluded to above, there has been a rush to attribute implicational characteristics to Dutch still lives, which have been deemed to show the affluence of the
Netherlands, the moral difficulties that affluence carried for Puritans, the domestic,
bourgeois nature of Dutch society, or the exotic and rare items possessed by
households in a mercantile land. By contrast, Cotán's might be said to be an image

devoid of implicature and almost entirely depictive. Does it tell the historian more than that quince, melon, cucumber and cabbage formed part of the diet of some people in seventeenth-century Spain? It could be argued that, used to thinking of art as something either less than reality – a painting of an object can never be as life-like as 'the real thing' – or more than reality – a depiction which also contains the essence of 'the thing itself' rendered through the eyes of the creative genius – historians look (too) keenly for the implicational in visual sources. Whilst possessing depictive qualities, describing the manner in which perishable foods were kept fresher in the searing heat by being hung (encouraging air circulation), in a clay larder called a *cantero*, the graphic, representational nature of the arrangement of items might suggest an aesthetic, implicational factor, the frame of the 'window' and the black background being compositional devices designed to invoke a response from the viewer.[37] The seeming disparity of these two approaches has been debated in terms of the techniques of painterly naturalism *versus* illusionistic *ingenio*: were the foods seasonal, were they fresh or prepared, were they already perishing, did life-size imply *trompe l'oeil*, does the 'window frame' exist to add illusional perspective, did some foodstuffs carry metaphorical meanings, and why did he so often paint the cardoon (contemporary Europe's forgotten vegetable)?[38] We can cross-reference two 'historical facts' – one descriptive document of Juan Sánchez Cotán's life and the other an implicational reading of this and other of his still lives – and arrive at a possible reading of these paintings which suggests movements in intellectual history. On the one hand, we know that in 1603 Cotán made a will and joined the Grenadan lay brotherhood of the Carthusian order.[39] On the other, commentators have noted the very precise placing of the items. In our chosen illustration, the items form a perfect parabolic curve. Hanging in the Prado is Cotán's *Still Life with Game Fowl, Fruit and Vegetables*, which may be a study of number: one whole cardoon, two francolins, three lemons, four birds at the centre-top, five carrots, six sparrows prepared on a cane for grilling, seven apples, eight stems of the cardoon. Research which might repay investigation could explore the intellectual history of post-Tridentine Spain to elucidate whether Cotán's paintings might be interpreted as pious studies of harmony: the juxtaposition of the perfection of God's creation with its geometrical or mathematical expression.[40]

Work which is ostensibly depictive may acquire implicational characteristics when compared across the production of an individual artist. In his early career as a portraitist in the second half of the eighteenth century, the British artist Joseph Wright of Derby, better known as a painter of the effects of light, painted a number of studies of married couples.[41] The paintings of Wright's own friends, when placed as a group together, allow us to make some comment about his view of society. There are studies of couples whose marriages were happy – *Mr and Mrs William Chase, Mr and Mrs Coltman: A Conversation* and *Rev. Thomas Gisborne and His Wife Mary*.[42] There are also pendants and pairs of paintings of couples whom we know to have enjoyed each other's company and found marriage an agreeable state, such as Robert Vernon Atherton Gwillym and his wife Henrietta Maria Legh, and the literary critic William Hayley and his wife Eliza.[43] We know that the couples in happy marriages were happy because of documentary context and pictorial implicature. Wright loved music, particularly the flute, which he played, and those couples with instruments represent the harmony of companionable marriage (Chase, Shuttleworth). He and his friends loved dogs and the hunt, and the inclusion of a dog is a sure sign of fidelity and companionship (Coltman and Gisborne). We know that his own marriage was happy, but that it was unpopular amongst his family because he married a woman of lower social status than himself, and that he was troubled in later life by mental illness. Coltman represented the marriage of a gentleman to a woman of humble means; Mary Coltman and Eliza Hayley were disturbed by mental illness. Wright saw marriage as a means to stave off physical and mental ill health, best achieved when the couple were not troubled by money, but the source of material comfort should always be the responsibility of the man. On the other hand, there are images of less happy unions. The example of which we have the most secure knowledge is that of cartographer *Peter Perez Burdett and his First Wife Hannah*.[44] Burdett's wife was from a more wealthy background than her husband, and the relative positioning of the figures in this painting allows us to infer the same relationship within the marriage of James and Mary Shuttleworth, though this is not shared by Egerton, who is at pains to stress James's relaxed manner.[45]

Paintings from a 'golden age' of cultural expression may be argued to have a very different relationship to depiction (description, representation, truth) than art produced after the development of the camera, although the degree to which a photograph represents reality is a debate had elsewhere in this volume.[46] Post-photography art, often with 'abstract' content, also erodes the association of art with 'high culture' and seriousness, while mixed media, installation art and so on blur the boundaries between the branches of the fine arts, and explode (though not for everybody) the distinction between the creative and the applied arts.[47] The artist, freed from any responsibility to include elements of representative depiction, foregrounds the implicational and art is increasingly defined by movements which judge how far it represents the 'spirit of the age' (*Zeitgeist*). The 1960s, for example, was the era of Pop Art, though its most famous exponent (because of the image used on the sleeve of the Beatles' *Sgt Pepper's Lonely Hearts Club Band* album, 1967), Peter Blake, deemed a failure the experiment to reach the same mass audience with art as with music, 'given that the sophistication of Blake's pictorial solutions would have been lost on such visually untutored spectators, for whom such pictures would probably not have conformed to their definitions of art'.[48] After his more famous Pop Art movement, Blake joined a group of artists who abandoned the city and deliberately migrated to the countryside, where, rejecting urbanism, they called themselves the Brotherhood of Ruralists.[49] One contextual implication which influences reading, therefore, is the homage to the mid-nineteenth-century Pre-Raphaelite Brotherhood, from which emerges the image of 'Ophelia', repeatedly painted by several of the Ruralists, both male and female.[50] 'Ophelia' (along with Alice in Wonderland, and Elgar) is a so-called 'thematic subject'.

In their estimation ('implicational content', artist intention) much of 'modern' art 'is, at once, both juvenile and self-regarding . . . to the extent of the worship of one's excretion, verbal and physical. The cult of the glory of self will no doubt give some amusement to future historians, though more for its curio value than as a relevant commentary on our humanity'.[51] In two respects, at least, therefore, this image engages with the implicational difference between artist intention and viewer interpretation. Blake's Ruralist phase might be considered at odds with the preceding Pop Art, but that is not how Blake sees it; using the metaphor of his art as a tree, with 'traditionalist' trunk, branching wherever 'art' takes him, all contain the same core essence of the artist.[52] Ruralist subject-matter has been derided as idealised and nostalgic (the opposite of realist).[53] The thematic-subject paintings have been analysed according to the same dialectic: claiming art as the only determinant of content – fellow Ruralist Graham Ovenden explains the youthful female form of Ruralist images as an example of pure aesthetic/depictive representation and a metaphor of projection towards mortality through an image of 'nature . . . spring . . . virgins'. Perception, however, is not within the artist's control, and a critical interpretation of this preoccupation 'reveals more . . . about the age than it does about him'.[54]

Historians cannot, therefore, afford to make art incidental illustration. The work must be illustrative but the historical enquiry must match the depictive content of the art-work. It is unscholarly to avoid difficult aesthetic value judgements: not even possible to escape the debate between 'good' or 'bad' painting, either because in depicting something it could illustrate something historical, or, with more nuance, that the more accomplished the painting, the more representational or representative will be the image. The aesthetic judgements which take in intention, execution and analysis are integral to the gaze and thus, if the viewer is a historian, the historian must engage with all of the components which might comprise the gaze, and must also be the gaze and stand full-square within the intersubjective triangle.

Notes

1 Aristotle, *Nicomachean Ethics* vi.4 (trans. W.D. Ross), Oxford: Clarendon Press, 1908.
2 Antony Flew and Stephen Priest, *A Dictionary of Philosophy*, London: Macmillan, 1979, reissued 2002; Immanuel Kant, *Critique of Judgment* (trans. J.H. Bernard), New York: Dover Publications, new edn, 2005.
3 A subject intimated in critiques of the Ruralist movement, see below pp. 26–7.
4 Francis Hutcheson, *An Inquiry Into the Original of Our Ideas of Beauty and Virtue* (4th edn), 1738, *Inquiry Into Beauty*, I.iv.i.; P.J.E. Kail, 'Function and normativity in Hutcheson's aesthetic epistemology', *British Journal of Aesthetics* 40.4, 2000, pp. 441–51; Peter Kivy, *The Seventh Sense: A Study of Francis Hutcheson's Aesthetics and Its Influence in Eighteenth-Century Britain*, Oxford: Clarendon Press, 2003.
5 William Hogarth, *The Analysis of Beauty*, London, 1753.
6 Jean Baudrillard, *Simulacra and Simulation* (trans. Sheila Faria Glaser), Ann Arbor, MI: University of Michigan Press, 1994, pp. 16–17.
7 J[ohn] L[angshaw] *Austin, How to do Things with Words: The William James Lectures delivered at Harvard University in 1955* (ed. J.O. Urmson), Oxford: Clarendon, 1962.
8 One contemporary philosopher who has applied this theory to the production of drawings and paintings is Catharine Abell, who uses Grice's theory of 'conversational implicature' – that is, of reading the non-literal meanings within speech acts – to argue that there is

also 'pictorial implicature' when the relationship between artist, object and viewer is such that the viewer is able to discern the intention of the maker through the object – the 'maker content'. Catharine Abell, 'Pictorial implicature', *The Journal of Aesthetics and Art Criticism* 63.1, 2005, pp. 55–66, 63; Abell, 'Pictorial realism', *The Australasian Journal of Philosophy* 85.1, 2007, pp. 1–17; Richard Wollheim, *Painting as Art*, Princeton, NJ: Princeton University Press, 1987; Robert Hopkins, *Picture, Image and Experience*, Cambridge: Cambridge University Press, 1998; Paul Grice, *Studies in the Way of Words*, Cambridge, MA: Harvard University Press, 1991; H.P. Grice, 'Meaning', in Peter Strawson (ed.), *Philosophical Logic*, Oxford: Oxford University Press, 1967.

9   Jacob Burckhardt, *The Civilization of the Renaissance in Italy* (trans. S.G.C. Middlemore, introduction Peter Burke), London: Penguin Books, new edn, 1990; Jacob Burckhardt, *Italian Renaissance Painting According to Genres* (trans. David Britt and Caroline Beamish), Los Angeles: J Paul Getty Trust Publications, 2004.

10   Peter Burke, *The Renaissance*, London: Longmans, 1964; Burke, *Culture and Society in Renaissance Italy, 1420–1540*, London: Batsford, 1972.

11   Simon Schama, *The Embarrassment of Riches: An Interpretation of Dutch Culture in the Golden Age*, Berkeley, CA: Vintage, 1988.

12   A. Th. van Deursen, *Plain Lives in a Golden Age*, Cambridge: Cambridge University Press, 1991.

13   Julie Berger Hochstrasser, *Still Life and Trade in the Dutch Golden Age*, New Haven, CT, and London: Yale University Press, 2007.

14   Ludmilla J. Jordanova and Deanna Petherbridge, *The Quick and the Dead: Artists and Anatomy*, Berkeley: University of California Press, 1997; Ludmilla J. Jordanova, *Defining Features: Scientific and Medical Portraits 1660–2000*, London: Reaktion Books, 2000; Marcia Pointon, *Milton and English Art*, Manchester: Manchester University Press, 1970; Pointon, *Strategies for Showing: Women, Possession and Representation in English Visual Culture, 1665–1800*, Oxford: Clarendon Press, 1997.

15   Marcia Pointon, *History of Art: A Student's Handbook*, London: George Allen and Unwin, 1980; Pointon, *Naked Authority: The Body in Western Painting 1830–1908*, Cambridge: Cambridge University Press, 1990; Kathleen Adler and Marcia Pointon (eds), *Body Imaged: Human Form and Visual Culture since the Renaissance*, Cambridge: Cambridge University Press, 1993; Marcia Pointon, *Hanging the Head: Portraiture and Social Formation in Eighteenth-century England*, New Haven, CT, and London: Yale University Press, 1993; J.B. Bullen, *The Pre-Raphaelite Body: Fear and Desire in Painting, Poetry, and Criticism*, Oxford: Clarendon Press, 1998; Penelope M. Gouk and Helen Hills (eds), *Representing Emotions*: *New Connections in the Histories of Art, Music and Medicine*, Aldershot: Ashgate, 2005.

16   Ludmilla Jordanova, *History in Practice* (2nd edn), London: Hodder Arnold, 2006, pp. 80–1; Theodore K. Rabb and Robert I. Rotberg (eds), *Art and History*: *Images and their Meaning*, Cambridge: Cambridge University Press, 1988; Michael Baxandall, *Painting and Experience in Fifteenth-century Italy* (rev. edn), Oxford: Oxford University Press, 1988; Svetlana Alpers, *The Art of Describing*: *Dutch Art in the Seventeenth Century*, Chicago: University of Chicago Press, 1983.

17   Burke, interviewed by Alan Macfarlane, part of a series of Social Science Research Council interdisciplinary seminars, ed. Martin Gienke and the Audio Visual Aids Unit, Cambridge. The British Film Institute transferred the tapes onto DVCAM, and they are now available to view through Cambridge University DSpace (digital repository), as MP4 films: http://www.alanmacfarlane.com/ancestors/burke.htm, accessed 15 July 2007. Students may also find useful the site developed by George Mason University, Center for History and New Media (CHNM), particularly the discussion 'Imaging the French Revolution': http://chnm.gmu.edu/revolution/imaging/, accessed 15 July 2007.

18   Jordanova, *History in Practice*, pp. 164–5.

19   Peter Burke, *Eyewitnessing*: *The Uses of Images as Historical Evidence*, London: Reaktion, 2001; Svetlana Alpers, *The Vexations of Art*: *Velázquez and Others*, New

Haven, CT, and London: Yale University Press, 2005, p. 9.

20 A case forcibly made by Nicholas Hiley, reviewing *Eyewitnessing*, *Times Literary Supplement*, 28 December 2001.

21 Francis Haskell, 'Review: Visual sources and *The Embarrassment of Riches*', *Past and Present* 120.1, 1988, pp. 216–26.

22 Ibid., pp. 224–5.

23 M.C. Scott Moncrieff, *Kings and Queens of England*, London: Blandford Press, 1966.

24 G.R. Elton and J.J. Scarisbrick, *Henry VIII: A Discussion between Geoffrey Elton and J.J. Scarisbrick*, sound cassette, Devizes, Wilts., Sussex Publications, 1971.

25 The image reproduced in Moncrieff, *Kings and Queens*, is a Holbein half-length of Henry VIII: National Portrait Gallery, London (NPG 157), after Hans Holbein the Younger, *King Henry VIII*, *c.*1536, oil on copper, 27.9 × 20cm. The cartoon of the mural, originally designed for the king's private chamber, but destroyed by fire in 1698, represents the left-hand side of the mural only: NPG 4027, Hans Holbein the Younger, *King Henry VIII; King Henry VII*, *c.* 1536–37, ink and watercolour, 257.8 × 137.2cm.

26 Pablo Picasso, *Guernica*, 1937, oil on canvas, 349.3 × 776.6cm, first exhibited in the Spanish Pavilion, World Fair, Paris Exposition, 1937, now held by the Museo Nacional Centro de Arte Reina Sofía, Madrid.

27 Panorama Mesdag is 120 metres in circumference and over 14 metres high: Panorama Mesdag, Zeestraat 65, 2518 AA, Den Haag, The Netherlands. Battles make excellent subjects for panorama, see http://www.panoramaonview.org/panorama_existing.htm, accessed 16 July 2007. The internet and photography have combined to offer a new means to understand art and architecture through the medium of the panorama, such as 360-degree views of Danish churches and their *kalkmalerier* frescos photographed by Hans Nyberg: http://www.panoramas.dk/church-murals/index.html, accessed 16 July 2007.

28 The reader may be interested to see the process in reverse, in the work of Graziella Tonfoni in devising CPP-TRS (Communicative Positioning Program/Text Representation Systems), a 'visual language based on a system of 12 canvas, 10 signs, 14 symbols and a wide set of visual dynamic schemes. Based on a very simple syntax, CPP-TRS is capable of representing meaning and intention as well as communicative function visually': G. Tonfoni, *Writing as a Visual Art* (with James Richardson and with a Foreword by Marvin Minsky), Oxford: Intellect, 1994.

29 Meindert Hobbema (signed near the foreground boat: m hobb()ma) (1638–1709), *The Haarlem Lock, Amsterdam*, National Gallery (NG6138), London, oil on canvas (77 × 98cm), Miss Beatrice Mildmay Bequest, 1953.

30 The *trekvaart* was the system of canals which connected the towns and villages of the Netherlands.

31 Hochstrasser, *Still Life and Trade*; Richard W. Unger, 'Dutch herring, technology, and international trade in the seventeenth century', *The Journal of Economic History* 40.2, 1980, pp. 253–80; Maarten Prak, *The Dutch Republic in the Seventeenth Century: The Golden Age*, Cambridge: Cambridge University Press, 2005, pp. 94–5.

32 See, for example, the work of father and son, Jan Pictersz Saenredam (1565–1607) and Pieter Jansz Saenredam (1597–1665); Hugh MacAndrew, *Dutch Church Painters: Saenredam's 'Great Church at Haarlem' in Context*, Edinburgh: National Gallery of Scotland, 1984; Angela Vanhaelen, 'Iconoclasm and the creation of images in Emanuel de Witte's "Old church in Amsterdam"', *The Art Bulletin*, June 2005. Analysis of individual art-works can be found at the Allen Memorial Art Museum, Oberlin College, Ohio: http://oberlin.edu/amam/, accessed 17 July 2007.

33 Cf. Meindert Hobbema, *A Wooded Landscape with Travellers on a Path through a Hamlet*, about 1665, oil on canvas, 38 × 51½ins, The Getty Center, Los Angeles; Meindert Hobbema, *A Wooded Landscape*, 1667, oil on panel, 24 × 33½ins, The Getty Center, Los Angeles; Meindert Hobbema, *The Travellers*, 166(2?), oil on canvas, 101 × 145cm, Widener Collection, National Gallery of Art, Washington DC; Meindert

Hobbema, *Woodland Road*, c.1670, oil on canvas, 94.6 × 129.5cm, Metropolitan Museum of Art, New York; Meindert Hobbema, *Entrance to a Village*, c. 1665, oil on wood, 74.9 × 110.2cm, Metropolitan Museum of Art, New York.

34   Cf. 'Dutch Italianisers at Dulwich – Inspired by Italy: Dutch Landscape Painting, 1600–1700', an exhibition at the Dulwich Gallery, London, 2002; Christopher Brown, *Dutch Landscape, The Early Years: Haarlem and Amsterdam, 1590–1650*, London: The National Gallery, 1986. The landscape painters went further in turning the descriptive landscape 'as it was' into Dutch landscape as a cause for national celebration, by painting within a deliberately restricted palette and range (the 'tonal movement'), epitomised by Jan van Goyen and Salomon van Ruysdael.

35   William B. Jordan and Peter Cherry, *Spanish Still Life: From Velázquez to Goya*, National Gallery Publications, London, 1995; Juan Sánchez Cotán, *Still Life with Quince, Cabbage, Melon and Cucumber*, c. 1600, signed lower centre: Juº Sãchez Cotan F., oil on canvas, 69.2 × 85.1cm, San Diego Museum of Art, http://www.sdmart. org/Image1/Index.html, accessed 17 July 2007.

36   Juan Sánchez Cotán, *Still Life with Game Fowl*, c.1600, oil on canvas, 67.8 × 88.7cm, The Art Institute of Chicago; Juan Sánchez Cotán, *Still Life with Cardoon and Francolin*, c.1600, oil on canvas, 66 × 62.2cm, Princeton, Barbara Piasecka Johnson; Juan Sánchez Cotán, *Still Life with Game Fowl, Fruit and Vegetables*, signed 'Juº Sãchez Cotan. F./ 1602', oil on canvas, 68 × 89cm, Museo del Prado, Madrid; Juan Sánchez Cotán, *Still Life with Cardoon and Carrots*, after 1603, oil on canvas, 63 × 85cm, Museo de Ballas Artes, Grenada (see the graphics for this museum's website also http://www.juntadeandalucia.es/cultura/museos/MBAGR/, accessed 17 July 2007; Felipe Ramírez (doc.1628–31), 1628, *Still Life with Cardoon, Francolin, Grapes and Irises*, signed and dated 'Philipe Ramírez/fa. 1628', oil on canvas, 71 × 92cm, Museo del Prado, Madrid.

37   Peter Cherry, 'Review of Sanchez Cotan at the Prado', *The Burlington Magazine* 135.1079, 1993, pp. 164–6; Jordan and Cherry, *Spanish Still Life*, p. 29; William Jordan, *La Imitación de la naturaleza. Los bodegones de Sánchez Cotán*, Madrid: Museo del Prado, 1992; W.B. Jordan, *Spanish Still Life in the Golden Age*, exhibition catalogue, Fort Worth: Kimbell Art Museum, 1985; M.N. Taggard, 'Juan Sánchez Cotán and the depiction of food in 17th-century Spanish still life painting', *Pantheon* xlviii, 1990, pp. 76–8.

38   Questions rehearsed by Cherry in 'Sánchez Cotán at the Prado', and *Spanish Still Life*; see also F. Marías, *El largo Siglo xvi*, Madrid, 1989.

39   D. Angulo Iñiguez and Pérez Sánchez, *Historia de la Pintura Española: Escuela toledana de la primera mitad del Siglo xvii*, Madrid, 1983.

40   The idea is in common usage in music, in that the baroque's intricate point and counterpoint replicated the music of the spheres, but in conversations with this author, the leading history of art expert on Cotán, Peter Cherry, is dubious about this reading, feeling that if this idea found artistic expression in Spain, a more likely example would be the architectural plans for Philip II's monastic palace at El Escorial.

41   Benedict Nicolson, *Joseph Wright of Derby: Painter of Light*, 2 vols, Paul Mellon Foundation, 1968; Judy Egerton, *Wright of Derby*, exhibition catalogue, Tate Gallery, London, 1990.

42   Joseph Wright, *Mr and Mrs William Chase*, c. 1762–3, oil on canvas, 54½ × 75ins, Private Collection, New York; *Mr and Mrs Coltman*, exhibited 1771(?), oil on canvas, 50 × 40ins, National Gallery, London, from Egerton, *Wright of Derby*, p. 72; *Rev. Thomas Gisborne and His Wife Mary*, 'I. Wright Pinxᵗ. 1786', oil on canvas, 73 × 60 ins, Yale Center for British Art, Paul Mellon Collection, from Egerton, *Wright of Derby*, p. 223.

43   Joseph Wright, *Robert Vernon Atherton Gwillym*, 1766, oil on canvas, 50 × 40ins, Saint Louis Art Museum, gift of Miss Martha I. Love in memory of Mr Daniel K. Catlin, and *Mrs Robert Gwillym*, 'J. Wright Pinxᵗ. 1766', oil on canvas, 50 × 40ins, Saint Louis Art

Museum, gift of Miss Martha I. Love in memory of Mr Daniel K. Catlin, from Nicolson, *Wright of Derby* i, p. 142; *William Hayley* and *Eliza Hayley* (both 1776), grisaille ovals, 13¼ × 11½ins, private collection, from Nicolson, *Wright of Derby* ii, plates 182, 183.

44 Joseph Wright, *Peter Perez Burdett and His First Wife Hannah*, 1765, oil on canvas, 57 × 80¾ins, 'I. Wright Pinx^t/ 1765', Národní Galerie, Prague, from Egerton, *Wright of Derby*, p. 87.

45 Joseph Wright, *James and Mary Shuttleworth with one of their Daughters, Mary*, 'Wright Pinx^t 1764', oil on canvas, 56 × 72 ins, The Lord Shuttleworth, from Egerton, *Wright of Derby*, p. 45.

46 See Derek Sayer, 'Photography', pp. 55–7.

47 Dadaism and then Surrealism introduced representation as conscious joke or subconscious image. A backlash against conceptual art and less representational creativity was launched in 1999 by thirteen artists called The Stuckists. Billy Childish was to leave the movement in 2001, but the name was coined by his then girlfriend, Tracey Emin, who chided him that his art was 'stuck': http://www.stuckism.com/index.html, accessed 18 July 2007. See also oral testimony interview, by Sarah Barber with Clifford Harper, London, Transcript 05/02, 22 November 2005.

48 Marco Livingstone, 'The first real Pop Artist?', in Christoph Grunenberg and Laurence Sillars (eds), *Peter Blake: A Retrospective*, exhibition catalogue, London: Tate Publishing, 2007.

49 Christoph Grunenberg, 'La mode retro: the Ruralist years', in Grunenberg and Sillars (eds), *Peter Blake: A Retrospective*; Christopher Martin, *The Ruralists*, London: Academy Editions, 1991; Jerrold Northrop Moore, Laurie Lee and Peter Nahum, *The Ruralists: A Celebration*, Cornwall: Ruralist Fine Art, [2003]. The work of the Ruralists achieved a wider audience collaborating to produce cover illustrations for the Arden edition of the works of Shakespeare; see, for example, 'Pericles', 'Romeo and Juliet' and 'The Poems'.

50 Peter Blake, *Ophelia*, 1977–2002, oil on board, work in progress, 139.1 × 96.8cm, Pprivate collection, from Grunenberg and Sillars, *Blake: Retrospective*, p. 117.

51 Ophelia in Moore *et al.*, *The Ruralists: A Celebration*, p. 25.

52 Martin, *The Ruralists*, pp. 35–7.

53 Matthew Riley, *Edward Elgar and the Nostalgic Imagination*, Cambridge: Cambridge University Press, 2007, pp. 82–6; Jeremy Crump, 'The identity of English music: the reception of Elgar, 1898–1935', in Robert Colls and Philip Dodd (eds), *Englishness: Politics and Culture, 1880–1940*, Beckenham: Croom Helm, 1986, pp. 164–90.

54 Martin, *The Ruralists*, pp. 34–5. The photographs illustrating Laurie Lee's essay, 'Understanding the Ruralists', *The Ruralists: A Celebration*, pp. 109–24, highlight the Pre-Raphaelite tradition, including the muse of women within the circle and their presentation with flowing, crimped tresses, and the legacy of Ruskin (looking like a Victorian family). The post-psychoanalytical world, which claims access to the subliminal intentions of the artist, has made the same points about the obsession with youthful female innocence of Charles Dodgson, a figure inspirational to the Ruralists; Alexandra Wood, 'Constructions of childhood in art and media: sexualised innocence', *Agora: an Online Graduate Journal* 2.2, 2003, 16pp., http://www.arts.ualberta.ca/agora, accessed 19 July 2007.

3   The Cartoon: the image as critique

Frank Palmeri

Modern caricature is generally dated to the late 1750s when the English amateur George Townshend began to draw satiric representations of public figures that exaggerated their features and figures. The use of the term 'cartoon' dates from about eighty-five years later when in the early days of the journal *Punch*, the word began to be used for the full-page drawing that appeared near the front of each weekly issue, and almost always referred satirically to some current political topic.[1] Because of their close connection to contemporary social or political issues, cartoons can offer an important resource for the historical investigator, and they have sometimes been used as evidence of how a wide spectrum of society lived. However, employing cartoons as sources in this way presents difficulties. Although they can provide evidence concerning institutions, practices, and events, many cartoons cannot be read straightforwardly to mean only what their overt message appears to say, nor can historical events or attitudes be read through them as though through a transparent medium. This is especially true of the most powerful cartoons and their artists. For example, for more than a century Thomas Nast's cartoons in *Harper's Weekly* in 1871 were taken to be responsible for the demise of William Tweed and the Democratic patronage machine that was centred on Tammany Hall. However, in the last few decades, this narrative of the heroic efforts of a lone cartoonist against an immensely powerful and corrupt ring of officeholders, which was based in part on Nast's own later account of the affair, has come to be questioned and revised. Thus, it has been shown that 'Boss' Tweed was not the leader of the political machine, that he was not the focus of Nast's attack on Tammany Hall during the first year of the campaign, that Nast was not acting alone but in line with the political sympathies and purposes of his own bosses, the Republican Harper brothers who owned the weekly for which he worked, and that exposés published by the *New York Times* contributed significantly to the bringing of corruption charges against Tweed.[2] Political cartoons, like satire and caricature generally, work by means of exaggeration: Nast exaggerated Tweed's importance in the machine and the extent of his takings in order to sharpen his focus and increase the effectiveness of his attack. His cartoons cannot be taken to represent accurately and straightforwardly the political situation in New York City after the Civil War.[3]

Still, like satiric works in other media, cartoons provide indirect evidence of and access to the attitudes of the artist and his audience. It is important in interpreting cartoons to remain attentive to context, including the form in which the cartoons appeared – for example, whether as single sheets or in journals – and, if they appeared in a periodical, to consider its character and history. One may also sometimes discern a divergence between the image of a cartoon and elements of its context, including the text accompanying the image. Reading in this way sometimes produces results that may have been outside the conscious intentions of the cartoonist, but may nevertheless be of value. It is also necessary to pay attention to the history of styles and techniques, to popular as well as to elite examples of the form, and to search out obscure artists who may produce illuminating or arresting images, even if these are not considered typical for the period in question.

The discussion in this chapter will begin with the 1790s and focus on English cartoons of the nineteenth century; many of the issues considered in relation to this material would also find a place in work on twentieth-century cartoons. In addition to considering the methodological questions raised above, we will also examine which theoretical approaches might be most helpful for historical researchers using visual satire. These will include Pierre Bourdieu's view of the different con-tributions to style and form made by individual artists on the one hand and the positions available in the field of cultural production on the other, as well as Antonio Gramsci's ideas concerning popular versus elite or hegemonic forms.

Determining the meaning or effect of a cartoon will usually involve examining the relation between the image and any accompanying text.[4] Occasionally, the author of the text and the maker of the image will not be the same, and in such cases tension may arise from divergence between the implications of the two.[5] This kind of divergence is uncommon but significant, because usually the artist writes his (occasionally her) own caption or text, and often includes his own title, but sometimes internal discrepancies arise between an image and text produced by the same hand. In addition, contradictory implications can be observed in the image itself; they then can serve as important indicators of ambiguities or ambivalences in the maker and/or audiences of the image, and thus constitute productive compli-cations in the satiric image, enriching our sense of its meaning and usefulness.

Such contradictions between parts or aspects of a drawing, often between an overt and an unaccented layer of meaning, or between an obvious first impression and a later implication, characterise many of the political satires of James Gillray.[6] We might take as an example a print by Gillray from 1798, 'New Morality; – or – The promis'd Installment of the High-Priest of the Theophilanthropes, with the Homage of Leviathan and his Suite' (Figure 3.1), published 1 August 1798, by the *Anti-Jacobin Magazine and Review*. The print presents a strong overt satire of the radical philosophers and writers of the preceding ten years in Britain, and of the doctrines associated with them. Amid a classicising background with massive columns that dwarf the human figures, stand statues of values associated with the radical philosophers – Justice, Philanthropy and Sensibility depicted as ugly old hags clothed in rags. Approaching the dais on which the statues stand

Figure 3.1 James Gillray, 'New Morality' (1798), reproduced with permission from the Yale Center for British Art (YCBA).

comes the train of thinkers and politicians themselves, amongst whom can be distinguished the caricatured faces of more than twenty public figures, some of whom retain their human form, while most appear as squat birds or as sea creatures, including the huge figure of Leviathan near the centre of the print, with Charles James Fox and two other Opposition leaders riding on his back and cheering. The radicals and their followers are thus represented as hybrid beings, part-human, part-animal, ugly, even monstrous. The publications of these thinkers are held aloft by their authors, others are strewn in a pile on the ground, and some come pouring out of a Cornucopia of Ignorance in the middle of the composition that carries on its whorls the names of liberal journals such as the *Critical Review* and the *Monthly Review*. One donkey kneeling over the books holds in his hand a volume of poems by Southey; another, representing William Godwin, sits on his hind legs and reads or brays out from *Political Justice*. The first effect is to represent the publications as the worthless trash produced by these gleefully misshapen, semi-human thinkers.

The print allows us to pay attention to the radical publications from another angle, however. In addition to those already named, the titles of these works legible in the print include *Glorious Acquittal of O'Connor*, *Whig Toasts & Sentiments*, Thelwal's *Lectures*, *Zoonomia* (by Erasmus Darwin), works of Tom Paine, (Wollstonecraft's) *Wrongs of Women*, Lauderdale on Finance, Tooke's *Speeches*, and Letter to Peers of Scotland. The text does not provide nearly as vivid an image of the products of the press, merely listing the names of well-known authors, with dashes substituting for vowels. However, the legible inclusion of the titles of almost fifty Jacobin or radical works in the print (even if some of them are purely satiric, such as poems by Toad and Frog) may serve to indicate the strength of opposition to the Tory government of Pitt, and the numerous publications in favour of the French Revolution in Britain during the 1790s, despite the suspension of habeas corpus and the deportation and silencing of the London Corresponding Society. The public sphere was not as unified in opposition to the Jacobins as the anti-Jacobins and the *Anti-Jacobin Magazine* liked to maintain. Although the proliferation of titles and authors in the train of the radical Leviathan suits the strategy of accumulating, cataloguing and listing the objects of satire, it also works to confirm that those who wrote the works included in the image constituted a considerable part of the intellectual community of the nation. On the one hand, they may have been numerous enough to be regarded as dangerous – and this is the overt implication of the print; on the other hand, they may come to appear more mainstream, less eccentric and monstrous than they are portrayed.[7]

In addition to observing such countercurrents in cartoons by well-known satirists, one can also work in the same direction by looking at cartoons by obscure artists. Many accounts of the 1790s suggest that Pitt's campaign against the radicals effectively silenced almost all opposition, and that war with the French Revolutionaries required most participants in the public sphere at least to downplay or moderate their criticisms of Pitt's ministry for fear of retaliation and charges of treason. However, several of the etchings of Richard Newton and William O'Keefe from the middle and even later years of the decade demonstrate the public existence of sharp personal attacks on Pitt comparable in intensity to the way Gillray's

Figure 3.2 William O'Keefe, 'Ducking a Pickpocket' (1797), YCBA.

attacked Fox and Napoleon. For example, in a print of 1794, Newton employs a play on words, using the call to 'support' the minister 'from above' to represent Pitt, the prime minister, hanging from a gallows. That he entitles the image 'The General Sentiment' indicates that Newton is at least able to claim that a wide portion of the public would like to see Pitt in such a plight. Similarly, in O'Keefe's 'Ducking a Pickpocket' (1797; see Figure 3.2), the citizens treat Pitt as a petty thief, dunking him in a pond and subjecting him to ritual humiliation, as one of the men urinates into the minister's mouth and bystanders cheer.[8] Newton and O'Keefe are not such accomplished draftsmen or as fertile in imagination as Gillray, nor do they call on the same range of cultural referents. But the strength of their courage and the directness of their political attack serve as some compensation for these deficiencies, and the intensity of their attacks on Pitt, like the unaccented implications of Gillray's prints, needs to be considered in accounts of the political public sphere in the 1790s. These images also serve to remind us that the sharpness and effectiveness of satire in images and text often derives from the violence, indignation and aggression it channels and expresses.

Some cartoons present another issue and opportunity for the historian as they move away from expressing such violent aggression and from the use of hard and sharp lines in the style of the 1790s. One of the questions raised by a shift of this kind has to do with how we should understand changes in dominant style from one period to another, as well as what are the bases of style. Here we can examine the cartoons that John Doyle signed as 'HB' and published from the early 1830s to the

Figure 3.3 HB [John Doyle], 'A Venerable Spider & a Buzzing Fly' (1832), YCBA.

mid-1840s. These lithographs have a very different look from the etchings we have been considering, an appearance that results from softer greys, thicker lines with less sharp edges, and indistinct facial features often appearing faint or smudged. In 'A Venerable Spider & a Buzzing Fly' (1832; see Figure 3.3), for example, a large fly with a human head buzzes towards the centre of a web where a white-haired spider awaits him with arms outstretched along strands of the web. Underneath the neatly lettered title, the print itself indicates its source: 'vide No. 629 of the John Bull', a reference to a passage in the newspaper *John Bull* which compares the French minister Talleyrand to a spider waiting to immobilise, wrap up and consume the English minister Lord Palmerston. The composition is extremely simple, including only the figure of the fly, the two heads, and some leaves; the features of Talleyrand remain extremely indistinct, as do the strands of the spider's web. Although the spider wants to eat the fly, no violence against or debasement of human bodies appears in the image. By comparison with the satiric images from the 1790s, or even with those by George Cruikshank and others from the 1810s and 1820s, Doyle's large series of *Political Sketches*, in which single sheets such as this were collected, seem tame and toothless. Still, his work was widely praised and popular in its day. It is difficult to decide how to account for such praise and for such changes in style and taste – to determine the extent to which they should be attributed to large shifts in social and cultural configurations, to individual artistic predilections, or to changes in technology and technique.

The technological change from etching to lithography had something to do with the shift to a tamer, less sharp style, at least in Britain. In etching, sharp lines are incised in a thin wax layer covering a copper plate, which is then dipped in an acid bath that bites into the lines left bare until the depth (and darkness) wanted is reached. In lithography, as the name implies ('lithos' = 'stone', from the Greek), the image is drawn directly on a flat stone surface with a wax crayon, and ink that adheres to the wax is applied directly to that image but repelled by the rest of the stone surface. The crayon tends to produce a broader and less sharp line than one produced by the etching process. Cross-hatching is not necessary to produce shadows, because they can be directly drawn in, and backgrounds can be much more hazy and atmospheric.

However, it is also clear that the appeal to technology or technique does not offer a complete explanation. Some graphic satirists of the time, unlike Doyle, did not work exclusively or primarily in lithography. For example, C.J. Grant, a radical and hard-hitting satirist, made some lithographic prints but often adapted them to the relief process of wood engraving, an old practice that had a period of renewed importance in the second third of the nineteenth century.[9] In this technique, lines are carved with a burin (a sharp instrument with an obliquely cut point) into the crosscut end of a thin block of wood and the surface that remains uncut is inked and printed. So in wood engraving what is to be printed remains uncut, while in etching, the lines that are cut are the ones to be printed and lithography is planographic (flat) – the image to be printed is directly on the surface, not raised or incised. A great advantage of wood engraving is that the process is not as expensive as etching or lithography. Moreover, the block can be set directly with a page of type, and the woodblock can last through the printing of tens of thousands of copies – more than an etched copper plate. Wood engraving is thus perfect for a mass audience, and for inexpensive periodicals such as the radical newspapers that during the early and mid-1830s sought to evade the stamp tax on periodical publications. Although wood engravings often possess a crude look, they can communicate an energetic satiric effect.

However, the same shift in technology supporting an art such as cartoons may produce divergent, even opposed results in different cultural and political contexts. Cartoonists began to use lithography in the US in the 1830s, the same time as in England. The appearance of lithography across the Atlantic thus coincided with the presidency of Andrew Jackson, a polarising time when democratising, populist elements were in the ascendancy. Lithographs could be produced and multiplied much more quickly than etchings, enabling cartoons to appear more quickly after an event. The fact that lithography did not require, and in fact did not allow, detailed depiction of backgrounds and settings led to a style of presentation that was more direct, more focused on the single figure who was the object of the cartoon's satire. Ironically, this was in some of the most memorable cases President Jackson himself, as in the anonymous print depicting him wearing a crown and other royal regalia as 'King Andrew I' (1832). In France, in the hands of Daumier and Philipon, the lithographic crayon produced effects that were even more striking because of the dramatic intensity produced by the single focus and stark lighting; one of the best examples of such a result is the image of a citizen lying dead on the floor of his own bedroom killed in his night clothes by the police in a raid ('Rue Transnonian', 1834). The criticism of the government in France led to the prosecution, censorship and eventually the prohibition of political cartoons by September 1835.

The writings of Pierre Bourdieu provide terms and lines of argument that can help us distinguish the roles played by technique, artistic personality and larger social or political developments in such cultural circumstances. For Bourdieu, there are at any time only a certain number of positions in a field of cultural production; these interact with the artistic personality or predispositions of individual artists and, I would add, the possibilities of technique at the time.[10] In England in the 1830s and 1840s, Doyle takes up a position in the wake of the Reform Bill of 1832 that defines itself against the free-wheeling, scabrous, anti-authoritarian graphic satire that had been dominant during the previous generation – the satire of the early Cruikshank, such as 'The Political House that Jack Built' (1819). It is no accident that when Dror Wahrman analyses the way a discourse of the centre became dominant in British culture in the 1830s, contrasting cartoons illustrate that argument: a cartoon from the 1790s depicts polarised groups in opposition to each other with no figures mediating between them; whereas one from the 1830s depicts figures in the middle ground that bridge or moderate opposed extremes.[11] Doyle also provides explicit representation of the middle way as desirable in a print entitled 'A New Way to Drive Over an Old Road; Now Alas! Sadly out of Order' (1847), where a carriage labelled 'Irish Measures' is driven by the minister Lord John Russell between declivities on either side, one identified as 'English Prejudice' and the other as 'Irish Improvidence'. One of the riders on the coach observes to the other, 'How nicely he avoids the ruts, on both sides of the road.' Such a cartoon hardly possesses any charge of satire or critique. Rather than pursuing the extremes of caricature, it celebrates the middle ground. Doyle's medium and technique reinforce the message of moderation: his softer lines and focus do not depict either government or opposition as monstrous or shifty embodiments of corruption or duplicity; rather, those on both sides of the political spectrum are represented inoffensively, with little if any caricatural exaggeration. Thus, Doyle occupies a position that accepts as legitimate the rule of the two parties, as well as the social dominance of the upper and middle classes, subject only to the mildest insider satire of the workings of the political order. It is a peculiarly moderate or bland form of satire that does not even recognise a need for continuing reform. It finds its audience among the upper classes, including the lords and national politicians whom it depicts without bile.

Cruikshank himself is changing direction and taking up a different position in the field of graphic satire during the 1830s. His early satire, especially the collaborations with William Hone during the Regency and the early reign of George IV, adopted the same use of parodic inversion and physical grotesquerie as had Gillray but with an opposition to the government that exceeded Gillray's in its intensity and consistency. However, in the late 1820s and 1830s, he moved away from such sharp attacks, producing only a few sheets during the crisis over the First Reform Bill in 1830–32. He then turned more towards social topics – satires of fashion, of women, and detailed but not sharply satiric observation of the life of the lower-middle ranks of people in the capital. Cruikshank thus occupied a position defined by the use of etching from the earlier period of the field, but he turned away from an indignant concern with the working poor to a more comical and affectionate observation of the daily life of the middle and lower-middle classes.

C.J. Grant, as we have seen, continued to use lithography, etching and especially woodblock prints in radical satire that provides the greatest continuity with the early Cruikshank. In the new political configuration of the mid- and late 1830s, his position is sympathetic to workers and artisans, and harshly critical of the rich and powerful, including the established church, politicians of the two dominant parties, the police and the army.[12] His work is closely and strongly related to what would become the Chartist position in 1839–40. Except for HB, all the other graphic satirists had to move away from the single-sheet satiric print. Sales at the lower end of the market no longer made it economically viable to issue graphic satires in this form, so almost all caricatures had to find publication either in periodicals or in loosely organised collections of an individual's work. While this held true for both Cruikshank and Grant, Grant continued to express his sharp critique of moderation and the middle classes through the mid-1840s, working for inexpensive periodicals and newspapers, as Cruikshank never consented to do. For example, on the first page of *The Penny Satirist* for 6 April 1844, which may be by Grant, the woodblock design is simple but effective in representing Cobden and the Anti-Corn Law League as the small force whose efforts might free the economic energies of the British lion from the constraints of grain tariffs.[13]

Punch began in 1841 and 1842 by taking positions that were also radical, both in its text and in its large and small woodblock prints (by artists such as John Leech) – attacking royalty (especially Prince Albert), expressing sympathy for the working poor and understanding the Chartist agitation, and pressing sharp critiques of hypocritical and corrupt politicians and churchmen.[14] For decades, the weekly continued to feature a large block woodcut in the front of each issue, but the edge of its satire became noticeably less sharp after the late 1840s. *Punch* moved to occupy a position based on inoffensive portrayal of the upper classes and national politicians of both parties, and on representations more comic than satiric of the peculiarities of social life, especially the speech and fashions of the world of manners. Such a focus meant that *Punch* was directing its mild comic satire to an upper-middle- and middle-class audience, and had removed itself far from the concerns with social justice that motivated most of its contributors in its early years. *Punch* depended for its long survival not on a sustained critique of the limitations and injustices of the British economic, social and political system, but rather on a decorous liberal view of the political and social establishment from the point of view of an insider. *Punch* became an established, respectable and self-satisfied institution. The careers both of Cruikshank and of the collaborators on *Punch* exemplify a general tendency for radical satirists to moderate their critique, and to shift from addressing a working-class to a middle-class audience. Cruikshank appealed more to a lower-middle-class audience, *Punch* more to an upper-middle-class segment.[15]

Bourdieu's ideas and terms can be useful in such an analysis because they enable us to avoid asserting a simple cause-and-effect relationship between external changes in the social and cultural realm and internal changes in the cultural field (such as shifts in the dominant style, genre, or medium). Taking into account the interplay of multiple factors can help us avoid the idea of the artist as an independent, autonomous creator or genius unaffected by social opportunities and constraints. Such an approach also makes it possible to avoid the external determinism of asserting that either an individual's social and economic place or the contemporary forms of publication alone define the position he takes in his graphic art. Rather, the dispositions of artists – their artistic personalities, so to speak, as well as their level of education and economic background – interact with the possible positions in the field in which the artist works. Only certain positions are available at any one time, and the artist must choose amongst them or stake out a new one. But he may also change positions, and the field itself may change in the course of an artistic career, as we have seen both that shifts in the field occurred and that individual artists changed paths during the 1830s and 1840s in Britain. The method sketched here also avoids one other kind of determinism – the idea that developments in technique or technology by themselves can provide explanations for changes in style and form. Thus, it is important to recognise, for example, that although lithography provided the medium during several decades in Britain for an unadventurous and inoffensive observation of the political scene, in France it was associated closely from the beginning of its use in caricature in 1830 and for several decades after that with the strong and discomfiting satire of Honoré Daumier, during most of whose career – 1835–48 and 1852–67 – political caricature was banned in France.[16]

In his discussions, Bourdieu gives little attention to shifts from one cultural or artistic period to another; he concentrates on analysing a particular configuration, most frequently that of late nineteenth-century France. In addition, Bourdieu's approach presumes that no instance of style or form in a particular medium is outside the field; if a particular position has found expression, then it is a position allowed or sanctioned by the field. However, another methodological approach can place the material examined here in a different perspective. Antonio Gramsci observes that certain genres or styles may be dominant at different periods in different cultures and that such forms can be taken as characteristic of a culture in a particular period. However, in his view, the dominant cultural configuration is not monolithic, but can be considered hegemonic, while at any moment dissenting, challenging and reactionary possibilities are also at work in the cultural sphere. Such counter-hegemonic forces often are expressed in sceptical strands of hegemonic culture (such as the covert implications of the Gillray print which was noticed near the beginning of this chapter), or in forms of popular culture. Rather than expressing an elite's view of itself, a work of popular culture may express the indignation, the fantasies, or the utopian ideas of a larger and less moneyed portion of a populace. Such fantasies in turn can ground inferences about the state of mind and attitudes of such people, which are otherwise very difficult of access. We have seen evidence of such a set of attitudes in the Radical satire of C.J. Grant in the 1830s and 1840s. However, several difficulties attend the study of popular material. For one, it has often not been taken seriously by historians of art or culture, sometimes because of a lack of sophistication in technique. In addition, popular materials are often more ephemeral than works of high culture directed to the upper or upper-middle classes, and they can disappear without leaving much of a record behind. This is true for the work of Grant, for example, about whom we know very little after his work in the mid-1840s.

From the 1850s to the 1870s, *Punch* dominated the culture of visual comedy and satire in Britain, as we have seen, with a liberal, self-satisfied and apolitical comedy of manners. This attitude was particularly pronounced in foreign affairs, where the magazine became strongly nationalistic and supportive of imperialist policies. Although *Punch* occupied a hegemonic place, its position was not monolithic or exclusive. One challenger, a weekly satiric magazine named *Judy*, provided a more conservative slant on the topical political and social issues; another, *Fun*, offered a more liberal alternative. In form and style, however, both *Judy* and *Fun* mirrored *Punch*, and thus confirmed its hegemonic position.[17] Little graphic satire challenged this position between the late 1840s and the late 1880s. One exception can be found in the weekly *The Tomahawk* (1867–70), edited and mostly written by Alfred à Beckett and illustrated with one large, double fold-out cut per week by Matt Morgan. The lead article on the first page, often an editorial, was usually concerned with the same topic as the one illustration. Thus, there sometimes arise the kinds of discrepancies noted at the beginning of this chapter between image and accompanying text.

If only because of the differences between the media in which they work, there will often be a tension between cartoons and the text that surrounds them, but whether it has to do with different emphases or even different topics, this relationship often helps determine the original effect of the cartoon. For this reason, as Corinna Peniston-Bird also points out, it is important to analyse the cartoons in context. Examining a succession of images without reference to the periodicals or newspapers in which they were first published removes them from the conditions that shaped their meaning and impact. The extensive series of visual portraits of well-known figures in political, legal and cultural life produced by *Vanity Fair* accompanied by verbal portraits of a paragraph or two provides a striking instance of the way both media contribute essentially to the effect of the whole.[18]

In the case of *Vanity Fair*, the effect is usually only mildly satiric; in the case of Morgan and à Beckett in *Tomahawk*, the collaboration between the editor and illustrator produces focused and powerful satire. After the first few weeks, most of the cartoons for the rest of the run were colour-tinted light green, blue, or even red. For example, in 'Couleur de Rose! Or Fancy and Fact' (3 November 1867), a large pair of eyeglasses, with both lenses coloured pink, dominates the cartoon. In one, a dying poor man is treated with respect and given the necessary medicines; in the other the poor are given a feast. However, around these rosy images are grouped representations of life for the poor as it really is: a young girl has drowned herself; infirm old men are made to crush rocks to obtain welfare relief; there is murder in a poorhouse. The article on the facing page is closely coordinated with the cartoon, and enhances its effect. Similarly, in 'The Real Guardian of the Poor! Or, A Change for the Better' (4 September 1869), a skeleton in a suit stretches out the bones of his hand over a poor, gaunt man who has slid off his chair to escape the grip, while in the distance two overseers converse smilingly. The lead article commends with bitter sarcasm the way the guardians of the poor take care to feed the hungry and clothe the naked, as both article and image confirm the implication of the print's subtitle that death brings the only true improvement in the condition of the poor.

Although the object of the satire is clear in both of these prints, some of Morgan's elaborate prints achieve a kind of visionary intensity. An atmospheric print tinted dark green presents a bird's-eye view of Paris in 'The Doomed City! Or, Life Beneath – Destruction o'er Head' (24 July 1869) (Figure 3.4). The Seine picks up a gleam from a storm overhead where striking white clouds pour out a stream of precipitation that spells 'Revolution'. The accompanying lead article criticises the emperor Louis Bonaparte, asserting that the memory of his past has taught his people to distrust and hate him. The apocalyptic atmosphere of the print predates and prophesies the emergence of a revolutionary regime in France a year before the establishment of the Paris Commune in 1870. The images and text in *Tomahawk* may not have been within reach of most manual labourers every week; the paper was not popular in that sense. But it did offer fantasies or prophecies of a popular nature, expressing widespread convictions and values that otherwise went unexpressed in public.[19] It also departed from the comical satire of *Punch*, *Judy* and *Fun*. However, the alternative provided by Morgan and *Tomahawk* to the hegemonic mild criticism of social manners could only be sustained for three years; after it ceased publication, Morgan moved to the United States for the rest of his career.[20]

We can consider two further counter-hegemonic challenges to the comic style and political position of *Punch* in the late 1880s. The first of these came from Martin Anderson, who signed himself Cynicus, and employed a non-dramatic allegorical style that personified, for example, Capital, Labour and the professions. But in his hands, such subjects differ widely from the allegorical stereotypes of the British Lion or the Russian Bear that John Tenniel employed uncritically and without satire in *Punch* at the same time. Rather, the institutions of social life prove in Cynicus's hands to be bloody, greedy and corrupt to the core. For example, in 'HISTORY' (no. 3 of *Cartoons, Social and Political* [1893]), a frowning woman in a sickly green toga wearing glasses that read 'Prejudice' sits on a throne with steps reading 'Falsehood' and 'Conjecture'. She writes in a book from an inkstand labelled 'Blood', and a bloodstained mitre and crown rest on the back of her throne. While it is not subtle, the design makes effective use of hand colouring to enforce its view of history as a blood-soaked pile of lies. Similarly, in 'JOURNALISM' (no. 23 of the same series), a red-faced, dishevelled man leans on a crutch reading 'Insurance' and 'Advertisements', carrying a bottle of gin in his pocket, and holding papers

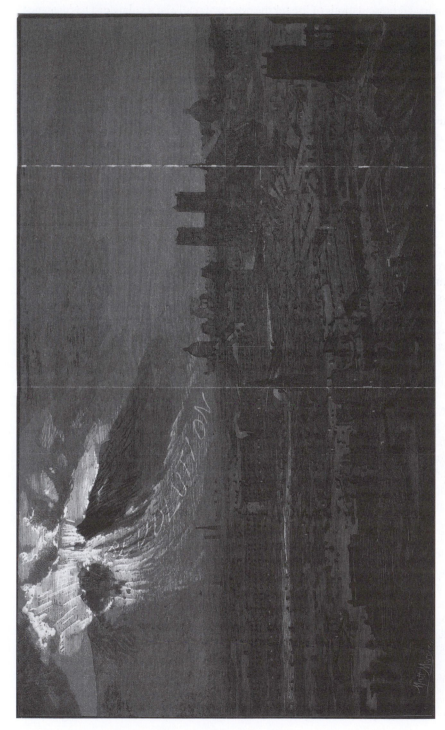

Figure 3.4 Matt Morgan, 'The Doomed City!' (1869), in *The Tomahawk*.

headed 'Crime', 'Slander', 'Murder', 'Divorce' and 'Fraud'. Under a table nearby sits a bucket of blood, and a bomb. The caption to this image sums up the cartoonist's view of journalism in four-beat alliterative verse: 'Bloating in gore and gruesome gabble / A paltry pimp who panders to the rabble.' Both of these images employ sharp, thick lines with little if any shading, which stand at the opposite extreme from the inoffensive comic satire that held sway for forty years in Britain.[21]

That Cynicus's work is not merely idiosyncratic emerges from comparing it with the images that Walter Crane published in socialist periodicals at the same time and collected under the title *Cartoons for the Cause* (1896). For example, in 'Signs of the Times, No. 1, Mrs. Grundy Frightened at her own Shadow' (originally published in a Supplement to *Commonweal* in 1886) (Figure 3.5), an unemployed young man stretches out his hand to help Mrs Grundy, an embodiment of propertied respectability, who is overburdened with the parcels she is carrying that read 'Land', 'Wages', 'Capital' and 'Profits', but she responds by threatening to hit him with her umbrella labelled 'Parliamentary Government'. Crane's draughtsmanship is far superior to that of Cynicus, but the two men share the use of allegorical figures depicted in thick dark lines, a focus on labelling the figures and objects in their prints, as well as an extreme disaffection from the political process and the capitalist system.

Earlier forms do not always disappear when they cease to be dominant but can persist for a long time afterward. Although the comic satiric periodicals ceased to constitute a hegemonic form of expression by the 1890s, *Punch* continued to be

Figure 3.5
Walter Crane, 'Mrs. Grundy
Frightened at her own Shadow' (1886),
in *Cartoons for the Cause*.

published for another hundred years. But even the occasional full-page cuts such as those of Cynicus and Crane did not define the newly hegemonic form and style. What came to replace *Punch* and the comic magazines was the daily editorial cartoon, which first began to appear in the *Pall Mall Gazette* in the early 1890s in the work of F.C. Gould.[22]

Analysis of the historical import of cartoons whether in the nineteenth century or since can profit from the approach discussed here: examining the relation, and in particular the discrepancies, between image and text. It can also open up otherwise hidden paths of argument to observe tensions within the image itself. We should try, as far as possible, not to read any individual cartoon in isolation, but rather to research the background, the politics, and the technique of the cartoonist, and the relation of his work to that of contemporaries who were working on related issues, perhaps from a different angle or in contrasting styles. Although it is difficult, we should try to be aware of what may not have survived, of the extent to which the hegemonic and the canonised tend to dominate the record. At this point, considerations that lead to the proper use of cartoons as historical sources join up with the logic behind the appropriate use of documents and other traditional materials. It is understandable, for example, to see in the weekly woodcuts of *Punch* or another long-lasting periodical a source of information about historical events, fashions, even opinion during its period of publication. But if we have recourse to satiric images to obtain access to the attitudes and beliefs of people of the time – and this seems to me to be perhaps the most compelling reason for consulting satiric cartoons – we must realise that there are no neutral images, just as there is no neutral discourse, from which we can read straightforwardly what life was like at the time, what those who lived then thought and felt. Images derive from and express a certain perspective, satiric images perhaps more clearly than other kinds. Therefore, it is important to remember that any cartoonist whose work was printed was making an image that would sell or be supported because it expressed the beliefs and attitudes of some (in most cases a dominant) part of the population, but there were other parts of the population with other perspectives and attitudes, who perhaps were not able to afford satiric caricatures, or, if they could, few of such inexpensive and ephemeral works may have survived their own day. Gramsci has good reason for maintaining that any moment in modern culture is shaped by a contest and struggle between alternate perspectives. Those who seek to appeal to cartoons in making arguments about historical attitudes should not only be attentive to frictions within and among cartoons, we should also attempt to search out those cartoons that in their own time fulfilled the important function of challenging the hegemonic perspective in style, form, or subject. Like historical sources of other kinds, those that survive do not necessarily tell the whole story.

Notes

1   In the US, 'cartoons' without a qualifier usually refers to animated short feature movies, sometimes satiric, almost always comic. 'Satiric' or 'political caricature' is the usage most often employed there for the nineteenth-century drawings known as cartoons in the UK. The term 'editorial cartoons' is used in the US for such politically satiric

drawings that appeared in daily newspapers from the end of the nineteenth century and throughout the twentieth century.

2 See the summary of the revisionary approach presented by Roger A. Fischer in *Them Damned Pictures: Explorations in American Political Cartoon Art*, North Haven, CT: Archon, 1996, pp. 2–17.

3 Donald Dewey makes a similar point about a series of related conjunctures, arguing that cartoonists and commentators have regularly exaggerated the impact that political cartoons have had on attitudes and elections. He points out that despite widespread and deeply antipathetic portrayals by cartoonists, Andrew Jackson, Franklin Roosevelt and Richard Nixon were all elected and re-elected to the presidency: Dewey, *The Art of Ill Will: The Story of American Political Cartoons*, New York: New York University Press, 2007. One would be hard pressed to explain such results if one took the political cartoons to be accurate reflections of the general attitudes of the times.

4 Text printed to accompany an image is often known as letterpress.

5 I have analysed such an instance in the *Comic Almanac* of the mid-1830s with illustrations by George Cruikshank: Frank Palmeri, 'Cruikshank, Thackeray, and the Victorian eclipse of satire', *SEL: Studies in English Literature 1500–1900* 44.4, 2004: pp. 753–77.

6 For an exploration of such tensions in the satires of Gillray, see Ronald Paulson, 'The grotesque, Gillray, and political caricature', *Representations of Revolution (1789–1820)*, New Haven, CT: Yale University Press, 1983, pp. 168–214.

7 Whether Gillray intended to produce such an undertow need not determine the issue in such a case: if the image can sustain the interpretation, if the implication is there in the work, then whether the cartoonist consciously intended to put it there does not matter. We should also keep in mind the difficulty, even the impossibility, of determining an artist's intention in a work apart from the evidence in the work itself.

8 On such ritual debasements in satire, which often bring figures of authority into contact with products of human elimination, see Mikhail Bakhtin, *Rabelais and his World*, trans. Hélène Iswolsky, Cambridge, MA: MIT Press, 1968, and *Problems of Dostoevsky's Poetics*, trans. Caryl Emerson, Minneapolis: University of Minnesota Press, 1984, chapter 4, on the carnivalesque in literature.

9 On the use Grant made of these various techniques, see Dave Cole, 'Grant's print techniques', in *C.J. Grant's Political Drama: A Radical Satirist Rediscovered*, London: University College London and the Paul Mellon Centre for the Study of British Art, 1998, pp. 19–21.

10 See Pierre Bourdieu, *The Field of Cultural Production*, New York: Columbia University Press, 1993, pp. 55–73.

11 See Dror Wahrman, *Imagining the Middle Class: The Political Representation of Class in Britain, c.1780–1840*, Cambridge: Cambridge University Press, 1995, p. 46.

12 On the objects of Grant's satire and the shape of the market at the time, see Richard Pound, '"Catching Follies as They Fly": C.J. Grant and the market for English political caricature in the 1830s', in *C.J. Grant's Political Drama*, pp. 3–14.

13 As in this example concerning the identification of the lion and the mouse, a short caption can serve an explanatory function, clarifying the allegorical or metaphorical significance of the cartoon. In some cases, the social comedy or mild satire of the cartoon resides almost entirely in extensive verbal material, such as elaborate dialogues that accompany the image; this is true for the cartoons of young people in stylish contemporary dress in du Maurier's cartoons in *Punch*, for instance. We might think that the text of captions usually serves to supplement and complete the meaning of the cartoon image, but both the allegorical image of Grant and the very different, stylish cartoons of du Maurier demonstrate the extent to which the text – whether brief or extensive – can be as essential as the image for communicating meaning, which is often not obvious by itself.

14 For a thorough consideration of the topics and strategies of *Punch* in its first decade,

see Richard Altick, *Punch: The Lively Youth of a British Institution, 1841–1851*, Columbus: Ohio State University Press, 1997.

15   For an analysis of this tendency towards moderation and comedy in Cruikshank and *Punch*, see Palmeri, 'Cruikshank, Thackeray, and the Victorian eclipse of satire'.

16   Political cartoons have also been subject to legislative proscription in the US. Both California (in 1899) and Pennsylvania (in 1903) enacted laws against political cartoons, although these remained ineffective and unenforced. However, the federal government, under the authority of the Espionage Statute of 1917, established a Bureau of Cartoons, which put strong pressure on cartoonists to support the Wilson administration's war policy. Using the same act and the Sedition Act of 1918, the Postmaster General prosecuted *The Masses* and other socialist journals for obstructing recruitment, in part because of cartoons they published. See Dewey, *Art of Ill Will*, pp. 37, 45–6.

17   In the US, the Democratic, liberal weekly *Puck* was not founded until 1876; its Republican, more conservative rival *Judge* was first published in 1881; and the third of the major magazines of humour and satire, *Life*, which was more interested in social than in partisan political issues, appeared in 1883. Although they came into print later than their corresponding periodicals in England, these three occupied positions that in many ways paralleled those of *Fun*, *Judy* and *Punch* in the last decades of the nineteenth century.

18   Donald Dewey is one of the few who write about the use of language in cartoons, but he focuses mostly on puns and on words that cartoons have contributed to the English language, such as 'gerrymander'. See Dewey, *Art of Ill Will*, pp. 20–5.

19   For the suggestive analogy between cultural artefacts and the dreams of a people at a cultural moment, see Jules Prown, 'The truth of material culture', *Art as Evidence*, New Haven, CT: Yale University Press, 2000, p. 223.

20   We should note here that the sequence of hegemonic forms and the shape of the cultural field in graphic satire in the US differed strikingly from those in Britain: rather than being a time when the dominant cultural and political trend was towards accommodation, the 1840s and 1850s were decades when regional political polarisation sharpened dramatically in the US. Even after the Civil War, American political caricature experienced a kind of golden age, as can be seen from the work of Nast for *Harper's Weekly* in New York. Morgan became an illustrator for *Frank Leslie's Illustrated Paper*, and finished his career as art editor for *Collier's*. For a wide-ranging survey of styles and artists in American cartooning, one can consult Harry Katz, *Cartoon America: Comic Art in the Library of Congress*, New York: Abrams, 2006. The work of Katz and his collaborators makes use of the Art Wood Collection, the largest of several collections of American cartoons held by the Library of Congress, dating from late eighteenth-century images to work of our time. See also Stephen Hess and Sandy Northrop, *Drawn and Quartered: The History of American Political Cartoons*, Montgomery, AL: Elliot and Clark, 1996.

21   David Low writes that Cynicus displayed 'the authentic later-eighteenth-century spirit': Low, *British Cartoonists, Caricaturists, and Comic Artists*, London: William Collins, 1942, p. 25.

22   On F.C. Gould as the first daily cartoonist, see under Gould in Simon Hough, *Dictionary of British Book Illustrators and Cartoonists*, Woodbridge, Suffolk: Antique Collectors' Club, 1978.

4 The Photograph: the still image

Derek Sayer

Beauty will be convulsive, or it will not be at all.

André Breton, *Nadja*, 1928

Modernity and the camera[1]

'The illiteracy of the future', wrote the Hungarian photographer László Moholy-Nagy in 1927, 'will be ignorance of photography.'[2] He was touching on a social change as profound as any that have characterised the modern era. It is ironic that for want of written documents historians of pre-modern societies are generally more inclined than their modernist colleagues to treat visual images as bona fide sources, for thanks to photography the modern world is awash with such images to an extent that is without historical precedent. Furthermore, this proliferation of images is as fundamental to what makes our world distinctively *modern* as electricity or the internal combustion engine. As Susan Sontag drily remarks, 'being a spectator of calamities taking place in another country is a quintessentially modern experience'.[3] Not for nothing have social theorists coined concepts such as 'the society of the spectacle' or 'hyperreality' in their attempts to grasp the distinctiveness of modernity.[4] Once the camera enabled reality to be duplicated as image and the printing press enabled the image to be played back, time and time again, as reality, it was inevitable that the lines between the real and the virtual – always a dubious boundary at best – would become increasingly blurred.

Much of what we today take to be reality has been made known to us only through the photographic image. Cameras on the Hubble Telescope show us galaxies and nebulae thousands of light-years away while microscopic photography lays bare the interior structures of bacteria, viruses and cells.[5] Marvelling at these pictures, we do not doubt that what we are seeing is *real*, even though what the camera reveals is invisible to the naked human eye. This is not the only respect in which photography extends the range of perception and alters the quality of experience. Since travellers first photographed distant lands in the 1840s, our planet and its peoples have become visible in a way that was previously impossible except for a privileged (or sometimes press-ganged) few.[6] Through the photographic image, endlessly reproduced on picture postcards, in illustrated magazines, travel brochures, films, TV and the internet, the unknown has become familiar and the exotic banal. We are as accustomed to the famine-stricken landscapes of Africa and the poverty-ridden slums of India as to the skyline of New York. Indeed, it has become difficult to visualise Africa without famine or India without poverty; these clichéd spectacles have become part of our own backyard. And nowadays we know our own backyard, or at least those parts of it into which photojournalists venture and most of us do not, a good deal better than we otherwise might. From the slums and sweatshops of Jacob Riis and Lewis Hine's America to the whores and hoodlums of Brassaï's *Paris by Night*, from Weegee's lurid New York crime scenes to the sunlit suburban porn studios of Larry Sultan's contemporary California, photography) has mapped what once remained, for most, the province of the imagination.[7] Be it the brothel, the deathbed (a commonplace of nineteenth-century photography, or the execution chamber, there is scarcely any sanctum the gaze of the camera has not violated; even the grisly rituals of lynching found their way onto picture postcards.[8] Our world has no more Dark Continents; today's travellers know exactly where they are going and what they can expect to see when they get there.

Photographs have habituated us to the sights of the hopelessness of poverty, the brutality of war, the horrors of natural disasters; from modest beginnings in Hermann Biow's daguerreotypes of the great Hamburg fire of 1842 and Alexander Gardner's *Photographic Sketchbook* of the American Civil War, human misery has become the visual staple of the morning paper and round-the-clock news. Glued to our TV screens, we could all *see* the collapse of the twin towers of the World Trade Center in New York on 11 September 2001 as it happened, in real time. But 9/11 also became the most photographed 'historic event' of all time, and through those photographs we can vicariously relive the tragedy again and again. We might ask whether without the camera 9/11 would have become quite so instantly 'historic'. The artist Damien Hirst got himself into trouble for telling BBC News on the first anniversary of the attacks that '[t]he thing about 9/11 is that it's kind of an artwork in its own right. It was wicked, but it was devised in this way for this kind of impact. It was devised visually'.[9] He was, of course, right. The possibility of creating an iconic *image*, laden with both visual spectacle and symbolic resonance, was integral to the terrorists' choice of target. One might go so far as to say that the entire spectacle was staged for the benefit of the cameras.

Critics differ as to whether photography's ability to record the suffering of others creates compassion, empathy and a will to act on their behalf – as the crusading Farm Security Administration photographers who documented the plight of American small farmers and rural workers during the Great Depression hoped – or whether, on the contrary, repeated exposure to such scenes merely blunts our sensibilities, turning the viewer into a jaded image-junkie who can only get high on ever-stronger fixes.[10] The sociologist Georg Simmel, writing at the beginning of the twentieth century, identified bombardment of the senses as a distinctive feature of the modern metropolis and saw a blasé attitude of generalised indifference as its inevitable corollary.[11] Photography virtualises this process of distancing, multiplying the stimuli to the point of ennui. Having seen the careworn face of Dorothea Lange's 'Migrant Mother', the skeletal corpses heaped up in Lee Miller's photographs of Dachau, or the terror on the face of the naked little girl at the centre of the frame in Nick Ut's Pulitzer Prize-winning 'Villagers Fleeing a Napalm Strike, Village of Trang Bang, Vietnam, June 8, 1972', reproduced a thousand times, can we be moved by these images any longer? [12] It is perhaps no coincidence that in French *cliché* is used to refer not only to a figure of speech rendered meaningless through endless repetition but also to a photographic image. Walter Benjamin's contention that reproducing works of art strips them of their aura, it might be argued, applies to more than just Old Masters; the camera enormously expands our vision but it does so only on condition that what we see is no longer *the thing itself* but its dead and deadening image. [13] From this point of view photography might justly be regarded as one of the most powerful instruments in Max Weber's apparatus of modern disenchantment, denuding the world of its remaining mystery and magic. [14]

But is it just that? Do photographic images not have an aura and a magic of their own, which is bound up precisely with their character as doubles? For it is just this uncanny ability to produce mimetic copies that gives photographs a totemic quality, making the absent present and reconnecting the viewer to the thing that is lost but the image recalls. The connection may be entirely virtual but the emotions it evokes are real enough. Why else do we carry portraits of absent lovers in our wallets, snap endless pictures of our children and pets and mount them in family albums, or pay exorbitant sums of money to wedding photographers and hang the resulting mementoes on our bedroom walls? We might wonder to what extent all our memories have become Kodak memories in which the image usurps the place of the event that occasioned it: is what we remember our own childhood or the photos mum and dad took of us playing in the garden, the vacation in Spain or the souvenir snapshots we have looked at again and again? It is also only thanks to the camera's duplicity (to return to Benjamin) that Renoir's bathers, Van Gogh's sunflowers, or Munch's scream have become familiar to all. Millions more people have seen Picasso's *Guernica*, whose reproduction can be bought at any IKEA from Warrington to Beijing, than have visited the Prado in Madrid where the original painting hangs. It is not, of course, Picasso's painting that they are seeing but its photographed and printed image, and with this comes an undoubted loss: loss of scale, loss of texture, loss of the play of light on the canvas, and much else. Nonetheless the image still has impact, and the painting has probably had its greatest impact as a photographic image. [15] This is one sense, among many, in which for good or ill photography is a profoundly democratising, not to say vulgarising, technology. Baudelaire distrusted it for that very reason, fearful that its facile mimicry would profane the temple of art. [16]

Not that the camera has not also consorted with power, and indeed changed the very terms on which modern power is exercised. Airplanes were first used during World War I, not for dropping bombs but for photographic reconnaissance behind enemy lines; today, spy satellites orbiting 100 miles above the earth's surface guide missiles on their way to their surgical strikes. This is the same technology that has given us the everyday miracles of SatNav and Google Earth. Diane Arbus's oft-quoted observation that one of the risks of appearing in public is the likelihood of being photographed has also taken on new meanings. Surveillance cameras (of which Britain has more per capita than any other country in the world) may catch serial killers and provide evidence in their trials, but are also the bane of every motorist.[17] Without the camera Michel Foucault's 'panopticism', which works through 'induc[ing] in the inmate a state of conscious and permanent *visibility* that assures the automatic functioning of power',[18] could scarcely be extended beyond the closed institutions (prisons, asylums) and emergency situations (towns quarantined because of plague) that provided its paradigm. Modern power, Foucault argues, individualises its subjects as agents and guarantors of their own conformity, and here too photography plays a crucial part. The photo-ID we dutifully carry in our wallets and purses, possibly alongside our dog-eared photographs of absent lovers, permits us to cross national frontiers, drive our cars, cash cheques and buy alcohol, while mug-shots have been the mainstay of police databases since the 1880s. The antecedent of the passport photo is the *carte de visite*, a small visiting card adorned with a photograph of the bearer which was much in vogue in fashionable circles in the 1850s.[19] 'Wanted' posters share a similar strange affinity with the pervasive images of celebrity integral to contemporary life. Where would commerce be without advertising and advertising without the camera? Images of David Beckham and Kate Moss gaze on us from billboards, magazines, computer screens and T-shirts the world over, glamorous embodiments of the dreams and desires that make the modern world go round.

The camera, in short, has changed the world as much as it has recorded it. The first thing the student of history has to recognise in this area is that photography does not merely document realities that would be the same if nobody took pictures of them. Photographic images constitute our reality in a way and to an extent that has no equivalent in earlier history. Increasingly, since the mid-nineteenth century, our perceptions of what reality *is* have been informed by photographic images, and it is on the basis of these perceptions that we – governments, companies, individuals – act. For historians, the resulting archive of millions upon millions of images is something of a mixed blessing. Photographs provide a source of information about the past that is without precedent in either its nature or its extent. But they also pose problems of analysis and interpretation which enormously complicate their use as historical sources. To paraphrase Karl Marx (who was writing of an equally pervasive feature of modernity, the commodity), the photograph seems, at first sight, a very simple thing, the image made by the action of light on a photosensitive medium. But on closer inspection it turns out to be a very queer entity indeed, abounding in metaphysical subtleties and theological niceties.[20] It is these subtleties and niceties that are the concern of this chapter.

The footprint of the real

On seeing the cave paintings of Lascaux soon after their discovery in 1940, Pablo Picasso is said to have exclaimed: 'We have invented nothing!'[21] Human beings have made visual images of the world around them since time out of mind. The Lascaux paintings themselves are estimated to be 17,000 years old. Regarding their modernist economy of line and flat swathes of colour, we might well agree with

Picasso that there is nothing new under the sun. But photography *is* new. The world's first successful photograph, Nicéphore Niépce's 'View from the Study Window at Gras', dates only from the summer of 1826 or 1827.[22] The new medium was not made public until Louis Jacques Mandé Daguerre and William Henry Fox Talbot announced their different photographic processes in Paris and London respectively in January 1839. The world's first photographic studio opened in New York City in March 1840; ten years later the city had fifty-nine studios (and over 100 by 1853).[23] Few, then, could have foreseen how thoroughly the little device Daguerre thought would aid 'collections of all kinds' and 'greatly please ladies'[24] would transform the world. But even if its ever-expanding range of applications was not yet clear, photography was recognised as a discovery that 'partakes of the prodigious' from its very inception.

Early commentators were remarkably perceptive about what distinguished the photograph from its artistic predecessors, such as the drawing, the painting, the engraving and the lithograph. 'M. Daguerre', wrote H. Gaucheraud in *La Gazette de France*,

> has found the way to fix the images which paint themselves within a camera obscura,[25] so that these images are no longer transient reflections of objects, but *their fixed and everlasting impress* which, like a painting or engraving, *can be taken away from the presence of the objects*. . . . Imagine the faithfulness of nature's image reproduced in the camera and add to it the work of the sun's rays which fix this image, with all its range of highlights, shadows and half-tones, and you will have an idea of the beautiful drawings with which M. Daguerre, to our great interest, displayed. M. Daguerre does not work on paper at all; he must have polished metal plates. We have seen on copper several views of boulevards, the Pont Marie and its surroundings and a lot of other places rendered with a truth which nature alone can give to her works. M. Daguerre shows you the piece of bare copper, he puts it in his apparatus before your eyes, and at the end of three minutes – if the summer sun is shining, a few more if autumn or winter weakens the strength of the sun's rays – he takes out the metal and shows it to you covered with an enchanting drawing of the object towards which the apparatus was pointed. It is only a matter of a short washing operation, I believe, and there is the view which has been conquered in so few minutes, everlastingly fixed, so that the strongest sunlight can do nothing to destroy it.[26]

The novelty of the photographic image is far more than just a matter of its being a relative latecomer on the historical stage. What the photograph does is also radically new. Though, tellingly, Gaucheraud still describes Daguerre's image as a 'drawing', that is precisely what it is not. Photography differs from all previous genres of visual representation in its ability to produce objective images of the visible world by purely mechanical means.

In the first book to be illustrated by photographs, which he titled *The Pencil of Nature* (1844–46), Fox Talbot boasted that 'the plates shown in this work have been produced solely by the action of light, without any help from the artist's hand'.[27] However faithfully rendered a Rembrandt portrait or a Vermeer interior may be, they remain, transparently, works of art – artefacts of the human hand whose resemblance to their subjects is entirely dependent upon the artist's knowledge and skill in manipulating materials. What is pictured in the photograph, by contrast, traces its own image by the action of light on a photosensitive surface. On seeing Daguerre's 'View of the Boulevard du Temple'[28] on 7 March 1839, Samuel Morse – the inventor of the electric telegraph – was astonished by both the fidelity of the image and the impossibility of producing anything comparable by traditional manual means:

> No painting or drawing could ever hope to touch it. For example, when looking over a street one might notice a distant advertisement hoarding and be aware of the existence of lines or letters, without being able to read these tiny signs with the naked eye. With the help of a hand-lens, pointed at this detail, each letter became perfectly and clearly visible, and it was the same thing for the tiny cracks on the walls of buildings or the pavements of the streets.[29]

The photographic image, we might say, is not a likeness of reality so much as its trace or footprint. Unlike a painting or drawing, which may be the product of nothing but the artist's imagination, we can be confident that what we see in a photograph *was once there*. That ghostly presence of the past in turn haunts its each and every reproduction. A photograph gives us the ability to recapture 'the decisive moment', as the photographer Henri Cartier-Bresson called it, at will. 'I prowled the streets all day,' he relates, 'feeling very strung-up and ready to pounce, determined to "trap" life – to preserve life in the act of living. Above all, I craved to seize, in the confines of one single photograph, the whole essence of some situation that was in the process of unrolling itself before my eyes.'[30] Along with the war photographer Robert Capa and others, Cartier-Bresson went on to found the world's most prestigious photographic agency, Magnum Photos, in 1947. 'When you picture an iconic image, but can't think who took it or where it can be found, it probably came from Magnum,' boasts the agency's website – with some justice.[31]

This uncanny connection between the image and its referent – the thing of which it is a photograph – provides the starting-point for one of the most celebrated of modern meditations on photography, Roland Barthes's last book, *Camera Lucida*. 'What the Photograph reproduces to infinity', he begins, 'has occurred only once: the Photograph mechanically repeats what could never be repeated existentially'.

> In the photograph, the event is never transcended for the sake of something else: the Photograph always leads the corpus back to the body I see; it is the absolute Particular, the sovereign Contingency, matte and somehow stupid, the *This* (this photograph, and not Photography), in short, what Lacan calls the *Tuché*, the Occasion, the Encounter, the Real, in its indefatigable expression.[32]

'A specific photograph,' he goes on, 'in effect, is never distinguished from its referent (from what it represents), or at least it is not *immediately* or *generally* distinguished from its referent (as is the case for every other image, encumbered – from the start, and because of its status – by the way in which the object is simulated).' While some professionals may be able to identify 'the photographic signifier', it takes an act of conscious reflection to do so. In the case of the written documents with which the historian usually deals, the status of language as a system of signifiers is clear. Nobody would confuse the words on the page with the objects or events to which they refer. We have developed an appropriate critical apparatus for dealing with textual sources, which embraces not only their provenance (which documents have been archived, how, why and by whom) but also their stylistics and contents. On looking at a photograph, on the other hand, what most of us see is not an assemblage of signifiers but simply the thing that it is a picture of. 'By nature,' Barthes continues, 'the Photograph . . . has something tautological about it: a pipe, here, is always and intractably a pipe.' He is alluding to René Magritte's painting *The Treachery of Images*, which portrays a meticulously painted pipe beneath which are written the words 'This is not a pipe' [*Ceci n'est-pas une pipe*]: a clear warning not to confuse images with things. Nevertheless, Barthes insists, '[i]t is as if the Photograph always carries its referent with itself, both affected by the same amorous or funereal immobility, at the very heart of the moving world . . . Whatever it grants to vision and whatever its manner, *a photograph is always invisible: it is not it that we see*. In short, the referent adheres.'[33]

This adherence of the image to its subject gives photography a unique documentary authority; the camera, in the popular dictum, does not lie. Every photograph, from Niépce's grainy and mirror-reversed view from his study window to Cindy Sherman's 'Film Stills' (in which the artist photographs herself in diverse wigs, costumes and settings, mimicking scenes from B-movies that never existed) or the fashion fantasias of Helmut Newton, Herb Ritts, or Guy Bourdin, is a *document* – and all photography, no matter what its subject-matter and irrespective of whether or not it is 'staged', is documentary photography.[34] What we see in a photograph – any photograph – was once in front of the lens. It might indeed be argued that photographs are among the purest documents that historians could possess. Which, we might ask, take us closer to nineteenth-century urban life, the descriptions in Friedrich Engels's *The Condition of the Working Class in England in 1844* or the images collected in Thomas Annan's *Old Closes and Streets of Glasgow* and Jacob Riis's *How the Other Half Lives*?[35] Which of these sources deserves to be regarded as the most primary, given that a photograph is by definition exactly contemporary with that which it depicts? Whatever difficulties might attend their interpretation, photographs would seem to offer the same advantages as hearing the recorded voice of the operatic divas Adelina Patti or Nellie Melba over reading a critic's review of the singing of Maria Malibran or Giuditta Pasta, both of whom died before the advent of sound recording. In both cases we are in the presence of the direct trace of the past, unfiltered by the wiles and guiles of language. Photographs, like gramophone recordings, are the literal records of realities from which all language, including the language of contemporaries, is always already at one remove.

Such considerations led the organisers of the exhibition *here is new york* to show more than 5,000 photographs of the attacks of 11 September 2001, shot 'with every conceivable kind of apparatus, from Leicas and digital Nikons to homemade pinhole cameras and little plastic gizmos that schoolchildren wear on their wrists', without attribution, titles, or framing. They believed that these photographs could stand as direct witness to what happened on that sunny morning, drawing our gaze and our minds back to 'the thing itself'. 'Photography', they comment, 'was the perfect medium to express what happened on 9/11, because it is democratic and infinitely reproducible . . . The guiding principle of *here is new york* is simple: if one photograph tells a story, thousands of photographs not only tell thousands of stories but perhaps begin to tell *the* story if they are allowed to speak for themselves, to each other, and to the viewer directly, not framed either by glass, metal, or wood, or by preconception and editorial comment'.[36] Given the mass of verbiage with which 9/11 was all too soon surrounded, one can see their point.[37] But unfortunately the magic of photography is more complicated than that. It is time that we turned our attention away from the referent and looked instead at the photograph itself.

Machine dreams

'For better or worse,' Dorothea Lange reminded her fellow-photographers in 1952 – by which time cameras had come a long way from Talbot and Daguerre – 'the destiny of a photographer is bound up with the destinies of a machine.'[38] Precisely because it is captured and reproduced by 'purely mechanical means' what is seen (as reality, remember) in the photographic image is affected by the characteristics of the entire technical apparatus through which it is produced, from shooting and developing to printing and duplicating. Let us look again at Daguerre's 'View of the Boulevard du Temple'. It is famous for being the first photograph to contain the image of a living human being: two human beings to be precise, which is rather odd, considering that this was a bustling Paris thoroughfare photographed in the bright light of day. Samuel Morse explained: '[m]oving objects leave no impression [on Daguerre's plate]. The boulevard, though constantly crossed by a flood of pedestrians and carriages, appeared completely deserted, apart from a person who was having his boots polished. His feet must, of course, have remained immobile for a certain time, one of them being placed on the boot-black's box, the other on the ground.'[39] The exposure-time, which at that date was still several minutes, was too long to be able to capture objects in motion (Niépce's 'View' had required several hours, so this was already a considerable advance). This famous image, then, tells the truth but by no means the whole truth. There is no doubt that the photograph carries the impress of the real, but what it portrays is equally certainly not what we ordinarily experience as reality.

The independent discovery by both Daguerre and Fox Talbot of the latent image – an invisible image that can subsequently be chemically developed – shortened exposure times considerably. These were further reduced between 1839 and 1841 through a combination of faster lenses and chemical improvements to the photosensitivity of the platform on which the image is recorded, though head-braces fixed to the sitter's chair long remained a fixture of nineteenth-century portrait studios, resulting in a rigidity in posture and facial expression that can easily be mistaken for Victorian stiffness – and may well have coloured our later perceptions of that phenomenon. The limitations of early photographic tech-nologies long continued to restrict what could be caught on camera. Up until the 1850s most studios produced daguerreotypes rather than calotypes (as Fox Talbot baptised his process when he patented it in 1841) because daguerreotypes were vastly superior in their detail. The major drawback of Daguerre's process, however, was that it produced a unique positive image, like a transparency, rather than a negative from which an infinite number of identical prints could later be made. This severely limited its commercial applications. Imperfect as Talbot's earliest calotypes were as images, the principles on which they were based would provide the foundation for all subsequent photography.

The wet-plate process discovered by F. Scott Archer in 1851 replaced Talbot's paper negatives with glass plates coated with silver salts in a viscous collodion binder that yielded a much clearer negative, seemingly offering the best of both worlds.[40] The plates were sensitised immediately before use and had to be developed quickly. The cost was the bulky paraphernalia of chemicals and plates the photographer had to cart around, as Roger Fenton's photograph of the wine wagon he converted into a mobile darkroom to photograph the Crimean War testifies. Fenton was not, as is often claimed, the first war photographer; around fifty anonymous daguerreotypes, including one of a (possibly re-enacted) battlefield amputation, survive from the Mexican–American War of 1846–48, while the British surgeon John MacCosh took calotypes during the Second Sikh War (1848–49) and the Second Burma War (1852–53).[41] But Fenton's images, many of which were quite obviously posed, do illustrate the difficulties that attended early combat photography. 'It was at this time', he writes, 'that the plague of flies commenced. Before preparing a plate the first thing to be done was to battle with them for possession of the place. The necessary buffeting with handkerchiefs and towels having taken place, and the intruders having being expelled, the moment the last one was out, the door has to be rapidly closed for fear of a fresh invasion, and then some time allowed for the dust thus raised to settle before coating a plate.'[42]

It is scarcely surprising that there are no 'action shots' in Fenton's *oeuvre*, though whether the reality of war is better communicated by Robert Capa's famous blurry close-ups of the D-Day Normandy landings or (for example) by Timothy H. O'Sullivan's static but eloquent 'Quarters of Men in Fort Sedgwick, Generally Known as Fort Hell' (1865) is moot. Fenton's most famous image is 'The Valley of the Shadow of Death' (1855, Figure 4.1) which shows the (purported) scene of the disastrous charge of the Light Brigade the year before. There is controversy over whether this picture, too, was faked: it exists in two versions, in the second of which there are many more cannonballs strewn across the road which stretches through low hills to the horizon, leading to speculation that Fenton might have strategically placed them there himself in order to lend greater 'authenticity' to the scene. What was not faked, but was not exactly real either, was the blank sky that adds immeasurably to the sense of desolation conveyed by the image: it was a side-effect of the collodion process whose sensitivity to blue gave the photographer the choice between an over-exposed sky or an under-exposed foreground. Professionals sometimes got around this problem by taking two negatives with different exposures, then artificially combining them to produce a more 'realistic' print.

It is worth mentioning in passing that we only know Fenton's photograph is a war photograph at all from its caption, which alludes to Tennyson's famous poem on the Charge of the Light Brigade ('Half a league, half a league, half a league onward, All in the Valley of Death, rode the six hundred'), and beyond that Psalm 23 – references that may make the image less immediately intelligible to many viewers today than it was to the God-fearing and poetry-reading Victorians. In looking at any photograph, and in particular in seeking to use it as documentary evidence, it is essential to distinguish the purely visual information contained in the image from associations deriving from its context. There is nothing in Fenton's photograph that shows us it was taken in the Crimea in 1855. We bring meanings to what we see in the image, guided in this case by the caption.

Similar associations are set up by juxtaposition of images with text, as in newspaper articles, or with other images, as in photo-essays or art exhibitions. An

Figure 4.1 Roger Fenton, 'The Valley of the Shadow of Death'. Salt print, 1855. Library of Congress, Prints and Photographs Division, Washington DC.

excellent example of the latter is furnished by the *Family of Man* exhibition that took place under the direction of Edward Steichen at New York's Museum of Modern Art in 1955. The exhibition, which travelled to thirty-seven countries over the next eight years, consisted of '503 photographs grouped thematically around subjects pertinent to all cultures, such as love, children, and death'. By focusing on 'the commonalties that bind people and cultures around the world', the blurb on the historical section of the MoMA website continues, 'the exhibition served as an expression of humanism in the decade following World War II'.[43] Steichen's introduction certainly suggests that the intention was to use photographs as 'a mirror of the universal elements and emotions in the everydayness of life – as a mirror of the essential oneness of mankind throughout the world',[44] but (as many critics have pointed out) this representation of human oneness effaced cultural, not to mention political and ideological, differences in favour of a very American universality. Were we to encounter the same images in another context they might impact on us altogether differently. It is a caution to be borne in mind approaching any photographic archive, including those that are now widely available on the internet. We need to be every bit as critical towards the categories that dictate the selection and ordering of photographic images ('American Memory', for instance) as we would be towards similar compilations of written documents.

In due course the kind of technical obstacles that beset Fenton would be overcome. By the turn of the twentieth century even amateurs could turn out decent images, leaving the business of development and printing to commercial companies: the Kodak roll-film box camera was launched in June 1888 under the slogan 'You press the button, we do the rest!' It would be easy to chart the history of photography as a story of unbroken progress, and assume that every improvement in technique – sharper lenses, the move from glass plates to film, the development of flash, the introduction of the 35mm camera, the multiplication of megapixels on digital cameras – brings the image that much closer to its subject. Such technical advances have undeniably permitted ever more accurate capturing of what is in front of the lens. Whether this means the image better reflects what we normally experience as *reality*, however, is a different matter. When in 1878 Edward Muybridge used high-speed sequential photographs to demonstrate that all four of a horse's legs leave the ground at once when it is galloping[45] – thereby settling a bet – his camera was revealing something invisible to the human eye, which is no more able to isolate such movements than Daguerre's apparatus was able to record the pedestrians and carriages on the Boulevard du Temple. The same is true of the razor-sharp images served up in today's sports photography of the athlete in full flight while the crowd behind is a blur; the opposite of what our eyes actually see if we are present at the event.

Perhaps less obviously, the so-called 'pure photographs' of American landscapes produced by Ansel Adams and other members of the celebrated f64 Group used aperture settings that produce a depth of field (the distance over which things are simultaneously in focus) that far exceeds the perceptual range of the human eye. Adams's beloved photographs of the Rocky Mountains, familiar the world over, show us the American landscape as we could never view it in 'reality'.[46]

Paradoxically, the closer that zoom and wide-angle lenses, fast film, variable aperture settings and shutter-speeds, artificial lighting and the rest of the technical gizmos of modern photography take us to 'the real', the further the image some-times gets from the reality of human experience – from what, that is to say, we would have taken to be reality had the camera not revealed it in a different light. The world as our senses experience it does not come in black and white (or more accurately in the graduated shades of Adams's grey scale) either, as it did in most photographs before the mid-twentieth century. Nor do we ever experience reality as a sequence of still images; photographs not only 'freeze' time, they abstract from the very dimension in which human lives are lived. Roland Barthes's remark on the photograph's 'amorous or funereal immobility, at the very heart of the moving world' needs to be taken seriously. In immobilising the moving world, the camera arguably distorts it.

Instead of attempting to chart a linear progression in the camera's ability to document reality, we need to recognise how different photographic technologies produce different kinds of image. Professional photographers have always made use of the range of possibilities offered by their equipment to achieve varied pictorial ends, of which the fidelity to Nature sought by Ansel Adams – or Henry Fox Talbot – is but one. Anyone who believes Daguerre's process was superseded because of its optical limitations would do well to look at Chuck Close's series of daguerreotypes of Kate Moss, produced in 2003. Close himself made it clear that 'I'm not interested in daguerreotypes because it's an antiquarian process; I like them because, from my point of view, photography never got any better than it was in 1840.' Among the features of the technique he believed were unmatched by any later photographic developments were 'a range from the deepest, darkest velvety blacks to the brightest highlights that reflect into your eyes. Each picture has unbelievable detail and very shallow depth of field.'[47] Every tiny line on the face, every pore and pock mark on the skin, is ruthlessly exposed, deconstructing the ubiquitous images of the supermodel with which we are all too familiar from billboards, TV advertisements and the covers of fashion magazines. Moss, whose fame and fortune have been built entirely on the camera's transmutation of her face and body into a mass-produced and mass-consumed image, is alleged to have commented that there were more than enough beautiful pictures of her out there already. Her favourite image of herself, she said in a recent interview, is Lucien Freud's very far from glossy oil painting of her naked and pregnant.[48]

Chuck Close is not the only modern photographer to have deliberately chosen to work with 'archaic' equipment and techniques. The period between the two World Wars was an explosive decade in the development of photography fuelled by technical advances (the 35mm Leica camera, whose combination of quality and portability revolutionised photojournalism, was invented in 1925), the mushrooming of popular illustrated magazines (*Life* first appeared in 1936), and an avant-garde sensibility determined to break with the artistic conventions of the past. At the same time as the militant young Soviet photographer Aleksandr Rodchenko was lam-basting 'navel level photography'[49] and developing a new visual vocabulary of breathtaking camera angles, bold compositions and exaggerated contrasts of light and shade, an old man named Eugène Atget was completing his lifework of photographing the streets, shops, statues, squares, parks and interiors of Paris – with a tripod-mounted nineteenth-century bellows camera that used by then very old-fashioned glass negatives. Atget modestly saw himself as no more than a producer of 'documents for artists', that is, images from which painters could paint their own landscapes. Like Daguerre's 'View of the Boulevard du Temple', his pictures are largely empty of people because he found it easiest, given the bulkiness of his equipment, to photograph early in the morning when nobody was up and about. The haunting simplicity of his work appealed to the Paris surrealists, and (largely through the efforts of Berenice Abbott, who bought and printed many of his negatives)[50] went on to exercise a major influence on 'the New Vision' – a style characterised by rejection of what were now seen as the excesses of *fin de siècle* pictorialism, which had aimed at producing photographs that were not merely mimetic documents but works of art in their own right.[51] Atget, who died in 1927, was an unlikely posthumous star of the 1929 Stuttgart exhibition *Film und Foto*, the largest showcase of avant-garde photography to take place in Europe between the wars.[52]

The one-armed Czech photographer Josef Sudek was another who chose to use an 1899 Kodak Panoram camera for his famous series *Panoramic Prague* (1959), which, like Atget's work, lovingly documents obscure corners of his city. Less well known, in part because the Czechoslovak communist authorities would not permit its exhibition or publication, is his series *Sad Landscape*, which he shot in the early 1960s.[53] Turning his back on the strong geometries, sharp focuses and heightened contrasts with which Jaromír Funke, Jaroslav Rössler, Eugen Wiškovský and others among his Czech contemporaries had dramatised the machine age (and he himself had employed in his stunningly modernist advertising photography of the 1930s),[54] Sudek used the same antique apparatus to photograph the ecologically devastated landscapes of Northern Bohemia, one of the most polluted areas in Europe. He took his pictures entirely in natural light, eschewed all zooming or cropping, and reproduced his images through contact prints taken directly from the glass plate negatives, refusing any enlargements. The prints reproduce every detail of the vast landscape in minutely graduated shades of grey, with no contrived or artificially emphasised highlights. 'Here is the silence of an unnatural landscape beneath a sky struck dumb with horror,' comments the critic Antonín Dufek. 'It is a parable for the dead end that is "rational" civilization, a metaphor that presents the other side of humanism.'[55] It is also a salutary reminder that much as the destiny of a photographer may be bound up with the destinies of a machine, that machine is always operated by the hand and mind of an artist. This brings me to the final set of issues I wish to consider here.

The language of images

Debates between proponents of the photograph as document and the photograph as art have divided photographers and critics since the medium's inception, with the pendulum swinging now this way and now that. During the first half of the twentieth century, advocates of what was (in some ways misleadingly, as the example of Ansel Adams shows) billed as 'pure' or 'straight' photography often linked their preference for unvarnished documentation to a political commitment to record and publicise unpalatable social truths. Walker Evans's teaming up with James Agee to produce the book *Let Us Now Praise Famous Men*, in which Evans's stark pictures of southern American sharecroppers' poverty illustrate Agee's inflammatory text, is a famous example.[56]

Such photographic 'realism' also had its champions on the other side of the Atlantic. Addressing 'The Tasks of Modern Photography' in an article of 1931, the Czech avant-garde leader Karel Teige praised the 'line of honest work devoid of artistic tricks . . . followed principally by reportage and documentary photography'. Alongside the work of the nineteenth-century Paris portrait photographer Nadar, he singled out Atget's photographs, which had recently been exhibited in *Film und Foto*, as being 'among the most beautiful works of the black-and-white chemistry of light'. 'It is characteristic of the images of this early era', he continues, 'that they are artistically undemanding, truthful in relation to the depicted object, and have a relatively high degree of technical perfection: honest work which is not glancing surreptitiously at painting and does not have to fear its competition'. He gives the experimental photographers of his own age – Man Ray, André Kertész, Berenice Abbott, Germaine Krull and Moholy-Nagy among others – their due for having 'enriched our visual experience and sharpened our ability to look and see', but warns of a slippery slope:

> W. Peterhans photographed, with masterly technique and miraculous perfection, cigarette butts, leftovers, fragments of objects, pieces of string: to show people facets of reality which they are unable to notice or unable to see? Why not? But enough is enough: to offer the thousand and first variation is not desirable. To demonstrate and study all the possibilities of photography, through manifold view angles, lens systems, negative prints, multiple printing, double exposure, etc.? Of course that is very important. However: have we acquired all these techniques just for the sake of using them, or to achieve a higher goal? Avant-garde photography, celebrating its successes by exhibitions and books, is slowly withering into a sick *l'art-pour-l'artisme*.[57]

Twenty years later Berenice Abbott, who had brought Atget's work to the attention of the world and attempted to emulate it in her own book *Changing New York* (1935–38),[58] took up the same cudgels in a denunciation of the 'super-pictorialists' (as she derided them) Edward Steichen – the future organiser of *The Family of Man* – Alfred Stieglitz, founder of the influential pictorialist magazine *Camera Work* (1903–17) and Paul Strand. She presents a remarkably similar history of the supposed highs and lows in the evolution of photography to Karel Teige's, albeit with an American rather than European slant. Like Teige she praises the unpretentious virtues of scientific photography, amateur photography and reportage. Her heroes (apart from Nadar and Atget) are the Civil War photographers Mathew Brady and Timothy O'Sullivan and the landscape photographer William Henry Jackson, while her villain is (the Englishman) Henry Peach

Robinson, whose 1869 book *Pictorial Photography* launched what she calls the 'terrible plague' of 'subjectivist' and 'sentimental' photography that ruled the roost at the turn of the century. 'A photograph', she insists, 'is not a painting, a poem, a symphony, a dance. It is not just a pretty picture, not an exercise in contortionist techniques and sheer print quality. It is or should be a significant document, a penetrating statement, which can be described in a very simple term – selectivity.' She goes on:

> [t]o chart a course, one must have a direction. In reality, the eye is no better than the philosophy behind it. The photographer creates, evolves a better, more selective, more acute seeing eye by looking ever more sharply at what is going on in the world. Like every other means of expression, photography, if it is to be utterly honest and direct, should be related to the life of the times – the pulse of today. The photograph may be presented as finely and artistically as you will; but to merit serious consideration, must be directly connected with the world we live in.[59]

As result of her assault on the American photographic establishment, Abbott found it impossible to exhibit her work or obtain magazine commissions for the next twenty years (which might remind us of the fate of Sudek's *Sad Landscape*).[60]

It would be understandable if historians were more drawn to the kinds of images Teige and Abbott championed than to, say, the romantic visions of a Julia Margaret Cameron or the surrealist fantasies of Hans Bellmer or Man Ray. They are more obviously and palpably documents. The documentary/pictorialist opposition, I would nonetheless argue, cannot finally be sustained. Notwithstanding all the tricks of the pictorialist trade, from soft-focus shooting to airbrushing of negatives to fanciful colour printing, the mechanical means through which the image is captured ultimately limit the artistic liberties that can be taken with it. A photograph can never be a pure product of the artist's imagination; it will always carry the imprint of the real. Equally, however, all photographs also remain images, and as such – like other works of art – they communicate as signifiers. Precisely because, to echo Gaucheraud's response to Daguerre, the photographic image 'can be taken away from the presence of the objects' it depicts, the same *différance*[61] obtains between the image and its referent as holds between signifier and signified within language. Photographs acquire meaning not – or at any rate not only – through their relation to their subject, but also from their multiple references to a wider culture. What they conjure up (connote) is as significant as what they portray (denote), and what they connote depends not on their relation to the real but to other signifiers. Dorothea Lange's 'Migrant Mother' – which some have claimed to be the most reproduced image in the history of photography – exemplifies the point well.[62] This celebrated portrait of a destitute itinerant pea-picker cradling her children, which became an iconic image of the Great Depression, works, in part, because of the way it evokes a long tradition of mother and child religious painting.

In this respect the elements of a photograph are analogous to the words in a written text and pose equally difficult problems of interpretation. A photograph may have a meaning for us even if we are completely ignorant of whom or what it is a picture of, or where and when the picture was taken. What the image connotes, suggests, recalls, or in a word signifies is independent of what it depicts. Photographic signifiers, to complicate matters still further, are neither simple nor stable; similar subjects may have quite different connotations for different viewers in different cultural contexts. Nick Ut's photograph of villagers fleeing the napalm attack at Trang Bang has become an iconic image of the Vietnam War largely because its central figure – and the photograph is composed to make her the central figure – is a naked little girl. In this context the conjunction of femininity, childhood and nakedness makes for an extraordinarily powerful visual symbol of vulnerability. In other contexts, however, a naked pre-pubescent female body would have other connotations entirely. In the infamous series of advertisements for Calvin Klein perfume shot by Mario Sorrenti, which featured in *Vogue*, *Vanity Fair*, *Elle*, *Rolling Stone* and *GQ* in the early 1990s, a naked and waif-like Kate Moss sends out unmistakably Lolita messages; Sorrenti's best-known image shoots her languorously stretched out face down on a sofa beneath the word 'Obsession', the breasts that would signify adulthood artfully hidden from view.[63] There is nothing comparably sexual, one might think, in Sally Mann's exquisite photographs of her own children in her book *Immediate Family*, which was first published to enormous acclaim by *Aperture*, one of the world's most respected photography magazines, in 1992. The children, Emmett, Jessie and Virginia, are often caught naked in the open air and at first glance their nakedness connotes no more than childish innocence: '[t]he withering perspective of the past, the predictable treacheries of the future; for the moment, those familiar complications of time all play harmlessly around them as dancing shadows beneath the great oak,'[64] Mann writes. But her work has been widely criticised since then in an increasingly puritanical America, and 'Venus After School' suggests why.[65] In this photograph, which was not included in *Immediate Family*, the naked pre-pubescent girl is posed in the exact position of the prostitute who posed for Manet's *Olympia*, a painting that scandalised Paris when it was first exhibited in 1863. Having seen 'Venus After School', we may be tempted to re-read, and newly sexualise, the 'innocent' images in *Immediate Family* itself.

The photograph, then, may always be a document, but it is never just a document. And (as Teige and Abbott both tacitly acknowledge) what allows the image to 'speak' – to revert to the rhetoric of *here is new york* – is not, or at least not just, the fidelity with which it captures the real but the facility with which it can signify within and across cultural contexts. Unfortunately for proponents of 'pure photography', this facility has everything to do with aesthetics: framing, angle, composition, balance of light and shade, focus, lighting – as their own work demonstrates perhaps above all. Lange was sufficiently concerned with 'artistic presentation' to take several trial shots until she had the little family posed in 'Migrant Mother' just as she wanted them, and to crop an intrusive thumb, which detracted from the symmetry of the composition, from the final negative.[66] Walker Evans is alleged to have rearranged the sparse furnishings of the shacks he photographed for *Let Us Now Praise Famous Men* to similar ends. Nothing fraudulent was going on here: these photographs remain authentic documents of the Dirty Thirties. But they are also more eloquent documents than most, because of the artistic skills deployed by their authors. Both photographers were professionals with an eye for what made a good image and an acute awareness that if their results failed as images, they likely would not work as messages.

The camera, then, does not tell nothing-but-the-truth either; everything about how the real is photographed and how those images are read derives from culture – the world of human reality, which is constituted in language, including visual languages. Empirically minded historians, all too inclined to cut to the chase of what is 'in the picture' and leave issues of semiotics and aesthetics to the cultural theorists, ignore such concerns at their peril. The symbolist vocabulary of *fin de siècle* pictorialism tells us as much about the sensibility of the age as the subjects of pictorialist photographs; so does the exuberant embrace of stripped-down, ornament-free modernism that characterised avant-garde photography between the wars, lending a common and instantly recognisable visual aspect to subjects as diverse as Moholy-Nagy's photograms, Rodchenko's propaganda montages of the building of the White Sea Canal, and Edward Weston's nudes.[67] This visual lexicon is part of – and constitutive of – the same modernity as Le Corbusier's architecture, Marcel Breuer's tubular steel chairs, or Harry Beck's map of the London Underground. Sudek's *Sad Landscape* differs from the photographs his Czech contemporaries were taking in the 1930s not in its subject-matter but in its vision, and in this difference there is much to be learned about how pre-war modernist dreams turned to post-war communist nightmares. In looking at photographs, in short, we need to attend to *the photograph itself* – the assemblage of signifiers Roland Barthes says is invisible – instead of focusing, as historians are wont to do, simply on what it depicts. The same might of course be argued of written sources, but that is an issue beyond the scope of this chapter.

In lieu of a conclusion: 'Falling Man'

Rather than end with a tedious academic recapitulation of main points, among them why students of history should make more use of the rich legacy of photography as a source than historians usually do, I would prefer to conclude with an image that encapsulates the two wings of what I have tried to argue here: on the one hand, the awesome power of the photograph to shape our perceptions of the world, which derives from its ineradicable origins in the real, and on the other, its equally inescapable entanglement in the realm of culture, which means that like all other images it is caught in the webs of signification through which it acquires and communicates meaning.

It is chilling, as well as salutary, to realise that of the thousands of photographs taken in New York on 11 September 2001 the one likely to become most emblematic of the event – to stick in, and therefore shape, the historical memory – will do so as much for its aesthetic qualities as for its subject-matter, which it comes perilously close to beautifying. I am speaking of Richard Drew's 'Falling Man', which I am sure most readers will have seen, even if they probably could not identify its author. If not, the photograph, which was first published in the *New York Times* and reproduced in newspapers all over the world, is readily available online. It shows one of hundreds of people – an anonymous man – who chose to jump from the upper floors of the stricken towers rather than be burned alive. Tom Junod describes the image as follows:

> In the picture, he departs from this earth like an arrow. Although he has not chosen his fate, he appears to have, in his last instants of life, embraced it. If he were not falling, he might very well be flying. He appears relaxed, hurtling through the air. He appears comfortable in the grip of unimaginable motion. He does not appear intimidated by gravity's divine suction or by what awaits him. His arms are by his side, only slightly outriggered. His left leg is bent at the knee, almost casually. His white shirt, or jacket, or frock, is billowing free of his black pants. His black high-tops are still on his feet. In all the other pictures, the people who did what he did – who jumped – appear to be struggling against horrific discrepancies of scale. They are made puny by the backdrop of the towers, which loom like colossi, and then by the event itself. Some of them are shirtless; their shoes fly off as they flail and fall; they look confused, as though trying to swim down the side of a mountain. The man in the picture, by contrast, is perfectly vertical, and so is in accord with the lines of the buildings behind him. He splits them, bisects them: everything to the left of him in the picture is the North Tower; everything to the right, the South. Though oblivious to the geometric balance he has achieved, he is the essential element in the creation of a new flag, a banner composed entirely of steel bars shining in the sun. Some people who look at the picture see stoicism, will-power, a portrait of resignation; others see something else – something discordant and therefore terrible: freedom. There is something almost rebellious in the man's posture, as though once faced with the inevitability of death, he decided to get on with it; as though he were a missile, a spear, bent on attaining his own end. He is, fifteen seconds past 9:41 a.m. EST, the moment the picture is taken, in the clutches of pure physics, accelerating at a rate of thirty-two feet per second squared. He will soon be traveling at upwards of 150 miles per hour, and he is upside down. In the picture, he is frozen; in his life outside the frame, he drops and keeps dropping until he disappears.[68]

The falling man, Junod might have added, not only bisects the picture perfectly but is positioned just above the centre of the frame, exactly as we would mount a photograph in a frame for hanging on a wall. I cannot believe the image was not cropped to achieve this end. Richard Drew is a professional; his earlier photographic credits include the assassination of Robert F. Kennedy (whose wife Ethel vainly begged him not to take pictures of her dying husband). Drew later told *Esquire* magazine that after shooting scores of photographs that morning he slipped the disk of his digital camera into his computer and on finding 'Falling Man' knew he need look no further. He had caught Cartier-Bresson's decisive moment. 'You learn in photo editing to look for the frame,' he explained. 'You have to recognize it. That picture just jumped off the screen because of its verticality and symmetry. It just had that look.'[69] This is the same look, the same frame, the same fearful symmetry, as Alexander Clausel's 1855 daguerreotype 'Landscape near Troyes, France',[70] whose compositional harmonies turn what might otherwise be an unremarkable bend in a river into an object of sublime and eternal contemplation.

Notes

1 This chapter is best read in conjunction with the images it discusses, but for reasons of lack of space (or cost of permissions) it has not been possible to reproduce them here. To facilitate access I have given online locations where most of these images can be found. General internet resources include: 'Masters of Photography' (http://www. masters-of-photography.com/, abbreviated as MP); the George Eastman House archive (http://www.geh.org/, abbreviated as GEH); and the 'Luminous Lint' site (http://www. luminous-lint.com/app/home/, abbreviated as LL). Wherever possible I have located the relevant images on these sites below.

2 László Moholy-Nagy, 'Photography in advertising' (1927), translated in Christopher Phillips (ed.), *Photography in the Modern Era: European Documents and Critical Writings, 1913–1940*, New York: Museum of Modern Art/Aperture, 1989, p. 90. The latter anthology is an excellent collection of primary source materials for the relevant period. See also Nathan Lyons (ed.), *Photographers on Photography*, New York: Prentice-Hall, 1966; Beaumont Newhall (ed.), *Photography: Essays and Images. Illustrated Readings in the History of Photography*, New York: Museum of Modern Art, 1980; and Alan Trachtenberg (ed.), *Classic Essays on Photography*, New Haven, CT: Leete's Island Books, 1980. There are a multitude of histories of photography; I would strongly recommend Mary Warner Marien, *Photography: A Cultural History* (2nd edn), London: Lawrence King, 2006, as a starting-point for students. The literature in photographic theory is similarly enormous. Here, I would suggest Susan Sontag's superb *On Photography*, New York: Farrar, Straus and Giroux, 1977, together with Roland Barthes, *Camera Lucida: Reflections on Photography*, New York: Hill and Wang, 1981, as a way into central debates. Robin Lenman (ed.), *The Oxford Companion to the Photograph*, London: Oxford University Press, 2005, and Michael R. Peres (ed.), *The Focal Encyclopedia of Photography* (4th edn), London: Elsevier, 2007, are comprehensive general works of reference.

3 Susan Sontag, *Regarding the Pain of Others*, New York: Farrar, Straus and Giroux, 2003, p. 18.

4 See, respectively, Guy Debord, *The Society of the Spectacle*, New York: Zone, 1995; Jean Baudrillard, *Simulacra and Simulation*, Ann Arbor: University of Michigan Press, 1995.

5 See the remarkable images reproduced at http://hubblesite.org/ (Hubble Telescope) or http://micro.magnet.fsu.edu/micro/gallery.html (examples of microphotography).

6 Early examples include Noël Lerebours's *Excursions Daguerriennes, représentant les vues et les monuments plus remarquables du globe* (1840–44), A. Schaefer's reliefs of the temple complex of Borobudur in what is now Indonesia (1845), Maxime du Camp's *Égypt, Nubie, Palestine et Syrie* (1852), Louis de Clercq's *Voyage en Orient, 1859–60: villes, monuments et vues pittoresques*, and Frances Frith's *Egypt, Sinai, Jerusalem* (1861). Much of the latter can be viewed at GEH and LL. The part played by photography in colonialism has been widely discussed; see, inter alia, James R. Ryan, *Picturing Empire: Photography and the Visualization of the British Empire*, Chicago: Chicago University Press, 1998; Eleanor Hight (ed.), *Colonialist Photography: Imag(in)ing Race and Place*, London: Routledge, 2002; Paul S. Landau and Deborah D. Kaspin (eds), *Images and Empire: Visuality in Colonial and Postcolonial Africa*,

Berkeley: University of California Press, 2003; and Christopher Pinney, *Camera Indica: the Social Life of Indian Photographs* (Chicago: Chicago University Press, 1997).
7 Work by Brassaï, Hine, and Riis can be viewed at MP. Both of Brassaï's volumes of photographs of 1930s Paris have been republished: *Paris by Night*, New York: Bulfinch, 2001; and *The Secret Paris of the '30s*, London: Thames and Hudson, 2001. For Weegee see http://www.getty.edu/art/gettyguide/artMakerDetails?maker=1887, and the virtual exhibition *Weegee's World: Life, Death and the Human Drama* at http://museum.icp.org/museum/collections/special/weegee/. Larry Sultan's work can be seen in his photo-essay *The Valley*, New York: Scalo, 2004. His artist statement for the companion exhibition at San Francisco Museum of Modern Art reads, in part:

> It is common for adult-film companies to shoot in tract houses – the homes of dentists and attorneys and day traders whose family photographs can be seen in the background, and whose decorating tastes give the films their particular look. It's as if one family went on vacation for a few days, leaving everything in the house intact, and another family, an odd assembly of unrelated adults, has temporarily taken up residence. While the film crew and talent are hard at work in the living room, I wander through the house peering into the lives of the people who live there. I feel like a forensic photographer searching out evidence.
>
> In these films, lazy afternoons are interrupted not by noisy children but by the uncontrollable desires of delivery boys, baby sitters, coeds and cops. They crowd in the master bedrooms and spill out onto the patios and into the pools that look just like our neighbors' pools, like our pool. And by photographing this I'm planted squarely in the terrain of my own ambivalence – that rich and fertile field that stretches out between fascination and repulsion, desire and loss. I'm home again.
>
> (http://www.tfaoi.com/aa/4aa/4aa422.htm, accessed 21 May 2008)

8 On lynching postcards see James Allen (ed.), *Without Sanctuary: Photographs of Lynching in America*, Santa Fe, NM: Twin Palms, 2000. Many of the images are reproduced at http://www.withoutsanctuary.org/.
9 Damien Hirst, as quoted in Rebecca Allison, '9/11 wicked but a work of art', *Guardian*, 11 September 2002, accessed 21 May 2008 at http://www.guardian.co.uk/uk/2002/sep/11/arts.september11.
10 See Beverley Brannan and Gilles Mora, *FSA: The American Vision*, New York: Abrams, 2006. FSA photographs can be viewed on the Library of Congress 'American Memory' website at http://lcweb2.loc.gov/fsowhome.html, and at the LL virtual exhibition http://www.luminous-lint.com/app/home/?action=ACT_VEX&p1=_THEME_Documentary_FSA_01&p2=1&p3=0&p4=0.
11 'The metropolis and mental life' (1903), in Georg Simmel, *On Individuality and Social Forms* (ed. Donald Levine), Chicago: University of Chicago Press, 1971.
12 Lange's 'Migrant Mother' (1936) can be seen at MP and LL. Some of Lee Miller's war photography is collected, along with her despatches, in Antony Penrose (ed.), *Lee Miller's War*, London: Thames and Hudson, 2005, as well as at http://www.leemiller.co.uk/. Nick Ut's photograph has been widely reproduced on the internet, including at http://digitaljournalist.org/issue0008/ng_intro.htm. His more recent photographic scoops include a sobbing Paris Hilton being returned to jail in June 2007.
13 Walter Benjamin, 'The work of art in the age of its technological reproducibility', in his *Selected Writings: Volume 4 1938–1940*, Cambridge: Belknap Press of Harvard University Press, 2003, pp. 251–83.
14 I discuss the theme of disenchantment, which is a central element in Weber's analysis of rationalisation – for him the defining feature of modernity – at length in Chapters 3 and 4 of my book *Capitalism and Modernity: An Excursus on Marx and Weber*, London: Routledge, 1990.

15 The circumstances whereby Picasso came to paint a scene of the bombing of Guernica, and a discussion of scale and image reproduction can be found in Chapter 2 of this volume, 'Art: the creative image', p. 21.

16 Charles Baudelaire, 'The modern public and photography' (1862), in Newhall, *Photography: Essays and Images*.

17 Surveillance cameras monitoring the movements of cars through Ipswich's red light district played a key role in identifying Steve Wright as a suspect in the murder of five young female sex workers in December 2006. Wright was convicted of the crimes in February 2008.

18 Michel Foucault, *Discipline & Punish: The Birth of the Prison*, New York: Vintage, 1995, p. 201.

19 For a range of examples, see the virtual exhibition *Cartes de visite* on LL, http://www.luminous-lint.com/app/vexhibit/_THEME_Carte_de_visite_01/1/0/0/.

20 Karl Marx, *Capital*, Volume 1, London: Lawrence and Wishart, 1967, p. 71.

21 Quoted in James Graff, 'Saving beauty', *Time Magazine*, 7 May 2006, at http://www.time.com/time/magazine/article/0,9171,901060515–1191806,00.html accessed 20 May 2008.

22 Nicéphore Niépce, 'View from the Study Window at Gras', http://www.hrc.utexas.edu/exhibitions/permanent/wfp/

23 Timm Starl, 'A new world of pictures: the use and spread of the daguerreotype process', in Michel Frizot (ed.), *A New History of Photography*, Cologne: Könemann, 1988, p. 43.

24 Quoted in Marien, *Photography: A Cultural History*, p. 14.

25 Known since antiquity, the camera obscura was a totally darkened room with a small hole drilled in one wall which used the diffraction of the light entering through it to project an upside-down image of the exterior scene on the opposite wall. A lens was added in the sixteenth century, and portable versions developed in the seventeenth. There was as yet no way, however, to make such images permanent.

26 H. Gaucheraud, 'The fine arts: a new discovery', *La Gazette de France*, 6 January 1839, translated in Newhall, *Photography: Essays and Images*, pp. 17–18. Emphasis added.

27 W.H. Fox Talbot, *The Pencil of Nature*, 1844–46, quoted in Frizot, *A New History of Photography*, p. 62.

28 Louis Jacques Mandé Daguerre, 'View of the Boulevard du Temple', http://upload.wikimedia.org/wikipedia/commons/thumb/1/1d/Boulevard_du_Temple.jpg/800px-Boulevard_du_Temple.jpg, undated.

29 Samuel Morse, undated letter, quoted in Frizot, *A New History of Photography*, p. 28.

30 Henri Cartier-Bresson, 'The decisive moment', in his *The Mind's Eye: Writings on Photography and Photographers*, New York: Aperture, 1999, p. 22.

31 http://agency.magnumphotos.com/about/about, accessed 20 May 2008.

32 Barthes, *Camera Lucida*, p. 4.

33 Barthes, *Camera Lucida*, pp. 5–7. Final emphasis added.

34 See Cindy Sherman, *The Complete Untitled Film Stills*, New York: Museum of Modern Art, 2003. Some of these can be seen at http://www.moma.org/exhibitions/1997/sherman/selectedworks.html, others at MP. Ritts' work may be sampled at http://www.herbritts.com/, Newton's at http://user.tninet.se/~ryk484d/newton/newton.htm, and Bourdin's at http://www.guybourdin.org/.

35 Friedrich Engels, *The Condition of the Working Class in England in 1844*, London: Swan Sonnenschein & Co., 1892; Jacob Riis, *How the Other Half Lives: Studies Among the Tenements of New York*, New York: Hill and Wang, 1971. See also note 7. Annan's *Old Closes and Streets*, first published in 1900, is reproduced in full on LL at http://www.luminous-lint.com/app/vexhibit/_PHOTOGRAPHER_Thomas__Annan_01/1/0/0/.

36 *here is new york: a democracy of photographs*, conceived and organised by Alice Rose George, Gilles Peress, Michael Shulan and Charles Traub, Zurich/Berlin/New York: Scalo, 2002, pp. 8–9. The entire archive can be seen at www.hereisnewyork.org.

37 See my article 'Wittgenstein at Ground Zero', *Space and Culture* 11.1, 2008, pp. 12–19.

38 Dorothea Lange, 'Photographing the familiar', in Lyons, *Photographers on Photography*, pp. 20–1.

39 Samuel Morse, undated letter, quoted in Frizot, *A New History of Photography*, p. 28.

40 Collodion is nitrocellulose (cotton wool soaked in nitric acid) damped down with butinol and dissolved in ether.

41 See Warner Marien, *Photography: A Cultural History*, pp. 46–9.

42 Fenton, quoted at http://www.rleggat.com/photohistory/history/fenton.htm, accessed 21 May 2008.

43 http://www.moma.org/research/archives/highlights/06_1955.html, accessed 20 May 2008.

44 Edward Steichen, Introduction to *The Family of Man*, New York: Museum of Modern Art, 1955, p. 4.

45 Muybridge's work (including 'Galloping Horse' and other studies of motion) may be sampled on MP.

46 Adams's pictures of the American West may be seen at MP.

47 'Chuck Close's best shot', interview by Leo Benedictus, *Guardian*, Thursday 19 April 2007, accessed on 17 May 2008 at http://arts.guardian.co.uk/art/photography/story/0,,2061258,00.html. Prints made from the daguerreotypes can be viewed at http://annemarchand.blogspot.com/2007/06/kate-moss-prints-by-chuck-close.html

48 'Supermom Kate Moss Reveals All!', http://www.thefashionspot.com/forums/f96/kate-moss-38658.html, accessed 28 July 2008. Freud's painting is reproduced at http://image.guardian.co.uk/sys-images/Guardian/Arts_/Pictures/2004/10/29/moss1.jpg.

49 See 'The paths of contemporary photography', in Aleksandr Rodchenko, *Experiments for the Future: Diaries, Essays, Letters, and Other Writings*, New York: Museum of Modern Art, 2005, pp. 207–12. Alexander Lavrentiev, *Alexander Rodchenko: Revolution in Photography*, Moscow: Moscow House of Photography Museum, is a comprehensive recent treatment. Rodchenko's work can also be seen on MP.

50 The story is told in Clark Worswick, *Berenice Abbott and Eugène Atget*, Santa Fe, NM: Arena, 2002, which (beautifully) reproduces many of Atget's images as printed by Abbott. His work can also be sampled at GEH, MP and LL (http://www.luminous-lint.com/app/vexhibit/_PHOTOGRAPHER_Eugene__Atget_01/1/0/0/).

51 LL has a good deal of pictorialist photography on display, including a virtual exhibit on the movement's American flagship magazine *Camera Work* (http://www.luminous-lint.com/app/vexhibit/_THEME_Pictorialism_America_Camera_Work_01/1/0/0/). For European work in the same tradition see Francis Ribemont and Patrick Daum (eds), *Impressionist Camera: Pictorial Photography in Europe, 1888–1919*, New York: Merrell, 2006.

52 Matthew S. Witkovsky, *foto: Modernity in Central Europe, 1918–1945*, London: Thames and Hudson, 2007, is a richly illustrated recent survey of the period which has the merit of treating previously forgotten Czech, Polish and Hungarian figures alongside their more familiar German counterparts. There is a very good accompanying website at http://www.nga.gov/exhibitions/2007/foto/preview.shtm.

53 Josef Sudek, *Smutná krajina/Sad Landscape* (2nd edn), Prague: Kant, 2004. On Sudek's work more generally see Anna Farova and Josef Sudek, *Poet of Prague: A Photographer's Life*, New York: Aperture, 1990.

54 See Maija Homa (ed.), *Josef Sudek: The Commercial Photography for Družstevní práce*, Helsinki: Alvar Aalto Museum, 2003.

55 Antonin Dufek, 'Memories of reality', in Josef Sudek, *Dialogue with Silence*, Warsaw: Zachenta Narodowa Galeria Sztuki, 2006, p. 67.

56 James Agee and Walker Evans, *Let Us Now Praise Famous Men*, Boston: Houghton Mifflin, 1988.

57 Karel Teige, 'The tasks of photography' (1931), in Phillips, *Photography in the Modern Era*, pp. 318–19.

58 For the latter see http://www.nypl.org/research/chss/spe/art/photo/abbottex/abbott.html.

59 Berenice Abbott, 'Photography at the crossroads', in Lyons, *Photographers on Photography*, pp. 20–1. See also her short essay 'It has to walk alone', in the same collection, pp. 15–17.

60 For details see Worswick, *Berenice Abbott and Eugène Atget*.

61 I employ Jacques Derrida's (untranslatable) concept here. Extending de Saussure's distinction between a signifier (the sound of a word) and a signified (the concept or idea it denotes), he argues that a signifier not only differs from a signified but also constantly 'defers' (alludes, invokes, brings to mind) other signifiers, creating an endless chain of signification. The implication is that meaning is always ultimately indeterminate; there is never a simple one-to-one relation between signifier and signified. I would argue that the argument applies even more strongly when visual rather than verbal signifiers are at issue. Whereas narratives can reduce the play of meaning of words, a single image is open to many readings from the start.

62 This is claimed, for example, on the website 'Pioneers of American Photography: Masterworks of the Pfeifer Collection', at http://www.lorrainedavis.com/Pfeifer%20 Catalog.pdf, accessed 20 May 2008.

63 Sorrenti's advertisements for Calvin Klein's 'Obsession' perfume can be viewed at http://www.katemosscollection.com/gallery/v/advertisements/CalvinObsession/.

64 Sally Mann, *Immediate Family*, London: Phaidon, 1992, unpaginated introduction.

65 Taken in 1992, 'Venus After School' is not included in Mann's *Immediate Family*. It may be viewed at the Pfeifer Collection website, location given in note 62.

66 See Hans-Michael Koetzle, *Photo Icons: The Story behind the Pictures*, Vol. 2, Cologne: Taschen, 2002, pp. 28–37, and introduction to Mark Durden, *Dorothea Lange*, London: Phaidon, 2001.

67 For Rodchenko see note 49 above. Examples of Weston's work may be viewed at MP; see also Edward Weston and Nancy Newhall, *Edward Weston's Book of Nudes*, Los Angeles: Getty Museum, 2007. GEH has an extensive collection of Moholy-Nagy's photographs (http://www.geh.org/fm/amico99/htmlsrc2/moholy-intro.html).

68 Tom Junod, 'The Falling Man', *Esquire*, 11 September 2007, http://www.esquire.com/ features/ESQ0903-SEP_FALLINGMAN, accessed 20 May 2008.

69 The interview quote from Drew can be found in Tom Junod, 'The Falling Man', *Esquire*, 11 September 2007, http://www.esquire.com/features/ESQ0903-SEP_FALLINGMAN, accessed 20 May 2008.

70 Warner Marien, *Photography: A Cultural History*, pp. 27–8.

5   Film and Television: the moving image

Jeffrey Richards

Visual sources – photographs, film and television – are important tools for the modern historian, potentially providing a more accurate record than paintings and drawings of buildings, transportation, costumes, work, war and public events from elections to coronations. But, like all sources, they present their own challenges of interpretation.

The twentieth century has been the century of the moving image just as the nineteenth was the century of the still photograph. But it was not until the 1880s that the technology had improved sufficiently to make candid camera shots possible rather than the posed and static scenes and portraits dictated both by the restrictive shutter speed on the camera and by contemporary ideas about the propriety of what should be photographed and how it should be photographed. From the 1880s onwards with the development of amateur photography, cheap cameras such as the Kodak and fast film techniques, photo-journalism of a modern kind and family snaps of weddings, funerals and holidays were made possible, adding to the store of visual evidence of both great national events and local family life. But photographs remain moments of time frozen for eternity. They do not move. Films move and they capture everyday life in action. Nonetheless, many of the questions associated with the interpretation of photographs carried over into the interpretation of film and later television: how and why subjects were chosen and handled in the way they were and what role an ever-changing and developing technology played in determining choices.[1]

The recent rediscovery of the short actuality films of Mitchell and Kenyon, the pioneer Blackburn film-makers whose work has been lovingly restored by the British Film Institute, demonstrates the power and immediacy of the moving picture. For seen one after another on a single disc, the films constitute a remarkable and rich panorama of life in Edwardian Britain. There is something profoundly moving about these scenes of workers streaming from factory gates, crowds attending football matches, holidaymakers at the seaside and, with the camera mounted on the moving vehicle, tramrides through busy city streets. These are not moments frozen in time, they are reanimated scenes of lives being lived a century ago, something we possess for no previous period of history. What particularly characterises them is motion and emotion. The motion was what caused Americans identifying the key quality of the new medium to nickname films 'the movies'. It is perhaps significant that the British nicknamed their films 'the flicks' or 'the pictures', suggesting that they identified the distinctive qualities of films as the flickering image and a static pictorialism. This distinction may well arise from the actual nature of the films produced in each country, with the Americans going all out for speed and pace and the British for a more stately exposition, influenced by the stage and by painting. The emotion these short films inspired in their original audiences was amazement and excitement, in particular in seeing themselves and their familiar haunts captured on celluloid. The emotion induced in present-day audiences is not dissimilar but the feelings are inspired by the idea of a lost world of people, their lives and work, their familiar scenes (many since destroyed by redevelopment and the ravages of time) brought to life before our eyes. Motion and emotion remain distinctive characteristics of film and television both factual and fictional.[2]

The early film pioneers believed that they were creating new sources of objective historical evidence. But almost at once it was demonstrated that this evidence needed as much stringent scrutiny as any conventional historical source, if not more. Between 1896 and 1910 the French film-maker Georges Méliès concocted a series of reconstructions of notable events of the day such as the coronation of King Edward VII and the assassination of President McKinley at which no film cameras had been present. They were recreated in the studio but sometimes deceived an innocent and not yet media-conscious public. Cinematographers regularly faked dramatic episodes from the Boxer Uprising, the Boer War and World War I, passing them off as authentic footage, to meet the growing hunger for moving images from the battlefront. Some of this footage has deceived experts ever since and the compilers of television series such as *The Great War*, crucially dependent on contemporary newsreel and documentary footage, had their work cut out establishing that all their material had been shot at the battlefront and not recreated, as some undoubtedly was, on the South Downs.

When in the 1960s historians first began to admit the use of film as evidence, it was to newsreel and documentary that they turned. Reassured by the presence of real people and real locations, they believed they were viewing 'reality'. But newsreels and documentaries no more presented 'reality' than did feature films which told stories, used actors and were often made entirely in studios. In the case of newsreel and documentary, what was seen on the screen was selected, shaped and placed there in pursuit of certain predetermined policies. Newsreel-makers and documentarists worked under the same constraint as feature film-makers, subject to interference from censors, sponsors and outside pressure groups. Newsreels and documentaries were always highly selective in what they showed and strictly controlled. As one British newsreel chief put it in 1938: 'The newsreel companies were always ready to give, and in fact frequently gave, assistance to the government in portraying matters which were deemed to be in the public interest.'[3] In Nazi Germany the newsreels came under the overview of the Ministry of Propaganda and Joseph Goebbels personally checked them out to ensure that they were promoting the government line. The value of actuality film, as discerned by historians, is that it can show what image is being presented of political leaders, what is the attitude of people at great public events and what version of contemporary history is being disseminated by the newsreel companies for public consumption. But in order to use newsreels as historical evidence, it is necessary not just to analyse the on-screen images but to go behind the screen, to look at the organisational structure, policies and personnel of the newsreel companies, their relations with government and censors and the limits imposed by technology on their ability to record events.[4] An exemplary study of the newsreels and the Spanish Civil War, Anthony Aldgate's *Cinema and History* did just this and provides a model of how to tackle the subject.[5]

Historians initially disdained the use of fictional films on the grounds that they were mere entertainment, involving actors, studio sets and 'unreality'. But the idea of a distinction between fictional and non-fictional films is essentially bogus. This is clearly evidenced by the fact that the greatest British film directors (Michael Powell, Carol Reed, Thorold Dickinson, Roy Boulting, David Macdonald, Pat Jackson, Lindsay Anderson, Karel Reisz among others) and the greatest American film directors (John Ford, William Wyler, Frank Capra and George Stevens among them), as well as the greatest Russian film director, Sergei Eisenstein, all moved with apparent ease between documentary and fictional feature film. Whether the directors were shooting on location with real people or on a studio set with actors, the resulting film was staged, framed and cut in such a way as to direct the viewers' attention where the director wanted it to go. The directors organised and constructed events to give them a narrative cohesion and order missing from everyday real life. They deployed lighting, movement, dialogue, music and colour to heighten mood and atmosphere, evoke an emotional response in the audience and to advance the story.

For historians, the study of the feature film became inescapable as from World War I until the late 1950s cinema-going was the principal leisure activity of the masses, particularly in Western and Eastern Europe, the Americas and the Far East. It occupied a place in people's lives which from the late 1950s to the present has been taken by television. The importance of the feature film was recognised and defined by the 1936 Moyne Committee Report into the workings of the Cinematograph Films Act:

> The cinematograph film is today one of the most widely used means for the amusement of the public at large. It is undoubtedly a most important factor in the education of classes of the community, in the spread of national culture and in presenting national ideas and customs to the world. Its potentialities moreover in shaping the ideas of the very large numbers to whom it appeals are almost unlimited. The propaganda value of the film cannot be over-emphasized.[6]

Nothing could more clearly justify the study of feature films and television programmes as historical evidence.

However, as historians in the 1970s and 1980s began to get to grips with the use of feature films as historical evidence, they were engulfed in culture wars as two principal alternatives to the study of film emerged: Film Studies and Cinema History. They grew out of different disciplines, each with its own emphases, methodologies and approaches. Film Studies developed out of English Literature and Cinema History out of History. Put simply, Film Studies has been centrally concerned with the text, with minute visual and structural analysis of individual films, with the application of a variety of sometimes abstruse theoretical approaches, with the eliciting of meanings that neither the film-makers nor contemporary audiences and critics – so far as we can tell – would have recognised. Cinema History has placed its highest priority on context, on the location of films securely within the setting of their makers' attitudes, constraints and preoccupations, on audience reaction and contemporary understanding. Recently there has been a rewarding convergence between the two approaches. Cinema historians and historians who use film as evidence have taken on board some of the more useful and illuminating of the theoretical developments, such as gender theory, and the Film Studies scholars have been grounding their film analysis more securely in historical context. The result has been that many scholars on both sides would now regard themselves more broadly as cultural historians. But there remains an unproductive hostility between some adherents of the alternative approaches, which takes the form of the cursory dismissal of works which deserve a more serious engagement with their ideas and approaches.

A regular criticism of Cinema History is that it is devoid of theory. It is worth pointing out to the proponents of that argument that empiricism, which underlies much Cinema History, is a theory and one that is longer established and more thoroughly tried and tested than some of the more fashionable but short-lived theories of recent years. The wholesale application to film criticism of the French linguistics theories associated with Saussure and the psychoanalytic ideas of Lacan, part of a bid to treat film analysis as a precise science, led for a while to the critical dominance of what David Bordwell called 'the sterile notion of the self-sufficient text', the idea that films possessed a meaning that was independent of the prevailing social, cultural, political and economic contexts.[7] This approach is now seen as both restrictive and ahistorical. Similarly restrictive was Marxism, as applied to culture by Louis Althusser, which insisted that 'every film is political' and that all other theoretical models were invalid. The empirical historian of film and the historian seeking to use film as evidence deal not in mere speculation but in solid archival research, the assembling, evaluation and interpretation of the facts about the production and reception of films with particular emphasis on the context, social, cultural, political and economic, within which the film was produced.

It is a truism that films change their meaning with the passage of time, with changes in the nature and assumptions of the audience. A film produced in 1930 necessarily means something very different to an audience in 2007 to what it meant to an audience in 1930. This can be demonstrated by two anecdotal examples. During the 1960s I watched with a student audience two films made in the 1940s, the British film *Brief Encounter* and the American film *She Wore a Yellow Ribbon*. The first film, a romantic drama about a suburban couple, both married to other people, who meet, fall in love, do not consummate the relationship and part for ever to preserve their marriages, was greeted with disbelieving laughter by the 1960s audience who simply could not understand why they did not just leap into bed together and who also found the accent, mores and attitudes alien. The second film, a celebration of the US cavalry and its battles against the American Indians, being viewed at the height of the Vietnam War, had the audience booing every time the cavalry appeared. What the historian seeks in feature films is evidence of values and attitudes from the time the film was made, the explication in story form of the contemporary ideas about the social and sexual roles of men and women, the concepts of work and leisure, class and race, peace and war. The great Victorian sage John Ruskin wrote: 'Tell me what you like and I'll tell you who you are.'[8] An analysis of the films people like can provide one way into the mindset of 'the silent majority' and challenge the interpretation of film critics.

To utilise film as evidence, three stages of investigation are needed. The first is to analyse the content of the individual film or television programme and ascertain how its themes and ideas are conveyed by the script, the *mise-en-scène*, the acting, the direction, the editing, the photography and the music. The second stage is to understand how and why the particular film or television programme was made, when it was made and how it relates to the political, social and industrial context in which it was produced. The third stage is to discover how the film or television programme was received – for instance, by reference to box office returns, television ratings figures, newspaper reviews and oral history surveys.

Aside from the basic questions – what is the film or television programme saying and how is it saying it? – the principal research questions include: What were the patterns of cinema-going or television-viewing and what was the actual experience of watching a film or a television programme in the period under investigation? What were the production strategies and policies of the film and television companies? What made up the contemporary debates within the culture about the influence of cinema and television? What were the aims, principles, operation and effects of censorship on cinema and television? What was the function, nature and appeal of the star system? What is the nature of the relationship between film and television on the one hand and the novels, plays and strip cartoons from which they have regularly drawn their material? How far can films and television be seen consciously or unconsciously to act as propaganda for some cause or other?

While many of the research questions and methodological techniques employed in film analysis can be applied to television programmes, there are some fundamental differences between the two media. Unlike film, much of television is live and therefore more immediate than film. This means that much of the output of television's early years is lost, just as a large proportion of silent films no longer exists, having been melted down for the silver content of their nitrate prints. So for those writing about early television and some silent films, scholars have perforce to rely on purely printed sources. Today with the latest developments in technology, almost all live programmes are preserved to facilitate the time-shifting preferences of viewers who can access them via computer. The actual absence of visual sources was compounded in Britain by a disastrous decision taken by the BBC in the 1960s. In order to save money, they decided to reuse the videotapes on which programmes were then recorded and so wiped many episodes of popular series such as *Doctor Who* and *Dad's Army*, which are now irretrievably lost.

Live television, by its very nature, is unpredictable and this has led to some sensational events. In the 1960s Kenneth Tynan caused a furore by uttering the then taboo word 'fuck' on live television and there was a similar reaction when an irate viewer physically attacked the critic Bernard Levin during a live broadcast of the satire show *That Was The Week That Was*. This can still happen today. Recently another sensation was caused when the columnist Matthew Paris 'outed' cabinet minister Peter Mandelson as gay on *Newsnight*.

The second major difference between films and television is the actual viewing experience, with television viewed primarily in the home and films traditionally in the cinema. This has important implications relating to the impact of the film or programme being viewed. The spectator goes out to the cinema, sits in a darkened auditorium and is focused directly on the large screen. Television tends to be viewed in a lighted room with life going on around it: people come and go, meals are eaten in front of it, conversations take place during it. Sometimes in some houses it remains on permanently as a kind of moving wallpaper, capturing the viewers' attention only intermittently. Even when television is being viewed in a concentrated manner, there are on commercial television in both Britain and America regular breaks for advertisements. This inevitably weakens the impact but also dictates the structure of the programmes, creating a different experience from film-watching in the cinema. Scholars need to take account of all these features in their analysis of the impact and influence of films and television.[9]

Historians no longer believe, as they used to, that films and television programmes are a straightforward 'reflection' of the world in which they were created. Fictional or non-fictional, they are constructed. So the first step is to analyse the nature of the construction and that requires a sophisticated approach to the visual analysis of the individual film or television programme. There are several useful guides to the complex process of reading a film. Two of the most useful – and they have by now acquired classic status – are James Monaco's *How to Read a Film: The Art, Technology, Language, History and Theory of Film and Media* and David Bordwell and Kristin Thompson's *Film Art: An Introduction*.[10] Between them they cover such topics as film form, cinematic language, genre, narrative, framing, editing, the fundamentals of film sound, aesthetics and technology. Monaco usefully includes a glossary of technical terms.

It is important for someone coming to film from a discipline other than Film or Media Studies to master the basic technical vocabulary for the purposes of detailed visual analysis. The most useful exercise to be undertaken is the in-depth analysis of a selected sequence from a film which facilitates better understanding of, for example, the use of the close-up for emphasis and the long-shot for spectacle, the rhythm of editing which dictates the pace of the film and the nature of the lighting which creates atmosphere. Such an exercise helps to reduce the dependence on plot and dialogue to which those unfamiliar with the technique of visual analysis usually turn first and on which they are sometimes over-reliant. It is also important when analysing a film or television programme to consider what is being left out as well as what is being included. For example, in the 1937 Warner Brothers biopic *The Life of Emile Zola*, which dramatised the defence by the French novelist of the wrongfully convicted army officer Captain Dreyfus, it is never once mentioned that Dreyfus was Jewish and that anti-Semitism was one of the reasons for his persecution. This was a deliberate exclusion, born of the fear of Hollywood movie moguls, many of them Jewish, that to highlight anti-Semitism might actually stimulate it in society.

The context within which the film or television programme was produced next needs to be established. Film and television are collaborative media and although the French *auteur* theory, which became fashionable in the 1960s, assigned to the director the principal creative input, in the heyday of Hollywood, for instance, it may have been the producer who had the decisive say, removing directors, re-cutting films, ordering reshooting and replacing stars. The full story of what went on behind the scenes can only be recovered from studio records. In America, many studios have deposited their records in university archives and they yield a rich array of letters, memoranda, story conference records and script rewrites, facilitating the reconstruction in detail of the production process. Selections of some of these memoranda have been published.[11] In Britain, no such record deposits have been made. But their absence can in part be remedied by consulting the trade press (*The Bioscope* and *Kinematograph Weekly* charted the day-to-day activity in the studios) and the private papers of directors, writers and producers where they have been deposited. In Britain, they are often to be found at the British Film Institute. In North America, directors' papers are, like studio records, routinely deposited at universities. For television, the BBC Written Archives at Caversham are an invaluable source. There is no accessible equivalent for Independent Television. There is also no such equivalent source for American television.

It is impossible to understand the functioning of cinema or terrestrial television in their heydays without an understanding of censorship. Every country censored films and many operated a policy of vetting scripts before they went into production. The aim of censorship universally was to maintain the moral, political, social and economic status quo and avoid anything smacking of controversy. The records of the British Board of Film Censors and the American Production Code Administration have yielded some fascinating studies of the way in which film-makers operated under continuing constraints. Censorship equally operated in television, and in Britain the statutory requirement for broadcasters to maintain balance was invoked when commissioned programmes such as Peter Watkins's anti-nuclear *The War Game* and Ian Curteis's *The Falklands Play*, deemed too sympathetic to Mrs Thatcher, were banned. Such bans invariably provoked furious debates in the press and parliament, centring on the issue of free speech.[12]

It is also important to understand what is happening socially and politically, as films and television programmes do not operate in a vacuum but respond directly to what is going on around them. For example, more feature-length films based on the Bible and/or the history of the Roman Empire were made by Hollywood between 1950 and 1965 than in any other period of cinema history. Why? One reason is technological – the rise of television. Television mounted a major challenge to cinema during the 1950s, plunging the industry into crisis. Between 1951 and 1958 weekly American audiences fell from 90 million to 42 million and the number of cinemas virtually halved. Hollywood's reaction was to do something not open to the small flickering black and white box in the corner of the average living room and that meant spectacular re-creations of the past, in particular the Ancient World. These subjects were enhanced by technological innovations during the 1950s in colour and screen size. But at the same time, the United States was engaged in the Cold War with the Soviet Union and its domestic by-product, the rise of anti-Communist paranoia and the McCarthyite inquisition against not just Communists but also liberals and radicals. So blockbusting epics such as *Quo Vadis* (1951), *The Robe* (1953) and *The Ten Commandments* (1956) explicitly painted ancient empires such as Rome and Egypt as godless totalitarian tyrannies, analogues of the USSR, and heroised their opponents as God-fearing democratic Christians and/or Jews, who represent the Free World. When the Cold War thawed out and the Ancient World cycle lost its box office appeal, it ceased.[13]

One of the most challenging areas for research is to assess the audience reaction to individual films or television programmes. There are cinema box office returns, both national and local, and television ratings which provide figures for spectator-ship.[14] Newspaper reviews can be helpful. Allowance has to be made for the attitude and readership of the various newspapers, but the critics were writing with the tastes and interests of their readers in mind. What they wrote was often heeded. As Winifred Holmes testified in a contemporary study of film-going in an unnamed southern town in the 1930s: 'Newspaper reviews of films are read with interest and play a large part in influencing people of all classes in an appreciation of the films shown.'[15] Newspaper reviewing was part of the wider popular culture and is a phenomenon in itself worthy of study. John Ellis's brilliant analysis of 1940s film reviewing in Britain uncovered the critical agenda and criteria to which 'serious' reviewers in the 'quality press' were working.[16] It is important to look at a wide range of reviews, however, and not isolated examples. It is known, for example, that Lord Beaverbrook admired the 1945 British epic *Caesar and Cleopatra* and instructed his film reviewer to praise it. So other reviews need to be consulted to balance this single opinion. It is also the case that audiences did not always heed the advice of critics. The Ancient World epics of the 1950s were critically excoriated but regularly topped the lists of annual box office winners.

A third source of evidence is audience surveys either based on questionnaires or on third-party observation of people reacting to the films. Mass-Observation, the anthropological social survey, was from its foundation in 1936 intensely interested in films. A questionnaire on their film-going habits and tastes issued to the patrons of three Bolton cinemas in March 1938 elicited 559 replies, 304 from men and 255 from women. A Mass-Observation directive in November 1943 asked which six films observers had liked best in the previous year and why. They received 220 replies. Mass-Observation reported on four feature films and, at the behest of the Ministry of Information, newsreels and short information films, to assess their efficacy and their contribution to national morale. They usually combined personal observation of the audience, questionnaires about individual reactions and analysis of newspaper reviews to check on the match between them and the popular reaction.[17]

The way in which such reports can throw light on audience reaction is evidenced by the case of *Ships with Wings* (1941), which, despite sequences shot aboard HMS *Ark Royal*, looks today like a highly romanticised and artificial tribute to the Fleet Air Arm. It featured a daredevil pilot, cashiered from the service for causing the death of the heroine's brother in a crash. He redeems himself by flying a suicide mission against an enemy-held island. It was mocked by the 'quality' press (*The Times*, the *Observer*, the *New Statesman*) as the stuff of outdated musical comedy. The *Daily Mail* ran an article by the war correspondent Noel Monks saying the film was a disgrace and should be scrapped. *Documentary News Letter* ran an editorial declaring: 'Films of this kind should not be made in wartime.' Michael Balcon of Ealing Studios, who had made the film, commissioned a report on audience reaction from Mass-Observation. The report revealed that the film had an 87 per cent approval rating, appealing equally to men and women, rich and poor, and all areas of the country. It was found to be thrilling, uplifting and emotionally satisfying. Nevertheless Balcon was so concerned at the original criticism that he initiated a switch in production to the sober and earnest reconstruction of real-life episodes from the 'People's War' that were to earn Ealing critical plaudits.[18]

A similar source exists for Nazi Germany in the *Sicherheitsdienst* (SD) security service reports on audience reaction to key propaganda films. Since these were not intended for publication but for the guidance of the Ministry of Propaganda in the implementation of its film policy, they can be assumed to be accurate. They certainly sound accurate. In preparation for the final solution, Goebbels authorised the production of three anti-Semitic films, one of them the documentary *Der Ewige Jude* (The Eternal Jew). The SD report on the film (dated 20 January 1941), based on evidence received from all over Germany, reads:

> Because of the very intensive publicity for the film and its impressive organisation of documentary evidence, the film's performances produced remarkably high audience figures. But in some places audience interest has often soon fallen off, because the film has followed too quickly on the feature film *Jud Süss*. Since a large part of the population had already seen *Jud Süss*, it was very often assumed – according to the information to hand – that the documentary film *Der Ewige Jude* had nothing to say. Reports received from, for example, Innsbruck, Dortmund, Aachen, Karlsruhe, Neustadt/Weinstrasse, Bielefeld, Frankfurt am Main and Munich all agree that it is often only the politically active sections of the population who have seen the documentary film while the typical film audience has largely avoided it, and that in some places there has been a word-of-mouth campaign against the film and its starkly realistic portrait of the Jews. The repulsive nature of the material and in particular the ritual slaughter scenes are repeatedly cited in conversation as the main reason for not seeing the film.[19]

One source of evidence that has never been properly exploited is letters to fan magazines. The fan magazines were a major part of film culture and there has been to date no systematic study of them. But J.P. Mayer in one of the earliest socio-logical studies of British cinema audiences, *British Cinemas and Their Audiences*, made very effective use of 200 cinematic autobiographies elicited by a competition in *Picturegoer* magazine. Typical is the account by a female medical student who recalled for Mayer her obsession with Deanna Durbin at the age of fourteen:

> She became my first and only screen idol. I collected pictures of her, and articles about her, and spent hours sticking them in scrapbooks . . . I adored her and my adoration influenced my life a great deal. I wanted to be as much like her as possible, both in my manners and clothes . . . She had far more influence on me than any amount of lectures or rows from parents would have had. I went to all her films, and as often as I could too.[20]

The role of cinema-going and films as part of cultural memory can be tapped by oral history interviews. The use of memory material is potentially problematic and requires a series of checks and safeguards. But two excellent studies which utilise oral history and successfully negotiate the potential pitfalls associated with it provide excellent templates for such work: Annette Kuhn's *An Everyday Magic: Cinema and Cultural Memory* and Jackie Stacey's *Star Gazing: Hollywood Cinema and Female Spectatorship*.[21] They deal with memories of cinema-going in Britain in the 1930s (Kuhn) and the 1940s and 1950s (Stacey).

There are a number of different theoretical arguments as to how the audience relate to film and the nature of the influence it has on them. The oldest argument is the so-called hypodermic argument which suggests that a passive mass audience is injected with the message of the film and absorbs it completely and that films as a whole reflect the psyche of the country producing them. The classic exposition of this argument is Siegfried Kracauer's *From Caligari to Hitler*[22] which saw Weimar cinema as specifically softening up the German audience for the Nazi takeover. This argument was subsequently challenged by many scholars who claimed that how a film affected an audience was likely to depend on the age, sex, class, health, intelligence, predisposition and ideas of each individual member of that audience. Sociologist Andrew Tudor proposed a more flexible model for the operation of film, suggesting that there was a reciprocal two-way relationship between the film-maker and the audience who both operated within a shared social and cultural structure, leading to more general rather than predominantly individual responses to particular films.[23]

A variation on the hypodermic model is the hegemonic model. Karl Marx wrote that the ruling class decide what is to be the dominant ideology and they impose it. This basic proposition was refined and expanded by Antonio Gramsci, whose ideas of 'hegemony' have been usefully applied to culture and the mass media by Stuart Hall.[24] According to this theory, the ruling class exert their authority over the other classes by a combination of force and the winning of consent. The ruling class's view of 'reality' comes to constitute the primary 'reality' of the subordinate classes, and the ruling class sets the limits, both mental and structural, within which the subordinate classes live. 'Hegemony' is maintained by the agency of super-structure – the family, the church, education, the media, culture, law, the police, the army – which contains the subordinate classes. Consent to 'hegemony' is gained by the promotion of consensus, and the mass media play a vital role in the creation and preservation of consensus.

The hegemonic argument was rejected by Richard Maltby who in his book on popular Hollywood cinema, *Harmless Entertainment*,[25] articulated a purely commercial view. He argued that within the reciprocal relationship between screen and audience, which permits the variety of individual interpretations to be drawn, the bulk of cinema effectively demands and secures a unilateral mode of com-munication, in which the spectator is encouraged to construct the fiction as intended by the film-makers because of the conventional arrangement of the fictional material. He calls this 'the cinema of consensus' and argues that its mechanisms were not concerned with the establishment of ideological hegemony or the imposition of a particular, ideologically conditioned system of perception. But it was rather a technological evolution geared to the production of more efficient entertainment. It was the desire to maximise profit that led Hollywood to project in its films the most acceptable and least demanding worldview, that is, the status quo. So conventions of storytelling built up based on genre, star personalities and visual style. Central to Hollywood's assumptions was a particular appreciation of the relationship between film and audience and of the reason why audiences attended the cinema, that is, to be entertained. So films were designed to be easily digested. The Hollywood narrative set out to engage the audience at the emotional level, the majority of the technical devices being engineered to encourage that level of engagement over all possible alternatives. So the point of view of the film is that of the hero and all spatial relationships, cutting, lighting, staging, are geared to direct the audience's involvement along the prescribed route. The narrative thus operates as a closed unit, endorsing particular characters, attitudes and actions from within a restricted framework which it alone defines. The way in which this worked is attested by no less a person than Marxist playwright Bertolt Brecht. To illustrate his argument that plays and films, whether good or bad, always embodied an image of the world which was transmitted to the audience, he cited the example of *Gunga Din* (1939), the Hollywood film celebrating the British Raj:

> In the film *Gunga Din* . . . I saw British occupation forces fighting a native population. An Indian tribe – this term itself implies something wild and uncivilized, as against the word 'people' – attacked a body of British troops stationed in India. The Indians were primitive creatures, either comic or wicked; comic when loyal to the British and wicked when hostile. The British soldiers were honest, good-humoured chaps and when they used their fists on the mob and 'knocked some sense' into them the audience laughed. One of the Indians betrayed his compatriots to the British, sacrificed his life so that his fellow-countrymen should be touched too: I felt like applauding and laughed in all the right places. Despite the fact that I knew all the time that

there was something wrong, that the Indians are not primitive and uncultured people but have a magnificent age-old culture, and that this Gunga Din could also be seen in a very different light, e.g. as a traitor to his people, I was amused and touched because this utterly distorted account was an artistic success and considerable resources in talent and ingenuity had been applied in making it.[26]

Interestingly, whether you adopt the hegemonic or the commercial interpretation of the operation of cinema on audiences, the net result is a cinema of consensus. This also operated in the age of television.

Soap opera is one of the staples of television. Thirty million people, about half the British population, watched the BBC soap *EastEnders* at Christmas 1986. The essence of soap opera has been defined by Hilary Kingsley:

> It must be a continuing story with a family background aimed largely at women. It must deal not with ideas but with feelings and emotions. Above all it must be seamless, endless. Problems arise, problems are solved. Danger appears, danger is averted. Love arises, love dies. But always the central story must flow on like a great river . . . In soap opera no eternal verities are questioned. Religion never plays a part in story-lines. Nor does politics . . . In soap conventional morality is never questioned. (It is often flouted, but the very flouting defines the morality.) In soap, the goodies and the baddies are clearly defined . . . Problems, of course, are soap's lifeblood. All drama is conflict; conflict causes problems. In soap the problems must be something like we have experienced ourselves, or problems we can imagine having . . . infidelity, money problems, paternity uncertainty, childlessness, loneliness, betrayal, worry about loved ones who have gone off to some other part of the world – all delve deep into our unconscious and conscious minds. *What soap does is to parade problems we either have or that we fear having.*

There is, however, a fundamental difference between British soaps, the most popular of which are set in a working-class environment, and American soaps, the most popular of which celebrate the lives of the super-rich. The audience response therefore is bound to be different: for the British soaps it is likely to be identification with 'people like us' and for the American, wish fulfilment fantasising about participation in a lifestyle way beyond the dreams of avarice. Writing in 1988, Hilary Kingsley saw soap opera as something binding society together:

> In the Middle Ages religion was the glue of society. Today television is the binding agent that helps us cohere. And the sticky quintessence of television . . . is soap opera. To watch soap is an affirmation of social piety, a declaration that we share the beliefs, hopes, fears and prejudices of the rest of Western mankind. People watch soap opera, talk and care about soap as a shared experience.

But a new element has now entered into audience reaction to, in particular though not exclusively, American soaps and that is postmodern irony. From *Dallas* to

Footballers' Wives, audience response has been split between those who took the stories seriously and those who sent them up. There has been a division along both class and gender lines. In the case of *Footballers' Wives*, sophisticated audiences treated the whole series as a glorious send-up of the lifestyles of the rich and famous; unsophisticated audiences took it seriously enough to name their baby daughters Chardonnay after one of the leading characters. This now has to be factored into audience analysis.[27]

The vital necessity of archival research in establishing the true story behind the making and reception of individual films can be demonstrated by the case of *Objective Burma* (1945). *Objective Burma* is remembered as 'the film in which Errol Flynn won the war single-handed'. It became notorious in Britain when it opened because there had been no major feature film set in Burma, the 14th Army was deeply sensitive about its neglect, becoming known as 'The Forgotten Army', and this film concentrated exclusively on a single American unit.

Both director, Raoul Walsh, and star, Errol Flynn, recalled the film in their autobiographies and in so doing reveal the danger of relying exclusively on the autobiographies of participants in a film. Walsh wrote in his autobiography:

> Though *The New York Times* called *Objective Burma* 'one of the best war films yet made in Hollywood', England banned it after the first showing and the British news media said a lot of nasty things. One newspaper depicted star Errol Flynn holding an American flag and standing on the grave of a British officer. Their resentment arose from the suggestion that American para-troopers, dropped in advance, single-handedly recaptured Burma from the Japanese.[28]

Errol Flynn's version appeared in his autobiography *My Wicked, Wicked Ways*, where he declared *Objective Burma* 'one of the few pictures of which I am proud' and recalled its good reception in America:

> The film got a different reception in England. In that country, which gave me my accent and my histrionic training and was my motherland until the time I took out American citizenship, you would have thought I was the repre-sentative of the State Department in Washington, telling the British that not only were Americans winning World War II, but that I, Flynn, was doing it single-handed. The Lord Chamberlain yanked the picture after the first showing – for the English press flipped in rage. Even so, a large crowd was out there, in Leicester Square, to see the picture the following night. Almost an international incident had begun. In a cartoon in one of the biggest news-papers in England, I was depicted standing triumphantly with the American flag, my right foot on the grave of a British soldier.[29]

Largely on the basis of these accounts, this story has been much retold. But in a model investigation of its time, film historian Ian Jarvie investigated it by going back to original sources and demonstrated that almost every element in both accounts was untrue.

It is possible to trace the development of the film through the Warner Brothers production files, now held at the University of Wisconsin. The film originated in a request by producer Jerry Wald to the writer Alvah Bessie to devise an original screen story set in Burma, and Bessie came up with the story detailing the exploits of a patrol of American paratroopers sent to knock out a Japanese radar station in the depths of the Burmese jungle. As Bessie recalled in his autobiography, after doing his research he reported to Wald that there were no American troops in Burma, to which Wald replied: 'It's only a moving picture . . . Put in some British liaison officers and stop worrying.'[30] Jarvie discovered that there were no British liaison officers in the script until after Bessie's story had been assigned to Lester Cole and Ranald MacDougall to be turned into a shooting script. But this conversation must have taken place at some stage.

The script was submitted, as was customary, to the War Department Public Relations Bureau and a memorandum came back to say that there were few American troops in Burma and it was largely a British operation, that there were no paratroop activities in Burma and the Japanese had no decent radar and no air superiority to capitalise on it. Warner Brothers agreed to add a newsreel prologue to the film stressing British involvement in Burma and to add a dedication at the end to the British, American, Indian and Chinese troops fighting in Burma. All this is detailed in the correspondence files of the War Department Public Relations Bureau.

Released in January 1945 in the United States, the film gained excellent reviews. But on 31 May 1945 several newspapers carried a Reuters report of an article by Colonel William Taylor, who had commanded American gliders in Burma, in *SEAC*, the daily newspaper of the South East Asian Command, describing the film as 'a sickening travesty'. Taylor's comments were extensively reported in the British press and when the film opened on 21 September 1945, the British press fell on it, denouncing it in outraged terms. The press reviews can be consulted at the British Newspaper Library, Colindale. Three popular papers (the *Sunday Express*, the *Daily Mirror* and the *Evening Standard*) called for it to be banned and it was denounced in an editorial in *The Times*. After a week, Warner Brothers bowed to the pressure from the press and withdrew the film. It was not seen in Britain until 1952. But it was not 'yanked by the Lord Chamberlain' (who had jurisdiction over the stage and not the cinema) nor was it 'banned by the British'. There were no crowds in Leicester Square, as Flynn claimed. Finally, the cartoon mentioned by both Flynn and Walsh did not feature Flynn. Ian Jarvie tracked it down to the 5 October 1945 issue of the *Daily Mirror*. The cartoon showed a typical Hollywood tycoon in a canvas chair, surrounded by scripts marked 'All American Burma Front', 'All American defence of London', 'All American Atomic Bomb'. A suited Englishman is politely pointing out: 'Excuse me – but you are sitting on some graves' and beneath the chair are a series of graves marked 'Britain's sacrifice for world freedom'.[31]

There is no doubt that the film was deeply resented by the British troops and the British public. When I wrote about the film some years ago, I received a telephone call from a woman whose father had managed a garrison cinema in British India.

She told me that after the film was shown there to an army audience, the audience rioted and several of them came back in the night and burned down the cinema. In 1954 when Alan Ladd came over to Britain to star in *The Red Beret*, playing an American serving with the paratroop brigade, he insisted on calling a press conference to stress that this was not going to be another film about another American winning the war single-handed but was about an American learning to fight from the British.[32] *Objective Burma* was still controversial when it was first shown on television in the late 1950s and had to be followed by a round table discussion by Burma veterans who largely dismissed it as hokum. Flynn's participation particularly irked people as although he was Australian, he spoke with an impeccable British accent, had starred in a series of heroic British roles (*The Adventures of Robin Hood*, *The Charge of the Light Brigade*, *The Sea Hawk*) but had taken out American citizenship in 1942 and was exempted from military service on health grounds (recurrent malaria and a heart ailment).

Aside from the controversy, what about the film? It is in fact an excellent example of a particular genre – the lone patrol film. It is not about the Americans taking Burma. It is the story of a single US army patrol and its fight against the jungle, the Japanese, the swamp, the heat, the flies, the fever, exhaustion and despair. In the end only eleven survive from the original fifty who set out. It is, typically for American war films, a multi-ethnic patrol, made up of Italian Americans, Jewish Americans and Irish Americans led by a WASP architect (Errol Flynn) and accompanied by a middle-aged war correspondent. The director is action specialist Raoul Walsh and he sets a relentless pace, stages the battles and attacks superbly and, aided by Franz Waxman's pounding score and James Wong Howe's atmospheric photography, delivers a tremendously exciting genre piece. Its generic nature is emphasised by the fact that Walsh himself essentially remade it in 1951 in colour as a Western, *Distant Drums*, with Gary Cooper leading a patrol against the Seminole Indians in the Everglades. The film exactly fits Richard Maltby's definition of the typical Hollywood film in structure and intent. But while it effectively dramatised the status quo for American audiences, it outraged the British. When fully documented, the story of the film and its reception is an important piece of evidence to illustrate the uneasy relations between the wartime Allies and the underlying potential for anti-Americanism to flare.

We are currently in the midst of a dramatic change in the media world. The multiplication of channels and the rapid development of new technologies which in Britain have added satellite, cable and digital channels to the existing five terrestrial channels has led to the prediction that there will soon be a thousand different television channels. This has had the effect of fragmenting the culture and atomising the audience. Television is no longer the unifying cultural force nationally it was from the 1950s to the 1980s and therefore of comparatively less value to the historian seeking to define the characteristics of a particular shared culture. This is evidenced by the fact that an audience of 25 million defined a hit television programme in the 1970s whereas now it is an audience of 6 million. The position is different globally as American television has continued the process of cultural colonisation of the world begun by Hollywood. At the same time more films are being watched than ever before but not primarily in cinemas. They are watched on television, video, DVD and computer and with global audiences running into millions. So we may be at the point where we turn from an exclusive reliance on television back to film for evidence about the national and, indeed, the international mood.

Notes

1 On photographs as historical evidence see Colin Ford and Brian Harrison, *A Hundred Years Ago: Britain in the 1880s in Words and Photographs*, Harmondsworth: Allen Lane/Penguin, 1983; Eric J. Evans and Jeffrey Richards, *A Social History of Britain in Postcards*, London and New York: Longman, 1980.
2 The significance of these films as historical evidence is explored in Vanessa Toulmin, Simon Popple and Patrick Russell (eds), *The Lost World of Mitchell and Kenyon: Britain on Film*, London: BFI, 2004. Compilations of Mitchell and Kenyon's films, *The Lost World of Mitchell and Kenyon* and *Electric Edwardians*, have been commercially released by the British Film Institute.
3 Quoted in Anthony Aldgate, *Cinema and History*, London: Scolar Press, 1979, p. 193.
4 For good general introductions to the problems of using film as evidence, see Paul Smith (ed.), *The Historian and Film*, Cambridge: Cambridge University Press, 1976; Pierre Sorlin, *The Film in History: Restaging the Past*, Oxford: Basil Blackwell, 1981; Nicholas Pronay, 'The moving picture and historical research', *Journal of Contemporary History* 18, 1983, pp. 365–95.
5 Aldgate, *Cinema and History*. Also on newsreels, see Raymond Fielding, *The American Newsreel 1911–67*, Norman, OK: University of Oklahoma Press, 1972; Luke McKernan, *Topical Budget*, London: BFI, 1992.
6 Cinematograph Films Act, 1927: Report of a Committee appointed by the Board of Trade Cmd.5320 (1936), p. 4.
7 David Bordwell, 'Textual analysis etc.', *Enclitic* 10–11, 1981–82, p. 135.
8 John Ruskin, 'The crown of wild olive', in E.T. Cook and Alexander Wedderburn (eds), *The Works of John Ruskin* vol.18, London: George Allen, 1905, pp. 434–5.
9 On television as evidence, see John Corner (ed.), *Popular Television in Britain*, London: BFI, 1991; John Fiske, *Television Culture*, London: Methuen, 1987; John Corner, *Television Form and Public Address*, London: Edward Arnold, 1991; Andrew Goodwin and Garry Whannel (eds), *Understanding Television*, London: Routledge, 1990; Greg Philo, *Seeing and Believing: The Influence of Television*, London: Routledge, 1990; Michele Hilmes (ed.), *The Television History Book*, London: BFI, 2003.
10 James Monaco, *How to Read a Film: The Art, Technology, Language, History and Theory of Film and Media* (rev. edn), New York: Oxford University Press, 1981; David Bordwell and Kristin Thompson, *Film Art: An Introduction* (rev. edn), New York: McGraw Hill, 2001.
11 Rudy Behlmer (ed.), *Memo from David O. Selznick*, New York: Viking, 1972; Rudy Behlmer (ed.), *Memo from Darryl F. Zanuck*, New York: Grove Press, 1993; Rudy Behlmer (ed.), *Inside Warner Bros. 1934–51*, London: Weidenfeld and Nicolson, 1986. Good examples of how the full story of the making of individual feature films can be told using studio records, memoirs and oral history evidence can be found in Aljean Harmetz, *Round Up the Usual Suspects: The Making of 'Casablanca'*, New York: Hyperion, 1992, and Aljean Harmetz, *The Making of 'The Wizard of Oz'*, New York: Alfred Knopf, 1978.
12 On censorship, see in particular James C. Robertson, *The British Board of Film Censors 1896–1950*, Beckenham: Croom Helm, 1985; James C. Robertson, *The Hidden Cinema*, London: Routledge, 1989; Anthony Aldgate, *Censorship and the Permissive Society*,

Oxford: Clarendon Press, 1995; Anthony Aldgate and James C. Robertson, *Censorship in Theatre and Cinema*, Edinburgh: Edinburgh University Press, 2005; Leonard J. Leff and Jerold L. Simmons, *The Dame in the Kimono: Hollywood Censorship and the Production Code from the 1920s to the 1960s*, London: Weidenfeld and Nicolson, 1990; Ruth Vasey, *The World According to Hollywood*, Exeter: Exeter University Press, 1997; Gregory D. Black, *Hollywood Censored*, Cambridge: Cambridge University Press, 1994; Anthony Slide, *'Banned in the U.S.A.': British Films in the United States and their Censorship, 1933–1960*, London: I.B. Tauris, 1998.

13   See Jeffrey Richards, *Hollywood's Ancient Worlds*, London: Continuum, 2008.

14   On individual cinema attendances, see Julian Poole, 'British cinema audiences in wartime: audience preferences at the Majestic, Macclesfield, 1939–46', *Historical Journal of Film, Radio and Television* 7, 1987, pp. 15–34; Allen Eyles, 'Hits and misses at the Empire', *The Picture House* 13, 1989, pp. 25–47; Sue Harper, 'A lower middle class taste community in the 1930s: admissions figures at the Regent Cinema, Portsmouth', *Historical Journal of Film, Radio and Television* 24, 2004, pp. 565–87; Sue Harper, 'Fragmentation and crisis: 1940s admissions figures at the Regent Cinema, Portsmouth', *Historical Journal of Film, Radio and Television* 26, 2006, pp. 361–94. National tables of cinema box office winners were published annually in the trade paper *Kinematograph Weekly*.

15   *World Film News* I, December 1936, p. 4.

16   John Ellis, 'Art, culture and quality', *Screen* 19, Autumn 1978, pp. 9–49.

17   Dorothy Sheridan and Jeffrey Richards (eds), *Mass Observation at the Movies*, London: Routledge, 1987.

18   Jeffrey Richards, 'Wartime British cinema audiences: the case of *Ships With Wings*', *Historical Journal of Film, Radio and Television* 7, 1987, pp. 129–41.

19   This report is reproduced in Erwin Leiser, *Nazi Germany*, London: Secker and Warburg, 1974, pp. 157–8.

20   J.P. Mayer, *British Cinemas and their Audiences*, London: Dennis Dobson, 1948, p. 90.

21   Annette Kuhn, *An Everyday Magic: Cinema and Cultural Memory*, London: I.B. Tauris, 2002; Jackie Stacey, *Star Gazing: Hollywood Cinema and Female Spectatorship*, London: Routledge, 1994.

22   Siegfried Kracauer, *From Caligari to Hitler*, Princeton, NJ: Princeton University Press, 1947.

23   Andrew Tudor, *Image and Influence; Studies in the Sociology of Film*, London: Allen and Unwin, 1974, pp. 20–102.

24   Stuart Hall, 'Culture, media and the "ideological effect"', in James Curran, Michael Gurevich and Janet Woollacott (eds), *Mass Communication and Society*, London: Edward Arnold, 1979, pp. 315–48.

25   Richard Maltby, *Harmless Entertainment*, Metuchen, NJ: Scarecrow Press, 1983.

26   John Willett (ed.), *Brecht on Brecht*, London: Methuen, 1964, p. 151.

27   Hilary Kingsley, *Soap Box*, London and Basingstoke: Papermac, 1988, pp. 1–3, 10. On audiences in general, see Nicholas Abercrombie and Brian Longhurst, *Audiences*, London: Sage, 1998; Andy Ruddock, *Understanding Audiences: Theory and Method*, London: Sage, 2001; Mark Jancovich and Lucy Faire with Sarah Stubbings, *The Place of the Audience*, London: BFI, 2003.

28   Raoul Walsh, *Each Man in His Time*, New York: Farrar, Straus and Giroux, 1974, p. 317.

29   Errol Flynn, *My Wicked, Wicked Ways*, London: Pan, 1961, pp. 251–2.

30   Alvah Bessie, *Inquisition in Eden*, New York: Macmillan, 1965, pp. 79–80.

31   The full story of the making and reception of *Objective Burma* is told in Ian Jarvie, 'Fanning the flames', *Historical Journal of Film, Radio and Television* I, 1981, pp. 117–37.

32   Beverley Linet, *Ladd*, New York: Arbor House, 1979, p. 179.

6 Music: the composed sound

Burton W. Peretti

Introduction

Young twelfth-century Bavarians capturing daily life, loves, and fears in song, in the vernacular Latin they shared with students across Europe.

Italian nationalists in the 1850s fervently celebrating the premiere of Giuseppe Verdi's newest opera.

King Oliver's Creole Jazz Band inspiring black and white teens in 1920s Chicago to become 'hot' jazz musicians.

The 'power chords' of heavy metal bands uniting a generation of disaffected youth in the 1960s and 1970s, on both sides of the Atlantic.

Lithuanian townspeople using traditional outdoor mass singing to mobilise successfully against Soviet sovereignty in the late 1980s.

These are a few examples of how music emerges as a factor – often an important factor – in the human past. If you pause to think of your own study of history, you might be able to think of other examples.

It is likely, though, that you cannot. Most history courses and texts make only the briefest mention of music. Textbooks on United States history might mention jazz in the 1920s, rock'n'roll in the 1950s, and rock music in the 1960s. Some of them also make note of colonial New England hymnody, antebellum blackface minstrelsy, ragtime and hip hop. Histories of Europe mention classical music at points where culture and politics seem to intersect, such as when Beethoven dedicated his 'Eroica' Symphony to Napoleon (and then withdrew the tribute when the general crowned himself emperor).

Historical authorities have tended to relegate music to the background. Specialised histories and monographs on narrower subjects rarely focus on musical subjects. (Studies on musical themes exist, but their small number indicates the general trend.) The reasons for historians' neglect of music are fairly clear. Modern historical scholarship remains grounded in politics and economics, as it has been for a century and a half. Music, also, is difficult to write about. Many words are needed to describe adequately the content or the impact even of a simple melody, and such description often invites the use of musicians' often highly technical terminology. Thus if music is included in history, it is often only a flourish, a light and colourful appendage to a 'serious' study of politics, warfare, or social upheaval. James M. McPherson titled his prize-winning history of the American Civil War *Battle Cry of Freedom*, the title of a popular song in the North, but in more than 900 pages McPherson has nothing at all to say about music. The same observation applies to Eugene Genovese's equally lengthy study of American slavery, *Roll, Jordan, Roll*. While music ought not to dominate histories of such subjects, the fact that songs lend their titles and their spirit to these books suggests that some coverage of music is warranted.[1] Few academically trained historians focus on musical topics. In the United States today there are Ph.D.s in history teaching in universities who write regularly on musical topics, but these scholars probably could be counted using the fingers of both hands. The situation is similar in Europe and in Oceania.

As the sample topics cited at the beginning of this chapter indicate, though, there are many anecdotal or fleeting indications that music has been central to the human past. If students look hard enough in scattered books and articles, they can intuit a rich and exciting musical presence in almost any historical period. Their chances of finding material improve in the literature of musicologists, whose field is centred on the study of musical activity, or ethnomusicologists, who examine this activity first-hand using the 'field' research methods of cultural anthropology. Many of these scholars have a keen interest in history. In fact, much of their work has struggled with the interpretation of the musical past. What major changes shaped this past? How can it be broken into periods or eras? How was music related to the general historical trends of the time? History students can gain a great deal of inspiration and insight from historically minded musicologists such as Paul Henry Lang, Carl Dahlhaus and Lawrence Kramer, and ethnomusicologists such as Bruno Nettl and Bonnie Wade.[2]

Musical topics provide a rich, largely unmined opportunity for history students. This chapter challenges these students to look anew at musical topics and sources. It will first give special consideration to the central issue of what music *is* – a deceptively hard definition to formulate. It will also suggest how music might be approached as a source for historical research and writing. (No such guide, to my knowledge, has appeared previously.) The chapter then will expand upon the difficulties of using music as a source – difficulties which, as we have already noted, account for music's low profile in history – and how they might be eased. Finally, we will examine some of the exemplary work that historians – as well as other writers who share historians' fundamental scholarly concerns – have recently produced on particular musical subjects, which might serve as models for future research and writing.

Defining and using music: ambiguities

Like other historical topics, music can be defined broadly or narrowly. It can allude to enormous categories such as 'Western music' or 'Chinese music' – centuries of compositions, composers, performers, organisations and performance traditions.

For many people, though, 'music' is what they hear in the background every day, on radio, television, or streaming over the internet – a lifelong pageant of sound, but one that is often experienced inattentively. Those who experience music intensely during regular religious services, by contrast, find it to be much more meaningful, but perhaps only on these occasions.

'Music' also denotes more specific units of creativity and experience. It may indicate the style of a particular musician during his or her career. It may also mean a discrete piece of music, or a limited number of musical works collected in a published folio or on a compact disk. 'Music' might also refer to isolated but significant bits of song or melody – 'Taps' played at the funeral of a US soldier, or the use of Strauss's *Also Sprach Zarathustra* at the beginning of the film *2001: A Space Odyssey*. People who write about music, especially music critics, tend to exacerbate this conceptual isolation of discrete artefacts. Like formalist literary critics, they analyse individual musical works (or concerts or CDs) in a social or cultural vacuum, making little reference to extra-musical contexts that may surround them.

The choice of a narrow or broad definition of music – like similar determinations of scope in an economic or a political topic, for example – forces the historian to choose particular sources. Like a music critic, the historian might choose to write about a particularly significant single performance. The Aeolian Hall concert by the Paul Whiteman Orchestra in New York City on 12 February 1924, which introduced George Gershwin's *Rhapsody in Blue* with the composer as piano soloist, is one example. A scholar might want to test the often-stated assumption that this concert was *the* moment when jazz strove to gain the respect of classical musicians. The music played at the concert would need to be surveyed. What did it sound like? What kind of ensemble performed it? The music itself provides clues, while the wider array of sources about the concert – such as newspaper reviews and reminiscences – would provide context. Conversely, a topic such as 'music in the English Civil War' requires the study of dozens, or perhaps hundreds, of musical texts, records of a certain number of performances, a wide geographical scope, and a large cast of characters. With the expansion of the topic, the sources that are needed multiply and diversify.

Both examples, though, fundamentally challenge history students to confront the music itself. Non-musical sources, such as newspaper reviews, tangential memoirs (say, by contemporaries in town who never heard the music), performer biographies and other sources all help to situate the music in historical context. But these sources usually just make passing reference to music, providing necessary but only supplemental threads that connect music with the rest of the past. Our goal is to perceive the connection most fully, by focusing historical study on music itself, in order to privilege it and to make it the central topic or problem of the historian's concern.

Beyond the basic definition of music, there is another obvious ambiguity that students must confront – an ambiguity music shares with other performing arts (as many recognise) and with traditional written historical sources (as recent 'post-modern' critics of history have noted). Music can be performed 'live', but it can also be *recorded*. 'Recording' here refers to all ways in which music can 'exist' outside live performance. Beginning in the thirteenth century, some European musicians began to compose not on their instruments, but with their pens. Musical notation ensured that music henceforth might be recorded – put down on paper – before it was performed (although in later centuries keyboard virtuosi such as Mozart reversed this, preserving their concert improvisations in written form). Composing on paper takes place with no audience present and is often, ironically, a silent procedure. Thomas Edison's invention of the phonograph in the 1870s, though, ensured that music could be recorded in a new and equally revolutionary way. Performed music was now reproduced and replayed electronically. Today, a live performance can be broadcast to millions, even billions, of listeners via the phonograph, radio, television, motion pictures, the internet and other electronic media.[3]

Written notation and electronic recording each raise profound theoretical issues that should be confronted by anyone seeking to write music history. Notated compositions are wonderfully stable and concrete representations of musical works. In the formative decades of their discipline, in the mid-1800s, musicologists (especially in Germany) made the analysis of written texts the foundation of their work. This preference was directly analogous to the fixation of the first professional historians, working at the same time (and, again, especially in Germany) on written records for research. Since that era, though, even musicologists have come to realise that written scores are only *representations* or 'recordings' of music, which capture just a few aspects of music history. At least since the Baroque era, in fact, composers have testified that scores are only starting points, 'sets of instructions' that do not dictate every nuance of live musical performances.[4]

Scores, though, are the best – and sometimes the only – record we possess of musical performances from the pre-Edison era. As I will stress later, the short-comings of written music as evidence do not absolve historians of the responsibility to learn to read them. Nevertheless, these shortcomings pose challenges to all historians who work with musical scores. Ironically, though, thanks to the 'critical turn' in recent cultural history, the kinds of doubts most of us harbour about written musical scores have also been applied to traditional written historical sources. In the postmodernists' estimation all texts must be 'interrogated' – doubted and deconstructed. Texts are to be referenced not for their supposed truth, but for their situation within fields of discourse – the debates, theories and biases of their time. Some contemporary musicologists have taken this critical turn and inter-rogate the sexist, racist and imperialist content of notated classical compositions. (Simultaneously, postmodernists have attributed textuality to every kind of cultural artefact – including live musical performances and musical recordings. This contention, potentially liberating for scholars but also deeply problematic, lies outside the scope of this chapter.)[5]

Electronic reproduction raises other theoretical concerns. To begin with, they are now seductively easy to use. CDs and MP3 audio make it incredibly easy to compile the entire recorded legacy of a major performer, or even a broad swathe of a geographical region or musical style. A well-produced CD set of an artist's complete recordings – gigabytes of pristinely restored sound, supplemented by detailed notes in a glossy booklet – may give even the most circumspect scholar the illusion of a complete sonic archive. That is, of course, precisely the sort of illusion that the postmodern theorists rail against.

The recordings that do exist should lead students of music to question exactly what they have inscribed for posterity. Recordings are always partial documents, capturing mere slices of a musician's creative activity. The same commercial forces that make recordings possible, for example, also restrict their value as historical testimony. Louis Armstrong's trumpet improvisations in nightclubs of the 1920s, for example, often stretched for dozens of song choruses, but the 78rpm disks of the day, limited to three minutes' duration, captured only one or two of them at a time. Chroniclers of jazz have been aware of these limitations since the 1920s, but many of them have proceeded to base 'jazz history' largely on this misleading recorded legacy. They also usually neglect under-recorded or unrecorded musicians and groups.

Of course, some records are much better than none, and like written scores, recordings allow scholars to make repeated and leisurely studies of music. A dependency on recordings skews the actual history of a music, but these sources certainly can help guide the historian, suggesting a hypothesis about that history that can be tested and refined with further research.

A third major theoretical concern for students involves classifications of music. Musicologists have always striven to divide music by styles and historical periods. The most fundamental classification in the West divides music into folk, elite and popular categories. Since the 1800s musicology has privileged elite or 'classical' music, traditions of European music that originated in the church and the royal courts and were later underwritten by capitalists and the bourgeoisie. Since 1900, in countries such as the USA, college music departments have also provided classical composers with employment. Also in the twentieth century, ethno-musicologists provided theoretical and empirical support for long-held notions about the music of 'the folk', the non-elites in all societies. Assisted by new recording technology, ethnomusicologists scoured the world for traditional peasant, rural and aboriginal music, much of it threatened by rising urbanisation and modern mass media. Those new forces, in turn, fomented the third major category, 'popular music' – material disseminated by commercial industries such as publishing, recording, touring circuits, motion pictures and television. Until very recently, most musicologists and musicians subscribed to this three-part model of the musical universe, and some still do so today.[6]

Historians in particular can appreciate the virtue of this model. Each of the three parts evokes a major cohort in modern Western history: aristocrats, peasants and the 'mass' industrial classes. As a heuristic model, in fact, the elite–folk–popular triad suggests very neatly how music might be incorporated further into standard histories of Europe, the USA and other modern or modernising regions. Periodisation in musical history also seems to align music with more general historical trends. Baroque music (*c.*1670–1740), for example, is inevitably associated with the architecture of the same designation, with which it shares certain aesthetic features (complex ornamentation, awe-inspiring contrast and scale), and with the similarly grandiose 'absolute' monarchies that patronised both arts. Cultural historians and musicologists alike have wrestled with the question of whether or not musical styles throughout history are aligned chronologically within the appropriate *Zeitgeist* – a distinct time period in which artistic, social and political trends cohere into distinct styles.

Almost all the models of musical periodisation, though, have been criticised for being inaccurate or too simplistic. The elite–folk–popular model also has been found to have plenty of flaws. Much 'folk' music in the era of recording, for example, is popular song from records and radio, adapted and transformed by people around their own hearths and doorsteps. 'Elite' musicians such as Caruso and Pavarotti have become popular celebrities. 'Popular' musicians such as Gershwin and McCartney delve into classical composition.

These flaws, though, should only encourage students of music history to investigate its relation to general history with more care. These heuristic models should encourage revisionism and greater sophistication. Music has accompanied military campaigns, courtship, rituals of leadership, the rites of passage of commoners and aristocrats alike, organised religious practices, personal mysticism, games and pastimes of childhood and adulthood, and numerous other major facets of the human experience. Scholars should at least try to remap human history along the contours of music history. Theoretical problems abound in the details, as we have seen, but the general promise of such a challenge should encourage us to get working!

What does music mean?

Enough about what music *is*. Another set of theoretical challenges arises when we consider the issue: What does music *mean*? Debates about music's meaning have spanned millennia and the globe. Ancient Chinese and Indian thinkers probably originated the study of the mathematical and acoustic properties of music – the approach to music that was emulated in the West by Pythagoras and his followers. Down to the present, the Pythagorean approach has allied music with mathematics and science. For medieval religious thinkers, such an approach reinforced their abstract notion of music as disembodied sound that mingled with angels to produce 'the music of the spheres'. Twentieth-century avant-garde composers echoed this attitude, treating music as a closed system to inoculate their work from the alleged unscientific and emotional distortions of mundane daily life.

The ancient Greeks pioneered other ideas about music's meaning as well. Plato and his followers considered music to be central to a philosopher's moral education. Other thinkers stressed the distinctiveness of music as an art and stressed the need to bring composition, instrumentation and other techniques to fruition over time (a 'progressivist' notion that later inspired medieval church music notation and the innovations of the Renaissance). Probably the oldest Greek notion, though, held that music was neither moral nor artistic, but rather the wild expression of the untamed human emotions, the cry of drunkenness, lust and other irrational urges.

The word 'music', ironically, derives from the term for 'the business of the Muses', who were thought to concern themselves exclusively with 'superior' arts – such as history – and to disdain singing and strumming.[7]

A science, a moral curriculum, a self-contained art, unchecked emotionalism – to a remarkable degree, these differing notions of music's meaning remain with us. Philosophers of music struggle to reconcile these conflicting interpretations. The unresolved nature of music's identity has helped to slow the incorporation of music into the story of the human past, and historians in general have made little effort to speed the process. Conversely, though, by initiating the thoughtful study of music in history, historians may be able to help settle some of these age-old confusions about music's meaning. Students who feel inclined to take up this challenge will discover exciting new avenues of exploration.

Those who investigate music in the West since the Romantic era (*c.* 1810–50) confront a special set of clashing theories, relating to the meaning of music within modern societal conflict. As Jacques Barzun and other historians have shown, classical music was central to the intellectual history of the 1800s, when thinkers puzzled over the new course of 'progress'. Idealists, the philosophical heirs of Kant and Hegel, saw music as evidence of the continuing synthesis of knowledge and society into ever-improving new phenomena – as the theme song, as it were, for modern progress. The young Nietzsche, intoxicated by Wagner, situated the 'birth of tragedy' in the cradle of music (which he considered the pre-eminent art form).[8] Attacking this notion of progress were materialists, ultimately led by Marx. In the early twentieth century, expressing the profound pessimism bred by the two world wars, Marxist thinkers such as Walter Benjamin and, above all, Theodor Adorno sought to strip music of its 'aura' of idealism. Although Benjamin and Adorno remained curiously attached to the notion of music as utopia-representing 'the promise of a life without fear', as Adorno called it – they also relentlessly exposed the corruption of music by the 'culture industry', the capitalist exploitation of music through commercial touring, radio, the phonograph and the motion picture.[9]

'Music' is a complex thing in any large society, but in the past century of electronic mass media, music's identity has been especially hard to grasp. Benjamin, Adorno and other members of the so-called Frankfurt School of cultural studies first noted how recordings seemed to threaten to overtake live music, supplanting 'the real thing' by virtue of their overwhelming ubiquity. More recently, though, beginning in the 1960s, students of popular culture – especially the new generation of British Marxist scholars – have rebutted this pessimistic criticism of mass-distributed music. These scholars discovered pockets of interaction and experience in popular music that help to liberate youth from oppressive industrial (or post-industrial) existence. Sociologists in the USA in these decades characteristically developed a less overtly ideological view, but they did especially reveal how musicians and listeners used jazz and the blues to define themselves as social deviants. Studies of punk rock, grunge, hip hop, reggae and other genres indicate that on both sides of the Atlantic (and the Pacific), despite the rise of an endlessly replicating mass culture, music retains its power to help people rebel against that culture and define their own corners of refuge, even of utopia.[10] These findings particularly suggest that historians would benefit from exploring the place of music within key discourses about progress and society in the modern era.

Music's ability to represent non-musical things has also been a source of theoretical debate. To what extent, especially, can music be said to represent social reality? This is a particular concern for historians striving to determine music's relation to society in general. Much music is fundamentally representational. Scholars have found that almost all aboriginal groups imitate the soundscapes of nature. In the same groups, music and language often develop simultaneously and share characteristics. Millennia ago this process nurtured tonal languages such as Mandarin and Lithuanian. Generally, though, as cultures developed, music's mimetic character was obscured; music usually developed a special identity and repertoire and became largely self-referential. Music, in short, came mostly to 'mean itself'.

However, in certain basic ways music remains powerfully representational. In virtually every human society music remains closely associated with spirituality. In shamanistic cultures songs are expressions of supernatural spirits entering human bodies, while in the major world religions music generally expresses faith and devotion. Music is also used nearly universally to signify and express deep emotion – despair, joy, amorous feelings and other passions – in ways that transcend the more information-heavy medium of spoken language.[11]

With regard to language, we must also consider briefly the fact that music is often difficult to divorce from the words attached to it, especially the lyrics applied to song melodies. Lyrics may be said to endow music with verbal information. If historians analyse, say, the lyrics of anthems of the French Revolution, are they still analysing music? A brief, common-sense answer might be that words and music can be studied separately, but that ignoring the one or the other detracts from the total artefact. No one would claim, for example, that written texts of the blues or freedom songs of the US civil rights movement capture the rich expressiveness of African American singing – in which musical notes and their style of delivery are chosen and the texts are integrated into a total artistic continuum. Similarly, although the music of Wagner's *Ring* cycle remains its most enduring element, we should never ignore the text (written by the composer himself) or the rich and diverse stagings of the four operas that have taken place since their premieres. Religious music cannot and should not be considered apart from the sacred or devotional texts with which they are paired. My point, then, is that historians should learn to understand and to evaluate music with the same facility which with they handle written-language sources, so that they can most effectively place music in the context of general human experience.

In summation, scholarly findings to date indicate that music should be a tempting topic for historical inquiry because it expresses certain human experiences and emotions, especially spirituality and passionate feeling, in uniquely powerful ways that elude the written and spoken word and other art forms. While music exhibits scientific and mathematical properties, its affective properties seem to define its honoured place in most, if not all, cultures. Finally, it is apparent that music attracts special interest in particular historical contexts – such as ancient Greece or industrial Europe – in which thinkers found it to be a notable embodiment of major philosophical notions.

Working with music

What, then, must a historian know about music? The technical jargon of Western music (to which I will confine myself in this section) is formidable. If historians want to be able to comprehend musicologists' analyses, they need to be conversant with the methods and terminology of the field. This is analogous to a historian gaining a strong understanding of particle physics in order to write a history of that topic, using terms and concepts from physicists' research and writing. (Historical writing is noted for its general freedom from jargon – even projects resulting from the most technically oriented research tend to be rendered in laymen's terms – but we are concerned now with research, not its final presentation.) Most historians and probably all history students, though, would not need to be so technical. The vast majority of musical phenomena can be researched with only a basic grounding in terminology, along with a general acquaintance with what musical practitioners do.[12]

Some of the terminology is quite familiar. *Rhythm* – the arrangement of notes over time – can vary considerably even in a short piece of music, but a basic, repeated rhythmic pulse or *metre* usually dominates. A *melody* is a tune that can either comprise virtually an entire short selection or serve as the inspiration for a longer composition. *Harmony* is the combination of different notes to produce satisfying *chords* or ensemble instrumentation. Various terms denote the structure of a work, which may be made up of sections, numbers, movements, or shorter musical passages. In the Western tradition various structures, such as *symphony*, *sonata*, *theme and variations*, and *rondo*, became common formal templates. A *scale* is an established sequence of notes – most commonly in the West they are seven notes in 'major' or 'minor' modes – in which a melody or work is anchored (in other words, the *key* in which it is set). Other musical terms might be less familiar to most historians. *Timbre* refers to the quality of a vocal or instrumental sound, described in everyday terms such as 'rough', 'smooth', 'resonant', or 'constricted'. *Consonance* (highly regular harmony) and *dissonance* (clashing tones) are opposing descriptions of the harmonic qualities of a work. *Modulation* refers to the change of key within a work.

Beyond these general terms, there are those pertaining to particular styles and instruments. Any historian writing about jazz ought to know (and explain) what 'comping', 'stop time' and 'riffs' are, while one discussing Western bowed instruments would refer to *pizzicato*, *arco* and *col legno*. (Much classical music vocabulary originated in Italy.)

Terminology allows historians to describe the music itself – how it sounds – and allows them to compare selections and styles. Compositions on paper offer abundant data about the music they contain. That is helpful, but it also invites the scholar to make much more complex and technical analysis. Compared to music performance, written composition is an introverted process, bound up in the complex symbology of notation. It is no surprise that musicological studies of scores often resemble literary scholars' painstaking analyses of poets' and novelists' sketches and drafts. If a historian chooses to discuss a composer's work in terms that go beyond basic description, training in music theory and its technical terminology is probably needed.

There are, however, other ways to interrogate musical phenomena. As with any 'labour history' (to use the term very broadly), historians of music can benefit from explorations of how music is actually produced. Method books by vocal or instrumental pedagogues – especially those from the relevant era – can provide information, as can histories of musical production by musicologists. The study of the musician's profession within a given culture – training, organisations, employment and the like – situates music wonderfully within concrete social, economic and cultural contexts. Similarly, acts of music-making – concerts, recitals, amateur expressions, spontaneous eruptions of song in unlikely settings – can be studied by historians by coupling their familiar technique of contextualisation (setting the time, place and circumstances) with the new understanding of music and how it is created that I have advocated here. Finally, of course, the historian can explore the relation between music and the broadest contexts of culture – the audience, the market, and discourses and social processes that make actual and metaphorical use of music. If such far-flung studies of music and society retain a focus on the fundamental musical stuff in question, I would suggest, tones and melodies would become much more healthily integrated into the general understanding of the human past.

Models for future historical work

In the field I know best, the history of music in the USA, some fine models of this kind of work already exist. Unsurprisingly, the ones that make the most detailed use of musical examples have been written by historically minded musicologists. Two works on Latino music make particularly effective use of songs as the foundation of historical study. Ruth Glasser's examination of Puerto Rican music during the mass migration to New York City in the 1920s and 1930s centres in part on 'Lamento Borincano', a 'Puerto Rican lament' that, for many migrants, poignantly expressed their feeling of separation from their homeland. Glasser notes that 'a musical analysis' of the song 'would show the influences of Italian opera, Puerto Rican mountain music, and Cuban popular sounds' but she does not make such an analysis, focusing instead on the social context surrounding it. 'The song', Glasser notes, 'was purely a New York product.' Composer Rafael Hernández claimed that while meeting friends in a Harlem restaurant, 'the nostalgia of that cold, sad, and melancholy afternoon drew my fingers to the almost-falling-apart piano in a corner, and I began to play the melody of "Lamento Borincano".'[13]

Steven Loza's *Barrio Rhythm* explores the musical culture of Mexican-American Los Angeles. Loza, a native of east Los Angeles, conducted oral histories with veteran musicians and accumulated an array of other sources on the topic:

recordings, playbills, school records, newspaper clippings and photographs. In several instances his exhaustive research revealed complex and rich cultural meanings in a musical artefact. One example of this is 'The Ballad of Pancho Lopez', a song in English written in 1956 by the veteran Los Angeles guitarist and songwriter Lalo Guerrero. The song, a parody of the recently popular 'Ballad of Davy Crockett', became the best-selling single record to date to come out of Mexican-American Los Angeles. Residents of the *barrio* accused Guerrero of pandering to Anglo record buyers with a song that perpetuated the derogatory stereotype of the lazy, slow-witted Mexican man. (Pancho Lopez does little but run a taco stand and take naps.)[14] In the late 1960s, as Latino rock bands aggressively espoused 'Chicano power', the song passed into oblivion. Loza's research shows, though, that Guerrero had strong credentials as a performer and composer in east Los Angeles. As his song's success shows, he also suffered from a cultural marginalisation that especially afflicted Mexican-American musicians, who were caught between their roots and the constraints of the mass market.[15]

Individual songs such as these can serve as windows into cultural complexities and predicaments. Like 'Danny Boy' (whose lyrics were written by an Englishman who never set foot in Ireland, and which is most popular among North Americans of Irish descent), the two Latino songs were not 'pure' or 'authentic' expressions of the cultures with which they are identified. Their musical qualities and lyrical narratives provide evidence of group experiences in particular historical contexts. Other examples are easy to cite. An ancient Jewish tune became the famed standard 'Havah Nagila' in 1918, as Zionists celebrated the Allied powers' apparent endorsement of a future Jewish homeland in Palestine. The brothers James Weldon and John Rosamond Johnson, African-American writers and performers, wrote the lyrics to 'Lift Every Voice and Sing' in 1899, and twenty years later it was adopted by the New York City branch of the National Association for the Advancement of Colored People (NAACP) as the so-called 'Negro national anthem'. Johnny Marks's 'Rudolph the Red-Nosed Reindeer' from the 1940s illustrated the power of corporate marketing as it moved from a department store greeting card into American commercial holiday folklore.

Historians have begun to align larger trends in music history with the more general contours of the past. An excellent example can be found in the story of how historians have come to explore African-American music. In the 1960s the US civil rights movement and other developments inspired young scholars to examine the black experience in depth, and to correct for the neglect, untested assumptions and occasional hostility of previous generations of (usually white) scholars.[16] Historians of this era inevitably turned much of their attention to black leadership and struggles for political and civil rights, but the most innovative studies sought to re-create the social history of average black people in slavery and in freedom.[17] Social historians needed help in order to be steered towards the history of black music. The few musicologists who had explored the topic, such as Eileen Southern and Dena Epstein, were of assistance,[18] but it was anthropology and folklore that provide historians with the most guidance. Pioneering students of West African and Caribbean cultures showed that African 'survivals' fundamentally shaped black religion, language, material arts, agriculture, family organisation – and music – in the New World.[19] Historians' new appreciation of the centrality of culture to our understanding of African-Americans of the past – who left few written records – drew them towards music. Lawrence W. Levine, in his pioneering *Black Culture and Black Consciousness* (1977), found the greatest and most revealing continuities in black culture from slavery to freedom in its music (which, he noted, was closely allied with spoken lore). Also, though, Levine noted that in the transition from spirituals to secular blues, music revealed the greatest cultural transformation that affected average African-Americans after emancipation.[20] In succeeding years, scholars have challenged and even debunked a number of Levine's arguments, but the centrality of music to our understanding of the African-American experience has not been dislodged.[21]

Professional historians as a group have been slow to emulate Levine's focus on music in the African-American past, but progress can be reported. We see this, for example, in the recent historical scholarship on jazz. Amateurs, usually critics or 'buffs', have written most jazz history. Few professional historians have helped write it, or have even used jazz seriously to illuminate American (or African-American) history as a whole. Among their number, though, we find pioneers such as Eric Hobsbawm and Neil Leonard and current practitioners such as Kathy Ogren, William Howland Kenney, David Stowe, Douglas Daniels, Sherrie Tucker, Joel Dinerstein and myself.[22] Our research into periodicals, oral histories, business records and photographs has helped to reveal jazz's importance to African-American communities, its precarious position as a multiracial music, its symbolic role as modernist, urban and 'democratic' music, and significance as an arena for changing gender roles.

Musicologists, though, are the scholars who have integrated jazz music itself into historical analyses of black America. While they rarely delve into social and political history to the depth that professional historians do, the interdisciplinary nature of their work especially helps to guide the rest of us in use of the music as a historical source. Ethnomusicology and postmodern critical theory have encouraged these musicologists to develop new approaches.[23] Notable among them are Paul Berliner (a veteran of African ethnomusicological fieldwork), who traces basic musical motifs in jazz literally note by note to tell the story of the lore of the music as a historical narrative. Mark Tucker, Scott DeVeaux and, to a lesser extent, Ted Gioia and Gunther Schuller (the dean of jazz musicologists) also have balanced historical context with analyses of the sounds of jazz. A culmination of this approach was Ingrid Monson's 1996 study, *Saying Something*. Monson uses exhaustive participant observation within the rhythm section of a professional combo (featuring the bassist, drummer and pianist) to show how the notes 'say something', as an elaboration of spoken communications between the musicians (and by extension within African-American culture). Her study especially breaks new ground in exploring the elusive relationship of music to language.[24]

The scope of *Louis Armstrong's New Orleans* (2006) by Thomas Brothers is larger than that of Monson's book. Jazz in New Orleans from 1900 to 1930 is a familiar topic in jazz history, but Brothers, like Monson, also aims to reveal what the music 'said' – expressing, in this case, profound cultural and historical change. Brothers's book is full of innovations in its scrutiny of New Orleans jazz and its greatest practitioner, Louis Armstrong. While these topics have attracted scores of chroniclers, they remain cryptic and paradoxical. The core mystery persists: how could this poor and racially oppressive city give rise to one of the most exciting, even revolutionary, popular musics of the twentieth century?

Brothers's study wisely shows just how unlikely Armstrong's rise to prominence was, and how close he often came to falling into obscurity. Poverty and racism conspired viciously to hold Armstrong down (and nearly succeeded), but black culture in New Orleans provided enough footholds for this optimistic and intelligent young man to solidify his artistry. In the end, though, Armstrong had to leave the city to realise his ambitions. Many of the obscure or anonymous musicians who influenced young Louis, such as the pedlars whose blasts on tin horns (to announce their presence in the neighbourhood) provided Armstrong with models for his cornet playing. It is a cliché that New Orleans was an invigorating 'gumbo' of diverse cultures, but Brothers shows how selective and often pernicious ethnic interaction and cultural sharing in the city usually were. The Holiness churches of poor blacks were disdained by other city residents, but they decisively shaped Armstrong's singing style (which became as influential as his trumpet playing). Also, by analysing a number of recordings, Brothers demonstrates convincingly that the light-skinned 'Creoles of color' in New Orleans did not contribute to, or (with some key exceptions) even learn, the blues-drenched 'hot' style that Armstrong championed. Only in later decades did some Creoles catch up artistically with the 'American Negro' players they shunned socially.[25]

Louis Armstrong's New Orleans, in short, depicts a cultural drama in which musical sounds and styles, championed by striving young men such as Armstrong, persisted and triumphed. Thomas Brothers blends musicological techniques with detail from written sources and oral histories to situate musical selections (usually Armstrong's) as convincing protagonists in the drama. While few musical stories possess the native pungency or improbable upward mobility of Armstrong's early life in New Orleans, almost any of them would be enlivened by such an approach.

Conclusion

Students of history should adopt these approaches as well. Like the scholars I have just discussed, they can employ gossamer melodic lines and 'inarticulate' drum-beats to show how music has helped to express and to cause cultural transformation, and has moved individuals, communities, or nations from one set of social realities to another. Generations of scholars from many disciplines have contributed diverse approaches to solving the riddle of music's meaning and its impact on human affairs, and today communications media allow us to gain access rapidly to vast arrays of written and aural musical texts. It is my hope that in the near future young scholars will do work which will help to construct a new and rich history of music's place in epochs throughout time and in societies around the globe.

Notes

1 James M. McPherson, *Battle Cry of Freedom: The Civil War Era*, New York, Oxford: Oxford University Press, 1988; Eugene Genovese, *Roll, Jordan, Roll: The World the Slaves Made*, New York: Pantheon Books, 1974.

2 See for example Paul Henry Lang, *Music in Western Civilization*, New York: Norton, 1941; Carl Dahlhaus, *Foundations of Music History*, Cambridge: Cambridge University Press, 1983; Lawrence Kramer, *Music as Cultural Practice, 1800–1900*, Berkeley: University of California Press, 1990; Bruno Nettl, *The Study of Ethnomusicology: Thirty-one Issues and Concepts* (2nd edn), Urbana, IL: University of Illinois Press, 2006; Bonnie C. Wade, *Imaging Sound: An Ethnomusicological Study of Music, Art, and Culture in Mughal India*, Chicago: University of Chicago Press, 1998.

3 An interesting exploration of the phonograph's impact on music is Evan Eisenberg, *The Recording Angel: Explorations in Phonography*, New York: McGraw-Hill, 1987. On the origins of notation, see Lewis G. Rowell, *Thinking About Music: An Introduction to the Philosophy of Music*, Amherst, MA: University of Massachusetts Press, 1983, chaps 3, 5.

4 On the origins of modern musicology, see 'Musicology', in Stanley Sadie (ed.), *The New Grove Dictionary of Music and Musicians* (2nd edn), New York: Grove, 2001, vol. 17, pp. 488–9, 492–4.

5 Useful introductions to postmodernism include Alan Megill, *Prophets of Extremity: Nietzsche, Heidegger, Foucault, Derrida*, Berkeley: University of California Press, 1985; Lynn Hunt (ed.), *The New Cultural History*, Berkeley: University of California Press, 1989; Terry Eagleton, *Literary Theory: An Introduction* (2nd edn), Oxford: Blackwell, 1996. Postmodernist musicological studies include Kramer, *Music as Cultural Practice*; Tia DeNora, *Beethoven and the Construction of Genius: Musical Politics in Vienna, 1792–1803*, Berkeley: University of California Press, 1995; Susan McClary, *Feminine Endings: Music, Gender, and Sexuality* (2nd edn), Minneapolis: University of Minnesota Press, 2002; Timothy D. Taylor, *Beyond Exoticism: Western Music and the World*, Durham, NC: Duke University Press, 2007.

6 For a survey of the history of musicology, see 'Musicology', in Sadie (ed.), *Dictionary*, vol. 17, pp. 488–533. On ethnomusicology, see for example 'Ethnomusicology', in Sadie (ed.), *Dictionary*, vol. 8, pp. 367–95; Timothy Rice, 'Toward the remodeling of ethnomusicology', *Ethnomusicology* 31.3, 1987, pp. 469–88; Bruno Nettl and Philip V. Bohlman (eds), *Comparative Musicology and Anthropology of Music: Essays on the History of Ethnomusicology*, Chicago: University of Chicago Press, 1990. On the theory of popular music, see David Brackett, *Interpreting Popular Music*, Cambridge: Cambridge University Press, 1995; Keith Negus, *Popular Music and Theory: An Introduction*, Middletown, CT: Wesleyan University Press, 1996.

7 See for example 'Philosophy of music', in Sadie (ed.), *Dictionary*, vol. 19, pp. 611–14; Rowell, *Thinking About Music*, chaps 1–2.

8 See for example Lang, *Music in Western Civilization*, chap. 16; Jacques Barzun, *Darwin, Marx, Wagner: Critique of a Heritage* (2nd edn), Garden City, NY: Doubleday, 1958, part 3; Kramer, *Music as Cultural Practice*, chaps 1–4; Friedrich Nietzsche, *The Birth of Tragedy*, 1875; rept. edn, Oxford: Oxford University Press, 2000.

9 Walter Benjamin, 'The work of art in the age of mechanical reproduction', in *Illuminations*, New York: Schocken Books, 1969 (rept. edn), pp. 217–51; Theodor Adorno, *Sound Figures*, Stanford, CA: Stanford University Press, 1999, pp. 2–14, and *Introduction to the Sociology of Music*, New York: Seabury Press, 1976; 'Philosophy of music', in Sadie (ed.), *Dictionary*, vol. 19, pp. 620–1. Ernst Bloch, who expressed a romantic and utopian vision of music's potential role in industrial society, was an exception among Marxist philosophers of the early twentieth century.

10 Representative of British scholarship are Simon Frith, *Sound Effects: Youth, Leisure, and the Politics of Rock'n'Roll*, London: Constable, 1983; John Clarke and Chas

Critcher, *The Devil Makes Work: Leisure in Capitalist Britain*, Urbana, IL: University of Illinois Press, 1985; Paul Chatterton and Robert Hollands, *Urban Nightscapes: Youth Cultures, Pleasure Spaces, and Corporate Power*, London: Routledge, 2003. American scholarship on deviance and jazz includes Morroe Berger, 'Jazz: resistance to the diffusion of a culture pattern', *Journal of Negro History* 32.4, October 1947, pp. 461–94; Neil Leonard, *Jazz and the White Americans: The Acceptance of a New Art Form*, Chicago: University of Chicago Press, 1962; Howard S. Becker, *Outsiders: Studies in the Sociology of Deviance*, New York: Free Press, 1963.

11 Three major explorations of music's relationship to language are Deryck Cooke, *The Language of Music*, Oxford: Oxford University Press, 1959; Leonard Bernstein, *The Unanswered Question: Six Talks at Harvard*, Cambridge, MA: Harvard University Press, 1976; and especially Joseph P. Swain, *Musical Languages*, New York: Norton, 1997.

12 The standard basic guide to the use of jargon or technical terminology in historical writing is Jacques Barzun and Henry F. Graff, *The Modern Researcher* (6th edn), Belmont, CA: Wadsworth, 2004, chap. 9.

13 Ruth Glasser, *My Music is My Flag: Puerto Rican Musicians and their New York Communities, 1917–1940*, Berkeley: University of California Press, 1995, pp. 163–4.

14 Steven Loza, *Barrio Rhythm: Mexican American Music in Los Angeles*, Urbana, IL: University of Illinois Press, 1993, pp. 73–6.

15 Loza, *Barrio Rhythm*, pp. 67–75, 162–5. See also Lalo Guerrero and Sherilyn Meece Mentes, *Lalo: My Life and Music*, Tucson, AZ: The University of Arizona Press, 2002.

16 Robert L. Harris, Jr, 'Coming of age: the transformation of Afro-American historiography', *Journal of Negro History* 67.2, 1982, pp. 107–21; Peter J. Parish, *Slavery: History and Historians*, New York: Harper & Row, 1989.

17 Important works include John W. Blassingame, *The Slave Community: Plantation Life in the Antebellum South*, New York: Oxford University Press, 1972; Genovese, *Roll, Jordan, Roll*; Robert William Fogel and Stanley L. Engerman, *Time on the Cross: The Economics of American Negro Slavery*, Boston: Little, Brown, 1974; Herbert G. Gutman, *The Black Family in Slavery and Freedom, 1750–1825*, New York: Pantheon Books, 1976; Leon F. Litwack, *Been in the Storm So Long: The Aftermath of Slavery*, New York: Knopf, 1979.

18 Eileen Southern, *The Music of Black Americans* (1st edn), New York: W.W. Norton, 1971; Dena J. Epstein, *Sinful Tunes and Spirituals: Black Folk Music to the Civil War*, Urbana, IL: University of Illinois Press, 1977. See also John Lovell, *Black Song: The Forge and the Flame*, New York: Macmillan, 1972.

19 Melville J. Herskovits, *The Myth of the Negro Past*, New York: Harper & Bros, 1941; J.L. Dillard, *Black English: Its History and Usage in the United States*, New York: Random House, 1972; Robert Farris Thompson, *Flash of the Spirit: African and Afro-American Art and Philosophy*, New York: Random House, 1983; Roger D. Abrahams, *The Man-of-Words in the West Indies: Performance and the Emergence of Creole Culture*, Baltimore, MD: Johns Hopkins University Press, 1983 (among other works by this author).

20 Lawrence W. Levine, *Black Culture and Black Consciousness: Afro-American Folk Thought From Slavery to Freedom*, New York: Oxford University Press, 1977, p. 6.

21 Direct rebuttals of some of Levine's arguments may be found in Gerhard Kubik, *Africa and the Blues*, Jackson, MS: University Press of Mississippi, 1999; Ronald M. Radano, *Lying up a Nation: Race and Black Music*, Chicago: University of Chicago Press, 2003, pp. 6–7. Henry Louis Gates, Jr, *The Signifying Monkey: A Theory of Afro-American Literary Criticism*, New York: Oxford University Press, 1988, epitomised a major new trend in African-American studies, whose impact on music scholarship is best exemplified by Samuel A. Floyd, Jr, *The Power of Black Music: Interpreting its History From Africa to the United States*, New York: Oxford University Press, 1995.

22 Francis Newton [Eric Hobsbawm], *The Jazz Scene*, New York: Pantheon Press, 1960;

Leonard, *Jazz and the White Americans*; Kathy J. Ogren, *The Jazz Revolution: Twenties America and the Meaning of Jazz*, New York: Oxford University Press, 1989; Burton W. Peretti, *The Creation of Jazz: Music, Race, and Culture in Urban America*, Urbana, IL: University of Illinois Press, 1992; William Howland Kenney, *Chicago Jazz: A Cultural History, 1904–1930*, New York: Oxford University Press, 1993, and *Jazz on the River*, Chicago: University of Chicago Press, 2005; David W. Stowe, *Swing Changes: Big-Band Jazz in New Deal America*, Cambridge, MA: Harvard University Press, 1994; Douglas Henry Daniels, *Lester Leaps In: The Life and Times of Lester 'Pres' Young*, Boston: Beacon, 2002, and *One O'clock Jump: The Unforgettable History of the Oklahoma City Blue Devils*, Boston: Beacon, 2005; Sherrie Tucker, *Swing Shift: 'All-Girl' Bands of the 1940s*, Durham, NC: Duke University Press, 2000; Joel Dinerstein, *Swinging the Machine: Modernity, Technology, and African American Culture Between the World Wars*, Amherst, MA: University of Massachusetts Press, 2003.
23 'Musicology', in Sadie (ed.), *Dictionary*, vol. 17, pp. 523–4.
24 Paul Berliner, *Thinking in Jazz: The Infinite Art of Improvisation*, Chicago: University of Chicago Press, 1994; Mark Tucker, *Ellington: The Early Years*, Urbana, IL: University of Illinois Press, 1991; Ted Gioia, *West Coast Jazz: Modern Jazz in California, 1945–1960*, New York: Oxford University Press, 1992; *The History of Jazz*, New York: Oxford University Press, 1997; Scott DeVeaux, *The Birth of Bebop: A Social and Musical History*, Berkeley: University of California Press, 1997; Ingrid Monson, *Saying Something: Jazz Improvisation and Interaction*, Chicago: University of Chicago Press, 1996.
25 Thomas Brothers, *Louis Armstrong's New Orleans*, New York: W.W. Norton, 2006, particularly chaps 2, 4, 6 and 7.

7 Oral History: the sound of memory

Corinna M. Peniston-Bird

Oral history is the historical source most greatly influenced by the passage of time. It rests on accounts of past experiences and events from the perspective of contemporaries, related after a time delay. Time not only permeates every word spoken, it also robs the historian of sources with every passing day. Ample reason, then, to encourage more historians to engage with this rich and challenging primary source, and to counter its detractors. The complexities of oral history begin with its definition. It is a multi-faceted term: in the singular with the indefinite article, an oral history refers to a spoken memoir, while 'oral history' describes a historical process and methodology; or, as Alessandro Portelli puts it, the term thus refers both to what oral historians hear and to what they subsequently write.[1] In the context of branches of history, the term can be misleading: rather than constituting a distinct type of historical investigation, oral history constitutes a methodology and source base which can be integrated into approaches to history such as social, political, cultural, economic, medical, legal or military history. One of the oldest sources, it predates the written word but gained momentum with the invention of portable recording devices in the 1940s, a momentum which has continued into the twenty-first century and the versatility of digital technologies. Further impetus has stemmed from shifts in historical focus: from the desire to capture the experiences not only of the 'Great Men of History', but of everyday life and experiences, for example the shift from consulting documentary sources to examining all records left by human life, and, more recently, a growing interest in memory, both collective and individual.[2]

When commencing a project, an oral historian needs to consider the following issues:

- the relationship between the research question and the source (does the question exploit the strengths of oral histories?);
- what type of interview is most appropriate (structured, semi-structured, free recall);
- how respondents will be identified and with what organisational logic. For example, unless the project is focused on specific individuals, what would constitute a 'representative' subject group; how many interview partners should be sought; who would the ideal respondents be, and (later in the process) how

does that ideal relate to the final selection which is likely also to exhibit random or circumstantial characteristics?

- what equipment to use (this changes quickly; within my lifetime from reel to reel to cassette recorders to digital recorders, but is also influenced by the intended location of the interview, the financial foundation of the project, and the longer-term intended use and destination for the recordings);
- what and how to transcribe, and will a data analysis package be employed – transcription is expensive, costing the researcher substantial amounts of either time or money, but early selectivity can be counter-productive.

For practical, up-to-date advice on these issues, readers are referred to the endnotes of some excellent guides, and should also explore the websites of the Oral History Society in Great Britain and the Oral History Association in the United States and in Australia.[3] The focus of this chapter will instead be on some of the key concepts which have engaged oral historians, and it will discuss the characteristics of oral testimonies and their relationship to other primary sources.

Oral history offers access to material that simply may not exist in any other form, from individuals who might otherwise leave little trace of the details of their existence. It has thus played a major role in what has been termed 'recovery history', recovering the voices of those who have been hidden, such as the working classes or women.[4] Oral history also alerts us to the strengths and weaknesses of the written record. For example, for a recent research project on homosexuality in the British Armed Forces in World War II, the written record included the medical discourse, the traces left by prosecutions and a minimal amount of material kept from debates within the Armed Forces, veiled behind allusion.[5] It was the oral testimony, however, which revealed how unrepresentative these sources were of the experiences and indeed the reception of homosexual men and women within the Forces.

Selectivity and gaps can be characteristics of oral history also, however, at a most basic level determined not only by the number of witnesses to draw upon, but also by their willingness to share their memories. In the case of the above-mentioned project, a very small number of homosexual men and no women responded to the multiple and repeated invitations to contribute. In consequence, the interview sample was much more selective than the ideal would have been. In terms of publication, many of the issues concerning selectivity and representativeness in oral histories are identical to those confronted by historians seeking to investigate any area in which source materials are limited, or by historians citing any source not reproduced in its entirety, or not readily available to all researchers. More specific to oral history are the ways that selectivity and silence resonate within oral histories, and this is discussed at greater length below.

Conducting oral histories is expensive, time-consuming and frequently unpredictable. Those are not the most common criticisms levelled against this source, however. The continued contention surrounding the value of oral testimony is surprising and sterile, dependent as it is on a false distinction between historical source materials. Most frequently, oral interviews have been criticised as inaccurate and subjective, prone to exhibiting all types of bias. Given that human memory is notoriously inaccurate, eye-witness accounts are easily construed as highly unreliable. As recently as 2001, the historian Arthur Marwick dismissed oral testimony as 'inherently (given the fallibility of human memory) a highly problematic source'.[6] Critics also point to the temporal gap between the experience and its relating, a time period in which memories are corrupted: reworked and impacted upon by subsequent life experiences and external interpretations of those events and their meanings.

Inaccuracy, subjectivity and time lag are not issues unique to oral histories, however, nor are the ways in which these characteristics can be responded to by the historian. The interview can be checked for internal consistency and inconsistencies, for example, and careful questioning can uncover contradictions, confusions or agendas. When factual accuracy is paramount, a skilled interviewer can find ways of helping their partner remember, without unduly influencing the data: 'What were you wearing?/Was it already dark?', for example, as a way of establishing what time of year is being described. Data can be triangulated, that is, cross-referenced against other sources so that material is found that complements, confirms or contradicts the memory. That should not be understood as suggesting that oral history is only of value when confirmed by documentary sources: if that were the case, it would be superfluous or, at best, an addendum. Instead, as Trevor Lummis notes, 'many of the problems of authenticity in oral evidence are simply the problems of documentary sources made plain and the value of any source depends, to some degree, on the quality of alternative sources.'[7] It may seem obvious, but the value of oral histories is dependent on the question being asked by the historian: many of the criticisms levelled against oral histories assume contexts in which they are being interrogated for material better found elsewhere (of which more below). Rather than setting sources up against each other, however, more usefully oral and documentary sources can be used in juxtaposition so that emphases, silences and interpretations can be cross-referenced and the different contexts of their creation used as an advantage. Rather than being dismissed for contradicting each other, or being positioned in a hierarchy of authenticity dependent not on content but on genre, these sources should instead be used for mutual illumination.

A distinction should be drawn between factual inconsistencies and interpretative shifts within interviews. In interviews conducted with veterans of the British Home Guard, for example, a home defence organisation set up in World War II, Penny Summerfield and I found that, over the course of the interview, some interview partners offered several alternative interpretations of the value of the Home Guard. As more memories were recalled and were met with an unjudgemental response, these interview partners became less likely to present their memories in the light of previous audience responses, less likely to reproduce the dominant cultural construction of the force, and more confident about asserting their own authority in interpreting the significance of the force.[8] Another genre of oral history encourages similar resilience: the life review, in which the meaning of selected experiences is placed into the wider context of character development over a life history. Conducted in the later years of an individual's life, the life review may take place well after the events being recalled but is typified by the desire to remember and, as Paul Thompson puts it, 'a diminished concern with fitting the story to the social norms of the audience. Thus bias from both repression and distortion becomes a less inhibiting difficulty, for both teller and historian.'[9]

The nature of the interview and the relationship between the interview partners is vital in this context. One dimension of the relationship between the interview partners is discussed in the concept of 'composure'.[10] Individuals compose memories in such a way as to be able to live with them, to permit a feeling of composure. Individuals also compose or construct memories using the public language and attitudes of their culture. Alistair Thomson pointed out the relationship between the two when he argued that 'our memories are risky and painful if they do not conform with the public norms or versions of the past. We compose our memories so that they will fit with what is publicly acceptable, or, if we have been excluded from general acceptance, we seek out particular publics which affirm identities and the way we want to remember our lives'.[11] This can also result in the silencing of certain memories, conformity through self-censorship. Luisa Passerini noted in her work on Fascist Italy that her interview partners had a tendency to jump from the aftermath of World War I to bombing in World War II, omitting the years under Fascist rule.[12] She concluded that the oral historian must engage not only with what is said, but with what is not: the tellingness of silences. These silences provide indications of the way in which what we remember is bound up with what we are supposed or allowed to remember and what messages we are given about what is trivial or significant. In this context, however, the passage of time may also be an advantage: dominant ideologies can change, and what could not be said at one point may become acceptable at another. 'Composure' is thus a process of becoming that is constantly under revision, never finally achieved, and always time specific.

The question of the reliability of oral histories can also be refined through greater consideration of the functioning of memory and recall. The labour historian Alice M. Hoffman, for example, conducted an experiment in which she interviewed her husband Howard S. Hoffman in 1978, in 1982 and in 1986 about his experiences as a mortar crewman in Company C, Third Chemical Mortar Battalion in World War II.[13] Cross-referencing against a detailed written log, Alice Hoffman found that her husband's memory of dates and physical conditions, such as the weather, were inconsistent and unreliable. This is hardly surprising: for one, individuals seldom organise memories according to their calendar date. As Paul Thompson points out, recognising this 'might reduce some of the suspicions of unreliability commonly aroused by oral evidence'.[14] Nonetheless, what struck both the Hoffmans was how consistent the narratives remained despite the passage of time. Howard concluded that 'certain memories can be so resistant to deterioration with time that they are best described as archival'.[15]

Factors relevant to the ability to remember include the amount of emotion attached to the event at the time (heightened emotion increasing the likelihood of recollection, although conversely, great suffering may be resistant to recall[16]); the significance of the event in relation to surrounding experiences, so that it can be seen as a 'first time', or as a turning point, for example; and the likelihood of the memory being re-visited because of its in/significance to the individual, or to his or her audience (the determination of which being itself of interest). If the interviewer interferes with the interviewee's preferred sequencing of events, this can also result in the loss of material. When memories pertain to general experience and recurrent processes in everyday life rather than specific events (such as daily routines, work patterns, leisure activities, etc.), these memories also appear resistant to mutation. The Hoffmans' emphasis is predominantly on which memories remained consistent over time, which they equate with reliability.

My experience listening to my grandmother's memories suggests that well-rehearsed narratives may well be most resistant to change, but that 'reliability' is a term which needs deeper consideration. As long as I can remember, my grandmother communicated through what I term 'frozen narratives': stories which were told in identical words at every repetition, whether on paper or in person, and repeated whenever certain stimuli triggered the memory. My mother's recollections of some of the stories told differed, however, from my grandmother's. My grandmother had a badly deformed back following a childhood accident: it had nearly cost her her life and meant that she received virtually no formal education. Her family assumed that she would never marry and her doctors that she would never be able to bear a child. My grandmother refused to let any of these hindrances define her life. In one story, she recounted how some young boys had seen her and shouted across the road, 'Look at that funny lady!' My mother, a fiery little girl of about six years of age, confronted them, retorting, 'That's not a lady, that's my mother!' My grandmother was proud of this protectiveness, and amused by the implied class humour, with its echoes of a music hall punch line. My mother, however, recalls her response as being 'That's not a funny lady, that's my mother!', a comment closer to that of the taunting boys, and one which retained the reference to my grandmother's disability. She remembers the incident vividly in terms of its location (which suggests the significance of the visual in the ability to recall) and above all, in terms of how shocked and angry she was. As she explained, 'It was the first time I'd seen her as other people saw her and it was a shock that she should be seen as funny.'[17]

I cannot know which version describes the related event more accurately. Through comparison with my grandmother's other stories I can conclude with some conviction, however, that her narrative had become frozen by repetition. Frozen narratives are repeated because they may have been met with a warm reception from their audiences (at least initially). For individuals experienced at being interviewed, they may well represent a survival strategy developed to cope with constant tedious repetition. Frozen narratives tend to follow certain narrative conventions, in this case, for example, by leading to a punch line. Finally, they present the narrator in a light acceptable to the narrator. When memories are selected as particularly meaningful to the individual, these are 'memories which define the self and constitute the persona which one retains, the sense of identity over time'.[18] The story of the taunt as told by my grandmother lies in its potential revelation of my grandmother's character, her relationship to her body and to her daughter, and her sense of humour, particularly the pleasure she derived from life imitating fiction. From my mother's point of view, it is the upsetting memory of the first time she saw her mother's disability as other individuals perceived it. The 'reliability' of these narratives lies therefore less in what is remembered than in how that memory is interpreted. Individuals may well exaggerate, reinterpret, confuse issues, err or even lie, yet this too reveals truth: the truth of the narration for the individual concerned. It is the oral historian's task to interpret the meaning of that narration and its end.

The critique of oral histories as subjective and inaccurate therefore risks discarding one of their greatest values, the insight they offer into subjective experience. This does more than merely add colour to history: few historians would refute, for example, that personal opinions, friendships and antipathies can make the difference between a successful military campaign and its failure, a consensual policy or a deep political rift. Indeed, the subjectivity of the interview has the power to transform what subject-matter is considered worthy of historical investigation. Thompson, for example, has drawn attention to the 'transforming impact of oral history upon the history of the family', pointing out that without it, 'the historian can discover very little indeed about either the ordinary family's contacts with neighbours and kin, or its internal relationships'.[19] Feminist historians have pointed out that subjective experience and emotional meaning has as much place in historical investigation as narratives of events.[20]

Oral testimony has other unique qualities. Within the restraints outlined above, oral historians can determine exactly whom they would like to interview, and what they would like to ask. No other type of primary source can be asked for illumination, challenge your interpretation, walk away from you, or feed you sandwiches. It is one of the few sources in which historians are confronted with the ethical considerations of working with live subjects. The relationship between the interview partners is crucial to the generation of material which will be determined by such variables as the mood and health of the participants, the rapport between them, the skill of the interviewer, and the extent to which the interview partners share a common language, in terms of both denotation and connotation. The oral interview is the product of two or more people relating to each other in conversation, for which there are well-established rules and conventions generally upheld through the co-operation of the interview partners. These conventions must be considered when the source is being interpreted, just as a historian must understand the historical conventions of portraiture in fine art, or the contemporary technological possibilities analysing a photographic representation. The researcher must consider, for example, how to phrase and pursue questions; how conversational conventions may favour emphasis on change rather than continuities; how to negotiate the likelihood of collusion; the significance of the contemporary context of the interview. The referencing conventions of oral histories allude to these aspects by the inclusion of both the interviewee and the interviewer (few sources are so explicit on the original audience), and the date of interview.

Spurred on by feminist historians sensitive to the power relations in the interview context and inspired by the desire to avoid approaching the respondent as an objectified other, oral historians have become increasingly aware of the inter-subjective nature of the interview, that is, its reciprocal nature. The narrative offered in an interview is, after all, dependent not only on the informant's memory but also on the researcher's skill in triggering memories, offering the space for corrections and reworkings, and being an engaged listener. This is not passive, static material being read and interpreted by the historian but a process of co-creation, in which the identity and approach of all individuals involved have a major impact on the material generated. As a young researcher, I was first made aware of this when I conducted an interview in which I found it very difficult to build any rapport with my elderly male interview partner. Within a minute of his opening his front door, I could feel him withdraw from me. This was the first time this had happened to me, and I was perplexed as to what had happened, especially as our letter contact prior to the interview had been relaxed and friendly. The indication happened, as so often, off tape. The respondent started looking around. I offered to help. 'I'm looking for my gla(h)-sses,' he responded. 'Ah, your glasses,' I said and started hunting around. 'Glar-ses,' he mimicked. It was my accent. As soon as he had opened the door and I had greeted him with 'How do you do? I'm Corinna', I had undermined the interview. Inadvertently I had dictated the tone of the interview, my greeting underlining a disparity in class and/or regional identity more significant in this particular context than that of age or gender.

There is a third level of composure, in which the composure of the interviewer must be taken into account as well as that of the interviewee, and the impact of this on the narrative considered. Oral historians may or may not share the same attitudes as their interview partners, as Gabriele Rosenthal had to negotiate in her interviews with SS veterans and perpetrators of the Holocaust.[21] They may be more or less comfortable being cast in particular roles, such as novice or expert, by their interview partner. They may have to contend with deeply disturbing and intimate stories, which may have some very private resonances. In an interview on agri-cultural labour for example, one respondent broke down in the middle of her narrative when she shared for the first time her experience of having been sexually abused at the farm where she worked. This memory took the interviewer into a very different situation from the one for which she had carefully prepared herself, as it evoked a similar experience undergone by a relative of hers. Such interactions cannot fail to impact on the co-creation of the interview, and forces the historian to take a much more self-aware and self-reflective position than other sources necessarily involve. The interview partners may on one level co-operate to ensure the composure – the establishment of an 'acceptable self' – of both participants, while the interview also has the capacity to stimulate but also destabilise through interrogation, or simply to provide a receptive audience to some of those memories and their interpretation.

The relative statuses within the relationship are complex. On the one hand, the interviewee is the expert, doing the historian the favour of giving their time and experience, determining what is shared and what is not, and their knowledge meriting both financial and temporal outlay. When I started interviewing, I believed that I had no right to expect somebody to speak to me if I was not prepared to offer details about the project and to share some personal details about myself. I quickly discovered, however, that my interview partners were not that interested or concerned, and that it was more respectful to respond only to curiosity when it emerged either in passing during the interview, or during breaks in the interview process. Responding to questions rather than volunteering unwelcome detail allowed me to avoid influencing the interview inadvertently. There can also be a tension that has to be negotiated throughout the interview between the interviewer's interest in generating material on a particular theme, and the interviewee's interpretation of what is significant. The consequences can range from the historian discovering hidden histories, being educated in much more productive questions, to knowing a great deal more about pet care than ever desired.

On the other hand, ultimately the power does not lie with the respondent. The historian initiates and opens the interview, thereby suggesting it is in his or her remit to determine who has the authority to speak and to contribute to the historical record. The interviewer determines the approach to the interview, ranging from the strictly structured to the free-flowing. Each has its own character: the first permits easy categorisation and comparison between large numbers of respondents on highly focused topics; the semi-structured and free-flowing interview permits the interview partner to determine the agenda from a lesser to a greater extent. The historian also often arrives with the weight of institutional support behind them, and, most importantly, leaves with material which she or he will interpret, and disseminate. Good practice involves discussing the conditions of the latter: ensuring the interviewee has the opportunity to negotiate how the material is used and in which context, while at the same time ensuring the interviewer is not hamstrung when writing up the material. The wording and the timing of discussion of release forms is part of this consideration, as is the legal right of individuals to be acknowledged as the authors of their own words, an issue which affects the use of pseudonyms.[22] These are not only an issue for the informant. In *Reconstructing Women's Wartime Lives*, Penny Summerfield notes that although most of her respondents were happy for their real names to be cited, in the monograph she gave all her interview partners pseudonyms in order to 'protect them from the embarrassment which my mediation between their words and "the public" might cause'.[23] As this suggests, interpretations of the meanings of the material generated in interviews are likely to differ between the interview partners, awareness of which challenges oral historians to reconcile their professional interpretation of the data with their awareness of the individuals who contributed to the research. Katherine Borland describes how she confronted 'interpretive conflict' when she chose to offer her interpretations of her grandmother's memories up to her grandmother's critical scrutiny.[24] In *Contesting Home Defence,* Penny Summerfield and I had to negotiate the tension between the focus of the story we were seeking to tell and the artificiality of our emphasis on the Home Guard for veterans reflecting on the meaning of their life journey as a whole.[25] The significance of the Home Guard experience was often minor compared with the importance of family, careers, pets, neighbours and gardens (not necessarily in that order), and our commitment to recover forgotten aspects of Home Guard history was not necessarily one shared with those individuals whose history we were supposedly recovering. That of course could be seen as confirming the importance of a study asserting the Home Guard's place in history and giving space both to the civilian male's experience and to the female membership, but it also required the reconciliation of different pulls – ethical, professional, financial and personal in both the interview and its subsequent analysis in prose.

Some historians choose to resolve the disjunctures of power and the potential for competing interpretations by purportedly leaving the testimonies to speak for themselves and refusing to interpret their content. This approach is problematic, however, when it renders indistinct or invisible the interventions made by the author. Even without an explicit interpretative framework, the editing and selection of the original text, and its juxtaposition with other testimonies, themselves suggest, interpretation, just as a painting is read in different ways depending on what is exhibited in its proximity. Oral historians should be explicit about how the source material has been treated and which editorial interventions have been made in the translation from speech into prose, and also about the goals, methodology and development of the research in relation to the interviews. Acknowledging the responsibility of the historian to interpret and analyse, Trevor Lummis argues that 'the process of using interviews to move from the biography of the individual to the social dimension of an historical account is, for me, also part of the definition and practice of oral "history"'. Thus 'to simply let oral evidence stand in its autobiographical form is to betray the contribution to the historical record which such evidence can make'. [26] The Oral History Association takes a similar stance: 'Oral history is a field of study and a method of gathering, preserving *and interpreting* [my emphasis] the voices and memories of people, communities, and participants in past events.'[27] There are three distinct genres of oral history – the individual biography, the collation and juxtaposition of multiple narratives, and the investigation of a particular historical issue through the interpretation and analysis of multiple interviews – but to be truthful to the process of oral history, all three require an acknowledgement of the explicit presence of the historian and their interventions in the text.

Thus far, the assumption has been that the interviews upon which the historian is drawing are interviews conducted by the author. This is, of course, often not the case. There are excellent sound archives upon which the historian can draw, with collections ranging from the memories of key individuals in national politics or the military to collections capturing the voices of less famous individuals. To name just a few, these include, in Britain, the BBC Sound Archive;[28] the Imperial War Museum Sound Archive;[29] the Liddle Collection;[30] the North-West History Sound Archive;[31] the School of Scottish Studies Archive;[32] the Sound Archive of St Fagans National History Museum, Cardiff;[33] and the British Oral Archive of Political and Administrative History.[34] In the United States, there are the Library of Congress Collections;[35] Studs Terkel's Conversations with America;[36] many university centres for Oral History (Alaska, Berkeley, Columbia, Hawaii, Indiana,

Nevada, etc.); the John F. Kennedy Library Oral History Project;[37] the Smithsonian Institution Archives;[38] the USC Shoah Foundation [39] and many more. Good starting places to identify these collections are the websites of the Oral History Societies or the British Library in Britain which offer lists of links.

These collections introduce further issues of methodology because the relationship between the interview and the interviewee is reduced to that which can be heard (or if on film, viewed; this is a format which can detract from the orality of the interview by asserting the power of the visual, however). Furthermore, the opportunities of returning to the interviewee are reduced or impossible. On the other hand, these archives can offer access to memories which would otherwise be lost to time, many of which have not been fully explored. They can save the researcher both money and time. Third-party interviews can also provide invaluable lessons in interview techniques, introducing the impact of effective or leading prompting, sensitive or perfunctory interactions, missed opportunities and unexpected treasures.

When the interview is only available as a transcript, the distance between the original and its representation is even greater. Oral history begins as the spoken word, but is seldom represented as such in its final form. By the time the words reach a wider audience, they have been transformed by transcription, editing and selection. Just as the interview itself follows certain genre conventions, so its representation in text also usually conforms to literary expectations: the rhythms of speech are represented through punctuation, and repetitions or over-speaking 'tidied'. Confronted with a script of their interviews in which these literary conventions had been imposed as little as possible on the transcription, our respondents were distressed by their perceived incoherence. This was an unfortunate consequence of attempting to be true to the spoken word, and undermined the intention to ensure that our interview partners had something to show (and share) for their investment of time (as well as double check for errors in transcription, a goal which our alternative solution, providing copies of the tapes, did not meet). Electronic publication and distribution possibilities permit sound files to be attached to written analysis, but the spoken word is nonetheless still most often represented as text. Represented in prose, the nuance and tone of the original are flattened or lost. Linguists have developed complex annotations to capture the pauses, emphases, etc. in the rendition of the spoken word to the page, but oral historians tend to keep these annotations to a minimum because they interrupt the flow of the text and can distract from the content, usually the primary focus of the discussion. Whenever possible, it is invaluable to listen to the interview alongside reading the prose and to note the impact of one upon the interpretation of the other. Similarly, it is invaluable after an interview to jot down one's impressions and overall sense of the interview, particularly when working as part of a team, so that these can inform any subsequent interpretation and possibly explain differences in perception of intended meaning and significance. Anderson and Jack noted that their project team 'found discrepancies between our memories of interviews and the transcripts because the meaning we remembered hearing had been expressed through intense vocal quality and body language, not through words alone'.[40] Making a note of impressions is equally valuable when working in the archive, where the researcher may remember even fewer of their impressions of the interview when reading back notes later.

Two brief excerpts from an interview I conducted with Lesley Revill, an agricultural worker and another veteran of the British Home Guard in World War II, serve to illustrate the characteristics of oral interviews covered so far.[41] The tape starts in the middle of a conversation begun by the interviewee in the corridor, who began by trying to date the founding of the Home Guard. It is a sad but frequent truth that the most fascinating or valuable parts of interviews often take place unrecorded: before the interview has officially begun, over the tea break, or in the concluding conversation in the doorway. The first statement on tape is as follows:

LR: But end of May, at the beginning of June, after the mass evacuation from Dunkirk.

CPB: Yes.

The interview concludes (several hours later):

CPB: Is there anything else that you think is important for people to know about this time? That I haven't asked you?

LR: . . . Well only that I'm, I'm sorry I just can't give you the exact dates but . . . [. . .] If, if you think of the end of May to the beginning of June in 1940, you've got a rough picture of, about the timing.

The interview, which covered a lot of ground in between these comments, thus began and ended with an attempt by my interview partner to narrow down the date of foundation of the Home Guard, although I never asked for this information. This material is readily available from other sources: after initial unofficial local initiatives, on 14 May 1940 Anthony Eden, the Secretary of State for War, called for volunteers for the new force in a BBC radio announcement. From 27 May to 4 June 1940, allied troops were evacuated from Dunkirk and the British forced off the continental mainland until D-Day: the foundation of the Home Guard, initially called the Local Defence Volunteers, thus *predates* the evacuation. Revill's dates may simply have pertained to his personal experience, suggesting when he joined up rather than when the force was founded.

Rather than merely dismissing Revill's information as close but inaccurate, however, his attempts to date the foundation offer rich ground for interpretation. The positioning of this information in the interview, at the very beginning and at the very end, is significant, and draws attention to the importance of considering not only extracts from interviews, but their overall shape, particularly as defined by the interviewee rather than by the sequence of questions posed by the interviewer. My initial 'yes' is a bland response: I was acknowledging his attempt rather than providing the information (which was not the way I wished to conduct the interview; it also was not a topic on which I wished to dwell). My final question was not an attempt to return to this issue but was intended to ensure my agenda had not over-shadowed his; nonetheless, the vexing issue of the date had clearly preyed on him. The age of my interview partner may be significant here: conscious of failing memory, elderly respondents may make a special effort to provide accurate information, particularly pertaining to time. I suspect the top and tailing of the interview was, however, also to do with my identity as a historian. In common perception, historians are associated with dates, and their expertise as lying in chronologies. The implication of the positioning of this dialogue at the beginning and end of the interview suggests to me that Revill assumed that this would be a matter of great importance for me. Interviewees hold a specific conception of a specific audience to whom they are directing their narrative, and this is determined not least by the perceived characteristics of the interviewer, in this case, an academic historian.

The desire to be accurate has a further impetus: the oral interview offers individuals the potential to contribute to the historical record, so that emerging from a relatively informal personal interaction; a shared memory becomes a public statement. There is a common desire exhibited by interviewees to get their information right: the responsibility of informing an individual and/or contributing to the historical record taken very seriously. A variety of strategies are employed by respondents to ensure or claim accuracy: finding artefacts; reading contemporary or secondary sources from diaries to histories and paralleling personal experiences with ones in the public record; running over the narrative with friends or relatives in advance of the interview, etc. Discussing the Northover Projector, a cheap weapon intended to launch grenades, F. Laws commented that 'Angus (Angus Calder in *The People's War* (but you know that)) Calder describes it as "a graceless weapon but fun to use" but I feel that in action it would be no fun at all'.[42] In this accurate quotation, Laws reveals himself to be informed by the historical record, but in a position to improve upon it, drawing upon personal experience to back up his judgement. His combination of research with experience serves to establish his credentials as an informed historical witness. His reference to the reader as an expert ('but you know that') avoids his comment being read as patronising and suggests a bond between those who recognise that 'Angus' is a reference to an eminent historian.

There is another dimension to the interpretation of Revill's narrative, however, and one which became more clear when his interview could be interpreted alongside interviews held with other Home Guard veterans: the association of the Home Guard with Dunkirk. Dunkirk is still a powerful signifier of World War II and British national character, and has cultural resonances in modern Britain, after nearly seventy years of interpretation and representation. The official function of the Home Guard was to meet the potential for invasion and guard against the activity of fifth columnists in the country. It was after Dunkirk, however, when the British Army had experienced a major defeat, and when the possibility of a pending invasion by German forces was at its greatest, that the Home Guard's function and value were at their most apparent. Hindsight tells us that the Home Guard was never called upon to fulfil this function to defend Britain against the invader. But in 1940 this was a very real possibility. The association of the Home Guard with Dunkirk therefore works on multiple levels. It suggests the importance of the Home Guard at that moment in British history, but also characterises the Home Guard through association with an event interpreted at the time and in retrospect as evidence of a British ability not to give in or up, and in which every individual could play a significant role. In that light, the value of the material provided in the interview depends not upon its adherence to fact, but precisely in its departure from it.

Interviews highlight for the historian the interplay of periods: memories of the past recalled in the context of the present. These periods have an intricate interplay in oral histories. Historians tend to place higher in their hierarchy primary sources created closest to the date of events described. A time delay may thus be viewed as problematic given the potential deterioration of memory in the interim. At a more complex level, any delay means that memories are subject to countless private and public influences between the experience and its recollection. As with the subjectivity of recollection, however, this patina can be integrated into the research rather than resulting in rejection. Nor should this patina be overstated. Interview partners can show a very acute awareness of differences between the past and the present, and the meaning of an experience at the time and in retrospect. Comparisons between 'now and then' are encouraged, for example, by comparisons between individuals' experiences and those of different generations (the interviewer, their children), awareness of personal development and change ('at that age, I really thought . . .'), the belief that society has changed ('very few people went to universities then'[43]) and holds different values ('it's not like that now'[44]), or changes in the physical landscape.

Life memories are also revised, however, in the light of both personal and public reworkings of the past. As we have seen, the 'acceptable self' is itself an internal dialogue between personal subjectivity and public constructions of the acceptable and unacceptable. Powerful cultural constructions have to be negotiated in relating memories. An oral history is a complex cultural product. The concept of the cultural circuit suggests that popular cultural accounts draw on the memories of individuals and, in turn, narrators draw on popular accounts in formulating and expressing stories of their own experiences.[45] The popular accounts find a much wider distribution through modern technology than the personal ones, however: many more people will have seen films set during World War II, for example, than will have talked to veterans. Graham Dawson suggested that because the public accounts are so powerful at 'defining and limiting imaginative possibilities', the individual's narratives cannot escape the powerful public representations, but must relate to and negotiate them.[46] Thus the accounts generated in an interview are, as the Birmingham Popular Memory Group put it, 'not simply the product of individual authorship' but 'draw on general cultural repertoires, features of language and codes of expression which help to determine what may be said, how and to what effect'.[47]

Home Guard veterans could not escape the dominant cultural construction of the Home Guard in the popular TV sitcom *Dad's Army* (1968–77, followed by frequent repeats). This is one of the most powerful public accounts of civilian participation in the defence of Britain. It influenced which narratives were encouraged and which silenced, and it had a powerful influence on audience reactions to shared memories.[48] An example of this is provided in an interview held in the Imperial War Museum Sound Archive, between a son and his mother, Marjorie Adams, speaking about her husband's service in the Home Guard. Asked when he first joined, Marjorie Adams responded:

A: You see Mr Tamner[?] lived at the end house. Percy Duick[?] was an old pal of his from the previous war. They were both in the army. They were asked to take over the organisation of the works Home Help, um the Works Home Guard. And um lived just down the road, just there, and they asked your dad, used to see him on the way to the office, to the bus and that sort of thing, and they had a chat, and 'what about you, Fred', and 'oh I don't mind'. You see. And so he joined, right at the very beginning. And they got the men interested, and they were very efficient. They organised it to have proper evenings for drill, and proper organisation all done on military lines, and your dad was made a corporal.

Q: Sounds more like Dad's Army. (*laughter*)

A: It was Dad's Army! But it was ever so efficiently run. All round Bradwell, Wolverton and Stratford there were lots of fire-watchers and Fire Service Men and the Works Home Guard was separate from them, see, and they had khaki uniforms. The fire-watchers used to meet in the water tower in this part of Stratford and they had, a, little hierarchies, and we used to see them learning how to put out fires with stirrup pumps and that sort of thing. Well the Works Home Guard they did all that but much more and they had, every Sunday, um, either all morning, sometimes going on into the afternoon, real proper, well like Territorial Armies, that sort of thing.[49]

In her opening response, Adams emphasises both the role of community, the significance of veterans, and the Home Guard's 'proper organisation all done on military lines'. Community and veteran membership is a key theme in *Dad's Army,* but the organisation along military lines is aspirational rather than achieved in the comedy. The son's immediate association with the sitcom thus triggers an ambivalent response. Although his mother appears in the first instance to agree with her son – 'It was Dad's Army', and they share a cosy laugh together, what she goes on to say refutes this immediately – 'But it was ever so efficiently run.' The interaction suggests the powerful desire to find points of contact in conversation, intensified here perhaps by the family connection. It also implies Adams understands and rejects the hidden assumption in her son's words, that this was an inefficient force. Lummis argues that 'unless the images of recent history reflect something of the reality of personal experience, individuals will reject it as unsound'.[50] As this extract suggests, however, unambiguous acceptance or rejection is not as simple as Lummis implies.

As this exploration of themes and case studies has suggested, being an oral historian requires the skills required of any historian: to seek and present appropriate sources, to evaluate, compare and draw conclusions in construction of a historical argument. But that identity also challenges historians to confront themselves as individuals and as historians, as words are transformed from an individual's memories, to a historian's memories of these memories, to the public domain.

Notes

I would like to thank Joel Morley and Emma Vickers for their comments on the penultimate draft of this chapter.

1 Alessandro Portelli , 'Oral history as genre', in Mary Chamberlain and Paul Thompson (eds), *Narrative and Genre*, London and New York: Routledge, 1998, p. 23. Portelli's writings on oral history are highly recommended; see, for example, 'The peculiarities of oral history', *History Workshop* 11, Spring 1981, pp. 96–107, and *The Battle of Valle Giulia: Oral History and the Art of Dialogue*, London and Madison: The University of Wisconsin Press, 1997.
2 Two collections are suggestive for developments within oral history: Thomas L. Charlton, Lois E. Myers and Rebecca Sharpless (eds), *Handbook of Oral History*, Lanham, MD, New York, Toronto and Oxford: AltaMira Press, 2006; Robert Perks and Alistair Thomson (eds), *The Oral History Reader*, London: Routledge, 2006.
3 The Oral History Society: http://www.ohs.org.uk/
   The Oral History Association: http://alpha.dickinson.edu/oha/about.html
   The Oral History Association of Australia: http://www.ohaa.net.au/
   A further online resource can be recommended: H-Oralhist is an international network for scholars and professionals active in studies related to oral history at http://www.h-net.org/~oralhist/
4 See, for example, Elizabeth Roberts, *A Woman's Place, an Oral History of Working Class Women, 1890–1940*, Oxford: Blackwells, 1996; Paul Thompson, *The Edwardians: The Remaking of British Society*, Bloomington: Indiana University Press, 1975, London: Weidenfeld & Nicolson, 1975, Routledge, 1992.
5 Research conducted by Emma Vickers, 'Homosexuality and military authority in the British armed forces, 1939–1945', unpublished Ph.D. thesis, 2008, Department of History, Lancaster University.
6 Arthur Marwick, *The New Nature of History: Knowledge, Evidence, Language*, Houndmills: Palgrave, 2001, p. 171.
7 Trevor Lummis, *Listening to History: The Authenticity of Oral Evidence*, London and Melbourne: Hutchinson, 1987, p. 73.
8 Penny Summerfield and Corinna Peniston-Bird, *Contesting Home Defence: Men, Women and the Home Guard in the Second World War*, Manchester: Manchester University Press, 2007.
9 Paul Thompson, *The Voice of the Past. Oral History*, Oxford: Oxford University Press, 1978, p. 113.
10 See Graham Dawson, *Soldier Heroes: British Adventure, Empire and the Imagining of Masculinities*, London: Routledge, 1994; Alistair Thomson, 'Anzac memories: putting popular memory theory into practice in Australia', *Oral History* 18.1, Spring 1990, pp. 25–31; Penny Summerfield, 'Culture and Composure: creating narratives of the gendered self in oral history interviews', *Cultural and Social History*, 1.1, January 2004, pp. 65–93; 'Dis/composing the subject: intersubjectivities in oral history', in T. Cosslett, C. Lury and P. Summerfield (eds), *Feminism and Autobiography: Texts, Theories, Methods*, London: Routledge, 2000, pp. 93–108. See also Corinna Peniston-Bird and Penny Summerfield, 'Women in the firing line: the Home Guard and the defence of gender boundaries in Britain in the Second World War', *Women's History Review* 9.2, June 2000, pp. 231–55, for discussion of the tension that can arise between the agenda of the interviewer and the composure of the interviewee.

11 Alistair Thomson, 'Anzac memories: putting popular memory theory into practice in Australia', *Oral History* 18.1, Spring 1990, p. 25.

12 Luisa Passerini, *Fascism in Popular Memory: The Cultural Experience of the Turin Working Class* (trans. Robert Lumley and Jude Bloomfield), Cambridge: Cambridge University Press, 1987.

13 Alice M. Hoffman and Howard S. Hoffman, 'Reliability and validity in oral history: the case for memory', reproduced at http://www3.baylor.edu/Oral_History/Hoffmans.pdf

14 Paul Thompson, *The Voice of the Past. Oral History*, Oxford: Oxford University Press, 1978, p. 131. There is some evidence that men and women create chronologies around different markers: women have been better able to remember family matters and the development of social networks and use these to help place events within a chronology, while men can place events into a chronological narrative through their relationship to the interviewee's occupational history. Such differences are obviously strongly context specific.

15 Hoffman and Hoffman, 'Reliability', p. 128.

16 Diana Gittins, 'Silences: the case of a psychiatric hospital', in Chamberlain and Thompson (eds), *Narrative and Genre*, p. 46.

17 Email from S.C.E. Peniston-Bird to the author, 23 February 2008.

18 Hoffman and Hoffman, 'Reliability', p. 125.

19 Thompson, *The Voice of the Past*, p. 7.

20 See, for example, Sherna Berger Gluck and Daphne Patai (eds), *Women's Words: The Feminist Practice of Oral History*, New York and London: Routledge, 1991.

21 Gabriele Rosenthal, *Erlebte und erzählte Lebensgeschichte. Gestalt und Struktur biographischer Selbstbeschreibungen*, Frankfurt a. M.: Campus, 1995; Gabriele Rosenthal (ed.), *The Holocaust in Three Generations: Families of Victims and Perpetrators of the Nazi Regime*, London and Washington: Cassell, 1998.

22 See the websites of the Oral History Associations for the possible wording on release forms.

23 Penny Summerfield, *Reconstructing Women's Wartime Lives: Discourse and Subjectivity in Oral Histories of the Second World War*, Manchester: Manchester University Press, 1998, p. 26.

24 Katherine Borland, '"That's not what I said': interpretive conflict in oral narrative research', in Gluck and Patai (eds), *Women's Words: The Feminist Practice of Oral History*, pp. 63–75.

25 Summerfield and Peniston-Bird, *Contesting Home Defence*.

26 Trevor Lummis, *Listening to History: The Authenticity of Oral Evidence*, London and Melbourne: Hutchinson, 1987, p. 28.

27 Oral History Association, 'About OHA', http://alpha.dickinson.edu/oha/about.html, accessed 28 February 2008.

28 http://www.bl.uk/collections/sound-archive/cat.html

29 http://collections.iwm.org.uk/server/show/nav.00g007

30 http://www.leeds.ac.uk/library/spcoll/liddle/

31 http://www.bl.uk/collections/sound-archive/ohlinks.html

32 http://www.celtscot.ed.ac.uk/archives.htm

33 http://www.museumwales.ac.uk/en/195/

34 http://library-2.lse.ac.uk/archives/handlists/BOAPAH/BOAPAH.html

35 http://memory.loc.gov/ammem/browse/ListSome.php?format=Sound+Recording

36 http://www.studsterkel.org/

37 http://www.cs.umb.edu/~serl/jfk/oralhist.htm

38 http://www.siris.si.edu/

39 http://college.usc.edu/vhi/

40 Kathryn Anderson and Dana C. Jack, 'Learning to listen: interview techniques and analyses', in Gluck and Patai (eds), *Women's Words: The Feminist Practice of Oral History*, p. 12.

41 Lesley Revill, interviewed by Corinna Peniston-Bird, 29 November 1999.
42 F.A.L. (Tex) Laws, correspondence with Corinna Peniston-Bird, 3 May 2000.
43 Lois Baker, interviewed by Corinna Peniston-Bird, 16 December 1999.
44 Winifred Atkins (pseudonym), interviewed by Corinna Peniston Bird, 23 March 2000.
45 Popular Memory Group, 'Popular memory: theory, politics, method', in Centre for Contemporary Cultural Studies, *Making Histories: Studies in History-Writing and Politics*, London: Hutchinson, 1982; Graham Dawson, *Soldier Heroes*; Thomson, 'Anzac Memories'.
46 Dawson, *Soldier Heroes*, p. 25.
47 Popular Memory Group, 'Popular memory: theory, politics, method', p. 229.
48 For detailed analysis of this, see Summerfield and Peniston-Bird, *Contesting Home Defence*, and Corinna M. Peniston-Bird, '"I wondered who'd be the first to spot that": Dad's Army at war, in the media and in memory', *Media History* 13.2/3, August 2007.
49 Marjorie Adams, interviewed by Roger Kitchen in 1983, Imperial War Museum Sound Archive (7295).
50 Lummis, *Listening to History*, p. 126.

8 The Internet: virtual space

Lisa Blenkinsop

> Can people find community online in the Internet? Can relationships between people who never see, smell, touch, or hear each other be supportive and intimate?
>
> Barry Wellman and Milena Gulia[1]

Though much research on the internet has been carried out in the areas of anthropology, computer science, cultural studies, health research, sociology and women's studies, the use of the internet as a historical source has not yet received the same attention.[2] The possibilities created by the internet as a source for inquiry in relation to history and diaspora studies are eloquently discussed by Ananda Mita, Patrick Manning and Radhika Gajjala.[3] However, just as the legitimacy and validity of oral history was attacked in the 1970s and 1980s, rebutted by Alessandro Portelli for holding a '*different* credibility', the use of the internet for the purposes of historical research is also misunderstood and regarded with some distrust.[4] Internet communities, virtual archives and commemorative sites represent a method of recording and communicating experience and feeling, a process whereby memory is constructed, and an understanding of the past presented. The internet, including chat forums, commemorative sites and virtual archives, offers new possibilities for historical inquiry precisely because these sites, like oral history interviews and retrospective writings, represent a construction of the past and add to, indeed create, public discourse. Furthermore, the potential influence of the internet to foster specific versions of the past should not be underestimated. These claims are not to ignore the selective nature of its creators or its audience: there are major global disparities in computer access and the demographics of internet usage. As Janusz Maciuba, a second-generation Pole, wrote when discussing my research project in correspondence with another society member, Barbara Kwietniowski:

> [t]here is also the problem with qualitative analysis as opposed to quantitative. If she [the author] uses the internet to gather surveys, she will get a certain type of Polish woman to reply: has a computer, educated, interested in her past, keeping up the traditions. The other 99 percent won't even know there is a survey.[5]

Selectivity and unrepresentativeness are not characteristics unique to the internet as a source, however, and the extent to which these constitute a problem is dependent on the research question the historian is seeking to explore, and the claims made for the conclusions drawn.

The internet has variable characteristics: sites can be static, or constantly under development; authorship singular or plural; access open or closed. The sites which constitute my case studies here are predominantly interactive, in a constant state of co-creation. This characteristic is suggested by the correct referencing format for websites which includes the date the site was accessed: an implicit acknowledgement of impermanence. The use of the internet as a medium to commemorate and archive memory takes its potential as a source a step further than Howard Rheingold's assertion that 'people in virtual communities do just about everything people do in real life, but we leave our bodies behind'. Particularly for some diaspora groups who use the internet to commemorate and memorialise, the internet allows people to do things that often they feel they *cannot* do in real life. For some, membership of a virtual community fills a need which cannot be met in the off-line world either because of the absence of a public discourse or because there is no available space in which to express a particular memory. As Rheingold makes clear, 'there is no such thing as a single, monolithic, online subculture: it's more like an ecosystem of subcultures, some frivolous, others serious'.[6] The aim of this chapter is to indicate the possibilities of the internet in the process of constructing the past. It is structured around the issues involved in choosing internet sites for research; considering the role of the moderator/s of individual sites in terms of mediating memory and presenting a particular construction of the past; how to use material generated in site guest books and archives; and ethical questions pertaining to using information gained from internet sites, particularly whether a researcher should obtain permission from site members before using posts in scholarly research. Practical examples are also offered of how to use information held on internet sites and how to reference emails and websites.[7]

The primary examples of internet sites drawn upon in this chapter are sites focused on the Polish experience of World War II, primarily *Kresy-Siberia* and *Poles in Great Britain*. These sites were founded by second-generation Poles but also include amongst their membership first-, third- and fourth-generation Poles. For some Poles the internet functions as a specific site of community whereby the Polish past is documented and commemorated. Indeed, the internet is a fundamental tool in the reconstruction of the Polish past, with many individual and organised sites dedicated to key historical moments in Polish history including the Soviet deportations during World War II,[8] the Warsaw Uprising 1944,[9] and the battle for Monte Cassino 1944.[10]

The *Kresy-Siberia* group, a restricted interactive internet forum, is dedicated to researching, remembering and recognising the experiences of Polish citizens deported from Eastern Poland to Siberia by the Soviet Union during World War II. The forum is primarily composed of those who were deported to Siberia and their descendants, but also includes those who are interested in this period of history for reasons of research, recognition and remembrance.[11] The ages of those active within the site range from members in their twenties to those in their eighties, although the largest age group is represented by those in their fifties. They are the sons and daughters of those deported as young adults or children. The *Poles in Great Britain* forum, another restricted membership forum, was founded on 3 February 1999 by Mike Oborski, a second-generation Pole. The chat forum was designed to bring all those interested in the Polish community together but, before the admission of Poland into the European Union, it was primarily used by British-born second-generation Poles to discuss being Polish, post-war Polish upbringing in the UK, and Polish rituals and culture.[12] Although the name of the group indicates that residence in Great Britain is the defining criterion of membership, non-British based members are active upon the site. Members who are not geographically resident in Great Britain include Australians who are interested in exploring their Polish ancestry, British citizens of Polish descent who are no longer resident in Great Britain and those who have been invited to join the group through cross-postings with other forums. Internet groups of this ilk have several important functions for their membership. As Debra Ferreday comments in her work on online pro-anorexia communities, for example, pro-anorexia internet sites facilitate communication between those with eating disorders and aim to construct a sense of community that is based on accessibility.[13] Their membership is thus self-selecting to a large extent, but the role of the moderator as gatekeeper should not be under-estimated.

Gaining access to some chat forums can be a difficult task, especially if a moderator desires to keep the site or forum exclusive. Arthur Edwards argues that the moderator does more than act as a filter and can enhance the quality of online discussion.[14] Whilst for some common interest groups this is indeed so, it cannot be ignored that, crudely put, the moderator has the power to act as the site censor, often without informing site members, screening out individuals who do not fit the founding principles of sites and sometimes even removing undesirable posts made by forum members. This effectively skews one's perception of the site because contributions are removed or doctored and the trace of those 'undesirables' who have accessed the site or forum is destroyed. Indeed, a methodological challenge when using chat forums is to trace potential members who are denied membership of particular sites and also those members who are asked to leave – this can often be done by searching for similar subject sites newly created and also replying to the introductory email posted by former group members. If a site or forum has the capacity to archive postings it can also be useful to read the postings in order to find the key threads of discussion where dissent may be found. The internet is not an open archive which embraces all users.

The internet is employed by some people as a virtual place where *the* truth of a particular experience can be deposited and accessed. By creating individual internet sites the founders are themselves at the centre of organising and maintaining a site of remembrance. In short, site founders act as the virtual custodians of what they regard as the experience, responsible for the preservation of *the* memory and the creation of a dominant narrative; that is, a singular version of an event or period commonly accepted as representative of it. Internet sites and chat rooms are static and fixed in the sense that they are grounded in and informed by the historical past, often replicating the dominant narratives and themes of commemoration found in more traditional forms. However, the facility for discussion and interaction by members indicates a fluid relationship between the members and the act of commemoration.

On the one hand, it can be claimed that the internet is a democratic space, offering what Jan Fernback regards as the new arena for participation in public life. It requires little technical expertise to contribute to sites, and even website design has become more accessible with increasingly user-friendly software. On the other hand, in the context of collective rather than individual sites, the internet can constitute an exclusive club of common interest groups where individuals attempting to access such groups are often at the mercy of site moderators.[15] Consequently, how a researcher accesses a site is as critical as what the site contains. In my own doctoral research focused on the Polish experience of World War II, I used the two sites mentioned above most frequently: *Kresy-Siberia* and *Poles in Great Britain*. Though a number of other forums existed, *Kresy-Siberia* and *Poles in Great Britain* were the largest groups with British membership. In addition, they were chosen for practical reasons as my application to join another forum, *UK Born Poles*, was rejected by the moderator, primarily because I was not a UK-born Pole.[16] A request to view only the archived postings was also rejected.

The criteria I used to determine which sites to include in my research were guided by the key research questions. Aside from my ability to gain basic access to a site, individual, autobiographical and community sites were also selected for use if the creator of the site was British-based and of Polish descent. Of the sites used, all were created and maintained by the first or second generation, with the exception of *Dzieje*, created and maintained by a third-generation British-born Pole.[17] I engaged in correspondence with all the site founders and moderators and have posted on all sites. I was open in my use of the sites and did not lurk or function as a silent member of a forum, which would, I contend, betray the founding principles of the sites used and allow one to be accused of deception. As Rheingold emphasises, not every internet group or forum is the same – the rules, etiquette and unwritten modes of behaviour which the researcher should learn and comply with differ between forums. How one approaches each subculture is thus determined by the subculture itself.

There are a variety of ways to identify online resources, some of them from off-line leads. In my project, I used in total twenty-six internet sites: eleven individual commemorative sites created and maintained by the first or second generation; seven chat forums created by the second generation; three sites based on published autobiography and/or oral history collections; three sites created by the organised Polish community; and two message boards found on the BBC site aimed at the Polish community in Great Britain, *Penley Poles* and *Staffordshire's Community Talk Board*.[18] Initially the sites were located from links provided on *A Forgotten Odyssey*, a site which is connected to a documentary film of the same name made by London-based film-makers Jagna Wright and Aneta Naszynska.[19] *A Forgotten Odyssey* led to the *Kresy-Siberia* forum from which links were posted to other sites by members, sites which included *Northwick Park Polish Camp*, *Shallow Graves in Siberia* and *Straws in the Wind*.[20] General searches were also made through Yahoo groups and Google, which yielded the *Poles in Great Britain* forum, *Polish Forces During World War II* and *Armia Krajowa*.[21]

After one gains access to a chat forum or internet site, four main bodies of information may be held within the internet site or chat forum: guestbook postings; virtual archives; visual images; and individual member postings. Each body of information tells the researcher something about the site users, the agenda behind the creation of the site and the key narrative of the site. The content of commemorative sites chosen by individual creators is telling in terms of the relationship between the creator and a construction of the experience marked; guest books indicate how viewers of the site relate to and connect with this construction of the past. Guest books should not be overlooked as they are often attached to websites and allow the viewer to make a contribution to the site through the presentation of their own experience related to the subject matter of the site. This provides instantaneous interactivity and also allows an individual to mark their presence on the site. Guest books also invite the viewer to offer general comment on the information, layout and concept of the site, and are thus of value to the researcher.

The guest books attached to the sites used for the purposes of my research into the Polish community represent a virtual collective confession by the second generation of their desire to uncover and trace their Polish roots. Guest books overwhelmingly indicate first-generation silence about World War II in the upbringing of the second generation. This silence appears to lead to a second-generation quest in adulthood to uncover and discover their Polish pasts. For example, in the old guest book of the *Sikorski Polish Club*, George Kempik wrote:

> It's approximately one year since I found out that my father was in the Polish 2nd Corps. 5th Kresowa, he died in 1969 when I was 12, he never spoke about his past, found out loads of information, been down to London for the 60th Anniversary Reunion, met lots of old soldiers, been back to Poland, found our family in Katowice, and best of all my old aunt is still alive, 80 years old, I feel I have been re born and I'm keen to speak to anyone who is like minded.[22]

Kempik's fervour is almost akin to a religious or spiritual experience, which allows him to reconnect with his dead father. One should not forget that Kempik shared his thoughts publicly with people he did not know. Yet Kempik assumed that those who read his entry were similar and would have a Polish connection because of the content of the site to which the guest book was attached. Kempik's posting indicates the significance of guest books, and also that it is just as important to consider how information is presented in terms of style and grammar as well as of the actual content. The absence of grammar and the amount of information contained in such a small entry indicates the emptying out of his feelings surrounding his Polish ancestry. Indeed, as discussed later, such raw emotion requires the researcher to consider the ethics of using such personal writings without asking for consent. Although these messages are on one level already public, their imagined audience on the website is different from the historian's academic audience, and furthermore, their meaning is transformed by a change of context from like-minded sharing to external interpretation.

Guest books offer an insight into how the site is used and what purpose it serves for its users. For example, second-generation Michael Kulik wrote in the guest book of *Stalin's Ethnic Cleansing*:

> My grandparents, Antoni Kulik and Stanisława Chiemelewska, were originally settlers on Osada Krechowiecka, District Rowne – before being deported to Russia on Feb 10th 1940. Unfortunately my grandmother later perished in Krasnavodsk although, thanks largely to her efforts, all her five children survived. Thank-you for helping me to understand my father's pain better.[23]

The experiences shared through the guest books move beyond merely expressing commonality in terms of the search for relatives in Poland or learning about the Polish wartime experience. Commemorative internet sites and the information they hold are constructed as life-altering experiences, here allowing the individual to claim an authentic Polish connection and to present that connection in an accessible Polish forum. Kempik and Kulik both indicate their motives for accessing the sites, which they express through the guest book.

Guest books encourage site users to respond to an understanding of the past as represented by the site to which the guest book is attached. As Jurek Narożański wrote in Paul Haver's Homepage guest book, a site focused on the geographic area of the Kresy:

> Many, many thanks for both your websites – Kresy + your homepage, in which your efforts, dedication and your polishness are so obvious. I feel I understand your motivation, as I'm on a similar quest to discover my roots, spurred on by the discovery of family (just last August by trawling the web!!) around Szczecin and Gdansk [*sic*].[24]

Narożański implies that commemorative sites are measured against criteria of Polishness constructed at other (off-line) locations. Commemorative internet sites and chat rooms do not stand alone as sites of commemoration, remembrance or memorialisation, but they constitute a reaction to exclusive and static acts of commemoration and remembrance. Site founders actively illustrate Polish identities and connections by maintaining commemorative sites; site users also want to prove their Polish credentials and do so through the interactivity offered by the internet, particularly by the guest book. For example, in the guest book of *Penley Poles*, Penley being a camp and hospital used by the Poles when they arrived in Great Britain during and shortly after World War II, second-generation Jurek Zdanko wrote:

> A great site and a very worthy one, too. I was born at Penley No 3 Polish Hospital in August 1947 – my Mother (Rozalia nee Zych, later Zdanko) came

from Maghull, near Liverpool, and I lived my formative years at Polish camps, including the famous Northwick Park Polish DP camp near Moreton in Marsh. I've retained a great deal of my 'Polishness' as befits someone who was born in a 'Polish Hospital' and to this date I am the chairman of the Polish Community in Redditch, a musician with Polish interests much in my repertoire, a charity fund-raiser with Polish matters much to the fore, and an activist in Polish related matters.[25]

For the researcher, both guest books and introductions offer spaces where contributors make explicit their reasons for attending the site and how they wish to position themselves vis-à-vis the other members. Thus the desire to indicate a strong Polish connection, as Zdanko illustrated, is also evident within introductions made to chat forums, which often perform the same function as a guest book entry. For example, in her introduction to the *300 Polish Squadron* forum, second-generation Janette Obuch wrote:

I am Janette Obuch the daughter of Warrant Officer, Franciszek Obuch, radio operator and middle turret gunner, a member of the 300 Polish bomber squadron who completed, in total 68+ missions flying from 1941–46. Dad was in air transport after the War.[26]

In a further post, one year later, welcoming a new member to the forum, Obuch wrote:

My father flew 68+ missions between 300, 301 Squadrons and Special flight 1586 flying out of the American airbase at Briindisi [*sic*], Italy. He crashed 5 times and went over Warsaw five nights in a row I think dropping supplies to the Polish Home Army during the Uprising. The Poles really were a thing apart in their prosecution of their duties and their ability to overcome fear and go up there time and time again. Considering that you have a 1 in 4 chance of surviving a bombing mission the luck of the devil was with him, and my brother Bernard and I are very lucky to have made it![27]

Obuch seeks to illustrate her Polish pedigree through her father's wartime experience as a member of the Polish bomber squadron. Commemorative sites permit the exchange of experiences and for individuals to demonstrate their identities, repeatedly if so desired. Cross-referenced introductions and postings thus permit analysis of which criteria are seen as significant to share, which provide signifiers of belonging, and whether there is any implicit ranking of criteria. Archived postings also allow the researcher to investigate the repetitive re-performance of a family story or life narrative. My investigation relied not only on what members communicated to me personally, but also what was repetitively communicated to the group as a whole.

Guest books cement the relationship between the viewer and the individual internet site, fixing the public relationship between the individual and the virtual space. The signing of guest books by the second generation had two functions: to mark visibly their Polish heritage and to create a lasting, virtual memorial through the written word by paying tribute to (often deceased) parents. For example, in the guest book of *Stalin's Ethnic Cleansing*, Susan Ann Smith (née Szyjka) wrote:

> I sign this book in the name of my father Jerzy Szyjka. A prisoner of the Russians during the WWII. He made it to England courtesy of Anders Army but his health was shattered and he died aged 39. He was a great Dad and my brother and I were blessed to have had him in our lives.[28]

The guest book provides a confessional space, and one which permits individual family members to pay tribute to a Polish parent. Guest books are fundamental because they allow collective confession, create a bond between site users, and function as the link between site user and site.

Internet sites do not only hold prose: they also act as a virtual archive for images of material objects. On the Polish sites, these holdings serve to legitimise the commemoration of experience through personal artefacts such as photographs, birth certificates and wartime identity cards. For descendants of Polish veterans and civilians, collecting and collating that which is deemed significant, such as photographs, identity cards and birth certificates, chart how far they have come in their search for information pertaining to the wartime experiences of relatives. Virtual archives provide online markers for what the moderators and users of the site associate with the particular subject matter of the site. The illustration of heritage through family wartime photographs, medals, badges and identity cards forges a link between the individual and the virtual space. Whilst artefacts represent a stationary moment in time and proof that predecessors had 'been there', they also represent a continuous and recycled performance of what it is to be, in this case, Polish and as expressed within the virtual world. Photograph albums archived on the *Kresy-Siberia* site, for example, trace the wartime journeys made by first-generation Poles and reveal how the first generation performed and sustained their Polishness during World War II, in religious processions, for example, but also how the second generation re-creates these photograph albums to share with other members of the site and assert their membership.

Symbolic images and photographs of physical objects used in website design or held within commemorative sites and forums serve as further key markers and signify the accessibility of the site, creating a feeling of kinship and inclusivity. These symbols have assumed almost mythic status in the Polish example. They include the train, the Polish Eagle and the insignia of the Polish Armed Forces which achieved their status off-line.[29] Thus, these sites can be derivative: recycling and reinforcing important off-line markers. A connection between the internet site and the viewer, and between the site and a specific narrative, is created by accentuating the familiar in both the written word and the visual image.

Individual member postings and guest book postings create ethical dilemmas for the historian using the internet as a historical source.[30] In conducting email research, Judith Sixsmith and Craig Murray have identified other ethical dilemmas including consent, privacy, and ownership and authorship of material.[31] Primarily, Sixsmith and Murray are concerned about what scholars do with the material they collect from postings and how the material is used. Though these concerns are very real and should impact on the design of a research project, many can be overcome by applying some of the skills and approaches used by oral historians. For example, before research begins one should decide whether one would be comfortable engaging in prolonged correspondence with site users, if one would want to reveal personal information to site users and then consider the potential effects of these decisions on the research process. Prolonged email correspondence necessarily creates a relationship that is more developed than simply using a single-member posting.

Radhika Gajjala suggests the difficulties of researching forum members within a 'cyborg-diaspora' who do not necessarily have an off-line relationship.[32] Gajjala's research centres on the exclusively female 'South Asian Women's Network', and highlights fundamental ethical problems with using member posts in scholarly research. For example, chat forum members do not join internet groups so that their words and interactions can be analysed and interpreted by academics. Furthermore, as highlighted above, the presence of such scholars upon chat forums potentially skews the relationship between the forum user and the site. Both *Kresy-Siberia* and *Poles in Great Britain* represent a 'place', albeit virtual, where members feel secure and comfortable and where personal information is revealed. Barbara Smolicz, who defined herself as a 'second generation Brit', wrote in her introduction, for example:

> My father died in 1999 with not having said very much about what he went through. My uncle is still alive and finds it hard to talk about these things. My father's best friend, who unfortunately died earlier this year, revealed some of the hardships of the camp. I don't know how much more I can tell you. I am hungry for information about that time in order to be able to understand better the pains and constrictions that my father lived with all his life.[33]

Whilst *Kresy-Siberia* provides a practical and an emotional support, potentially representing even a form of therapy for the children of the deported, my motivation for joining the group was to gain research material. Although members can choose to maintain some sense of anonymity by withholding 'real' names, the *Kresy-Siberia* site in particular acts as a method of reuniting families lost or separated as a result of World War II and, more often than not, members posted with their full names and place of residence. Indeed, this was encouraged by the moderator. For example, Anna Coates, whose grandmother, mother and aunt were deported to Siberia, wrote in her introduction to the *Kresy-Siberia* site: 'I am a Polish Citizen through my mother, and I would like to trace her two brothers, whom she has not seen for almost 60 years, they were teenagers when World War II started'.[34]

The site acts as a space in which the second generation in particular can request information about family members with whom other posting entries may have served during the War or lived during deportation. Archived postings and introductions to the group might act as what Michele Wilson terms the 'historical trace of a character', reducing the sense of anonymity, and the attempt to trace individuals through the *Kresy-Siberia* forum roots each member within the group.[35] Although my place within the group met the defining criteria of membership based on research, recognition and remembrance, I had no familial experiences to report or name to submit to the *Kresy-Siberia* Memorial Wall. Although it would be wrong to say that I felt like an impostor, I occupied a grey space between outsider and insider.

Elizabeth Reid makes the point that the physical boundary between cyberspace and an individual's day-to-day life helps to create the perception of safety.[36] Indeed, it is easy to appreciate that posting from the domestic private setting of home to a restricted membership forum which has a trusted moderator at the helm creates a false sense of privacy. The use of posts within an academic study potentially ruptures the distinction between the virtual and the real, leading to discomfort and insecurity for some forum users if they read back in their off-line life what was written during their online life. One solution to this is to post any work written using research gained from chat forums in the archives of individual sites for members to read, and to invite discussion amongst members of the work. This has the effect of including those researched in the whole research process. I invited site users to respond to my posts privately rather than to submit a response to the whole site. In addition I kept interested members abreast of my work, posted conference papers on the site and invited comment. Another way to address these issues is to consider how internet and email research is referenced. Though it is becoming increasingly common to find private individual email addresses as part of referencing email correspondence, I contend that this is unsafe and unnecessary. If one was engaged in letter correspondence, the postal address of each corres-pondent would not be included in the reference. I argue that the same rule should be followed when referencing email correspondence and that it is sufficient to include a name, subject title and date.

There is much debate within the social sciences focused on whether informed consent of posters is required before an email post can be used in research. Though some argue that consent is not required because posts exist in the public domain, the counter argument claims that not to gain consent makes members wary and distrustful of cyber-communities. I contacted members individually or through the list if I wanted to use private material posted upon the site, which had the added advantage of introducing me to new respondents. In addition, when I engaged in prolonged correspondence with site moderators or users, I made clear that the material generated would potentially be included in the finished research project. However, when it came to individual posts on chat forums and guest books, I used them without gaining the consent of each individual poster and credited them as any other source. In all correspondence to the sites I made it clear that I was a Ph.D. student engaged in research in preparation of a thesis. Furthermore, I did not 'lurk' upon the two forums, but made frequent posts and was a familiar name in the virtual community. Indeed, at times I felt mobilised by the *Kresy-Siberia* group and wrote to my then Member of Parliament, Hilton Dawson, suggesting that he push for an apology from Michael Howard, who had publicly referred to 'Polish concentration camps'.[37] What this alerts us to is the possibility that the historian's interaction with living individuals may create ties between them and their sources: in this case, for example, I became part of a virtual community and experienced its potential as a mobilising force.

Respondents did not only engage with the subject of my research, but were also interested in my methodological approach and were keen to correct approaches which did not match their understanding of the Polish community. Concerned about the demographic profile of the respondents my work was reaching, Janusz Maciuba queried my conceptual methodology in what Gajjala terms 'talking back', defined as the questioning of methodological assumptions.[38] I responded to Maciuba by making clear that I was utilising four different sources and encouraged this kind of dialogue with my respondents. Only one other member on the *Poles in Great Britain* forum expressed concern when I asked members why they had joined the forum:

> Perhaps others feel differently but I would want more details as to the background to the project, the exact subject matter and terms of reference before making a decision about giving out any personal views. Personal opinions can so easily become misrepresented in such projects.[39]

Silence, however, was the most effective way of not contributing to my research. I received only three replies from the *Poles in Great Britain* forum and there was no interaction amongst members pertaining to such questioning. In contrast, my appeal upon the *Kresy-Siberia* forum reaped eleven replies and sparked debate amongst members who did not necessarily direct their comments at me. Whilst this difference can be explained by the differing mandate of both groups – one conceived as a site for 'research, recognition and remembrance', and the other as a site for anyone interested in Polish culture – it might also relate to the extent to which I was accepted by both groups. Though an absence of Polish heritage seemed to have no consequence on the *Kresy-Siberia* site, my outsider status and non-Polish British upbringing on the *Poles in Great Britain* forum could not be overcome.

As one might expect, the use of an interactive medium focused on internet forums, commemorative sites and virtual archives reveals and allows the researcher to acknowledge variations in the construction of memory. The internet provides a space for the development of common interest chat forums and discussion groups relevant to particular experiences and represents a convenient and fluid way for history to be discussed, debated and constructed. Indeed, it is the interactivity and evolution of internet sources which distinguishes them from other sources and allows the researcher to move beyond the recovery of a hidden voice to consider the relationship between dominant and silenced narratives and the processes by which this relationship is played out.

Notes

1 Barry Wellman and Milena Gulia, 'Virtual communities as communities: Net surfers don't ride alone', in Mark Smith and Peter Kollock (eds), *Communities in Cyberspace*, London and New York: Routledge, 1999, p. 65.

2 Radhika Gajjala, 'Cyberfeminism, technology and international development', *Gender and Development* 7.2, 1999, pp. 8–16; Siriporn Panyametheekul and Susan Herring, 'Gender and Turn Allocation in a Thai Chat Room', *Journal of Computer Mediated Communication* 9.1, 2003; Marjorie D. Kibby, 'Home on the page: a virtual place of music community', *Popular Music* 19.1, 2000, pp. 91–100; David Trend (ed.), *Reading Digital Culture*, Oxford: Blackwell, 2001; Katherine Walker, '"It's difficult to hide it": the presentation of self on Internet home pages', *Qualitative Sociology* 23.1, 2000, pp. 99–120; Andrew Winzelberg *et al.*, 'Evaluation of an internet support group for women with primary breast cancer', *Cancer* 1.97, 2003, pp. 1164–73.

3 Radhika Gajjala, 'An interpreted postcolonial/feminist cyberethnography: complicity and resistance in the cyber field', *Feminist Media Studies* 2.2, 2002, pp. 177–93; Patrick Manning, 'Gender in the African diaspora: electronic research materials', *Gender and History* 15.3, 2003, pp. 575–87; Ananda Mita, 'Virtual commonality: looking for India on the internet', in Steve Jones (ed.), *Virtual Culture: Identity and Communication in Cybersociety*, London: Sage, 1997.

4 Alessandro Portelli, 'The peculiarities of oral history', *History Workshop* 12.1, 1981, p. 99.

5 Janusz Maciuba to Lisa Blenkinsop, email correspondence, 17 June 2003.

6 Howard Rheingold, 'The virtual community', in Trend, *Reading Digital Culture*, p. 274.

7 There are multiple ways of referencing electronic media, but the following include the most important elements. Email correspondence should include author and recipient, subject line and date of email. Websites should include author if known, the title of the page, the date the latter was created (if available), and the date it was accessed. Messages on discussion boards should be referenced with the author, the subject of the message, the title of the discussion list followed by the phrase 'Online posting', the address through which the posting is available, and the date of posting.

8 Eugene Krajewski, *Straws in the Wind*, http://www.strawsinthewind.com, accessed 9 May 2008; Krajewski's site, *Straws in the Wind*, is based on his published auto-biography of the same name, which details his wartime experiences. The site was created and is maintained by Krajewski's second-generation British-born daughter, Julia Krajewski, and explains Krajewski's motivation in writing his autobiography, provides a brief biography explaining his settlement in Great Britain, and offers an interactive map of his journey from Poland to Great Britain. Michael Krupa, *Shallow Graves in Siberia*, http://homepages.tesco.net/theprophecy/SGIS/index.htm, 2004, accessed 9 May 2008. *Shallow Graves in Siberia*, based on the autobiography of the same name written by Michael Krupa, was created by Krupa's second-generation British-born daughter, Danuta Lawson, and is maintained by his third-generation British-born grandson. Although the site, founded in August 2004, details Krupa's journey from southern Poland to a Soviet prison and then escape to join the Polish Forces via Kazakhstan and Uzbekistan, its primary purpose is to publicise the autobiography and to indicate public reaction to this account of Krupa's journey and wartime experience.

9 *Poland At War* is a photographic tribute founded and maintained by British-born second-generation Stefan Mucha. The site was founded in 2003 and contains photographs of Warsaw at war, the Jews of Poland, the Warsaw Uprising 1944, Poland 1939–45 and the Warsaw Ghetto. Stefan Mucha, *Poland at War*, http://www.thornb2b.co.uk/Poland_at_War/, 2003, accessed 9 May 2008.

10 Julian Hoseasman, *Poland in Exile*, http://www.polandinexile.com/, 2002, accessed 9 May 2008. *Poland in Exile* was founded in 2002 by British-born second-generation Julian

Hoseasman. Hoseasman's father, Zenon Krzeptowski, joined the Polish Independent Carpathian Rifle Brigade in Palestine in 1941 and arrived in England in January 1942.

11 The *Kresy-Siberia* group has functioned informally since early 2001 and is a restricted membership forum with the motto 'recognition, remembrance, research'. It was officially founded on 18 September 2001 by Stefan Wiśniowski, a Canadian national who now lives in Australia, after he visited Polish relatives in Krakow and London who relayed their wartime experiences to him. This led to Wiśniowski, son of a Siberian survivor, wanting to put the story of his family forward to the world. Stefan Wiśniowski to Lisa Blenkinsop and Kresy-Siberia@yahoogroups.com, 'Who founded the forum?', 17 June 2003.

12 *Poles in Great Britain*, http://groups.yahoo.com/group/polesingreatbritain/, created 3 February 1999.

13 Debra Ferreday, 'Unspeakable bodies: erasure, embodiment and the pro-ana community', *International Journal of Culture* 3.6, 2003, pp. 277–96.

14 Arthur R. Edwards, 'The moderator as an emerging democratic intermediary: the role of the moderator in Internet discussion', *Information Policy* 7.1, 2002, pp. 3–20.

15 Jan Fernback, 'The individual within the collective: virtual ideology and the realization of collective principles', in Steven Jones (ed.), *Virtual Culture: Identity and Communication in Cybersociety*, London: Sage, 1997, p. 37.

16 Yahoo Groups Notification to Lisa Blenkinsop, email correspondence, 'Request to join ukbp denied', 17 October 2004.

17 Waldemar Werbel, Dzieje 2-go Korpusu Inacej http://dspace.dial.pipex.com/town/pipexdsl/r/arar48/dzieje/, created 1 November 2003. The site is dedicated to Werbel's grandfather who was a member of the Polish Second Corps and is based on a book published in 1969 and on illustrations of Mieczysław Kuczyński, a survivor of Monte Cassino.

18 *Penley Poles*, http://www.bbc.co.uk/wales/northeast/sites/wrexham/pages/penley.shtml, last updated 18 February 2008; *Staffordshire's Community Talk Board*, http://www.bbc.co.uk/stoke/have_your_say/polish.shtml, 2003.

19 *A Forgotten Odyssey*, http://www.aforgottenodyssey.com/, 2001.

20 Zosia Biegus, *Northwick Park Polish DP Camp*, http://www.northwickparkpolishdpcamp.co.uk/, 2005, accessed 9 May 2008; Mathew Lawson, *Shallow Graves in Siberia*, http://homepages.tesco.net/theprophecy/SGIS/index.htm, accessed 9 May 2008; Eugene Krajewski, *Straws in the Wind*, http://www.strawsinthewind.com/, accessed 9 May 2008.

21 Mike Oborski, *Poles in Great Britain*, http://groups.yahoo.com/group/polesingreatbritain/, accessed 9 May 2008; *Polish Forces During World War II*, http://groups.yahoo.com/group/polishforces/, created 16 August 2001; *Armia Krajowa*, http://groups.yahoo.com/group/armiakrajowa/, created 23 March 2000.

22 George Kempik, *Sikorski Polish Club*, http://www.sikorskipolishclub.org.uk/oldguestbook.htm, 1 February 2002, accessed 29 October 2004.

23 Michael Kulik, *Stalin's Ethnic Cleansing*, http://www.stalinsethniccleansing.com, accessed 10 October 2004. *Stalin's Ethnic Cleansing*, a compilation of oral testimony originally published in book form in Polish in 1996, also commemorates deportation, along with the relationship between the actual experience of some of the first generation and the inherited experience of the second generation.

24 Jurek Narożański, 'New Guestbook', http://www.theguestbook.com/read.php/375442, accessed 28 October 2004.

25 Jurek Zdanko to *Penley Poles*, http://www.bbc.co.uk/wales/northeast/sites/wrexham/pages/penley.shtml, 21 January 2006.

26 Janette Obuch to *300 Polish Squadron*, 'From Janette Obuch: new member', 6 March 2005, http://groups.yahoo.com/group/300polishsquadron/message/52.

27 Janette Obuch to *300 Polish Squadron*, 'Please welcome our new member Mike Markut', 4 March 2006.

28 Susan Ann Smith, 'Guest book – Stalin's ethnic cleansing', http://www.stalinsethnic cleansing.com, accessed 10 October 2004.

29 The most powerful symbol of the Polish wartime struggle is that of the train. It represents the forced removal of Poles from the Kresy to the Soviet Union. It also represents freedom since it was the mode of transport used by the Poles to reach the Polish Army in southern Russia after the Amnesty was granted in 1941. This is the significance of the visual image used on the home page of the *Kresy-Siberia* forum, which is a photograph depicting two young girls gazing out of the window of a train.

30 Sarah Flicker, Dave Haans and Harvery Skinner, 'Ethical dilemmas in research on internet communities', *Qualitative Health Research* 14.1, 2004, pp. 124–34.

31 Judith Sixsmith and Craig Murray, 'Pearls, pith and provocation: ethical issues in the documentary data analysis of internet posts and archives', *Qualitative Health Research* 11.3, 2001, p. 424.

32 Gajjala, 'An interrupted postcolonial/feminist cyberethnography', p. 178.

33 Barbara Smolicz to Kresy-Siberia@yahoogroups.com, 'Welcome Barbara Smolicz', 15 August 2003.

34 Anna Coates to Kresy-Siberia@yahoogroups.com, 'New on-line member', 24 October 2003.

35 The 'historical trace' relates to the traceable presence of members accessing forums. Michele Wilson, 'Community in the abstract: a political and ethical dilemma', in David Holmes (ed.), *Virtual Politics: Identity and Community in Cyberspace*, London: Sage, 1997, p. 68.

36 Elizabeth Reid, 'Hierarchy and power: social control in cyberspace', in Mark A. Smith and Peter Kollock (eds), *Communities in Cyberspace,* London and New York: Routledge, 1999, p. 113.

37 Lisa Blenkinsop to Hilton Dawson, email correspondence, 'Michael Howard and Polish concentration camps', 28 July 2004. My email to Hilton Dawson read:

> I am a research student (Ph.D.) at Lancaster University working on the Polish community in Great Britain. Recently Michael Howard is reported in the press to have stated that his grandmother died in a Polish concentration camp. Of course, this was a Nazi concentration camp in Nazi occupied Poland and not a 'Polish' concentration camp. I am sure the Polish community feels insulted by this comment. As far as I know an apology has not been issued – I would urge you to push for one.

The following reply came: 'I appreciate your feelings about this but you can never rely on anything quoted in the Press in this fashion. Frankly I'd also quail at the prospect at raising allegations of the complicity of some Polish people in the Holocaust.' Hilton Dawson to Lisa Blenkinsop, email correspondence, 'Michael Howard and Polish concentration camps', 28 July 2004.

38 Gajjala, 'An interrupted postcolonial/feminist cyberethnography', p. 182.

39 Ania to polesingreatbritain@yahoogroups.com, 9 August 2004.

9   Landscape: the configured space

Tom Williamson

What is landscape history?

Landscape history or landscape archaeology – the two terms are virtually inter-changeable – has enjoyed phenomenal growth over the last four decades. The subject first emerged in the 1950s: its inception is usually associated with the work of the economic historian W.G. Hoskins, whose immensely successful *The Making of the English Landscape* was published in 1955,[1] although a number of other scholars were also influential in its development, most notably the historian Maurice Beresford and the historical geographer Harry Thorpe. During the 1960s, 1970s and early 1980s the subject grew steadily in popularity, although initially for the most part among those involved in the extramural sector. Indeed, many authors of the volumes in Hodder and Stoughton's county-based *Making of the English Landscape* series – essentially a spin-off from Hoskins's original book – were tutors in extramural departments, including Trevor Rowley (*Shropshire*), Lionel Munby (*Hertfordshire*) and Michael Reed (*Buckinghamshire*).[2] But this period was also marked by the growing involvement of individuals from outside the ranks of economic history or historical geography, especially field archaeologists and historical ecologists. Among the former should be mentioned Christopher Taylor, effectively the second founder of the subject, whose books included *Fields in the English Landscape*, *Village and Farmstead*, and *The Archaeology of Gardens*.[3] The most important of the ecologists were Max Hooper, whose work on hedges was to influence a generation, and above all Oliver Rackham, whose *Trees and Woodland in the British Countryside* of 1976 was followed in 1986 by his *History of the Countryside*, which twenty years on still remains a standard text.[4] Since the 1980s the subject has seen both further growth, now more in the mainstream of British university life, and the increased involvement of archaeologists, especially those involved in the study of prehistoric landscapes. Today, landscape history can boast a number of specialised undergraduate and MA courses at British universities, and two academic journals (*Landscapes* and *Landscape History*). Each year a substantial array of books is published with (appropriately or otherwise) the word 'landscape' in their title.[5]

The above account simplifies the history of the subject considerably, and in particular neglects the complexity of its relationship with other disciplines, especially local and regional history and the study of vernacular architecture. It also, perhaps, suggests a more coherent bundle of ideas and concerns than really exists. But, most importantly of all, it fails to explain just what it is that all these people actually *do*. In essence, landscape history is concerned with the historical interpretation of the physical structures and spaces which make up the environment: roads, field systems, settlement patterns, buildings and the various semi-natural habitats such as woods, heaths or hedges. It seeks to explain their character, both now and at various points in the past, in terms of social, economic and ideological processes and influences. But at the same time, it tries to use this physical evidence to contribute to wider debates in history and archaeology. Landscape historians employ a wide range of documentary sources (although especially maps) but, more importantly, they use physical evidence, such as earthworks, standing buildings and vegetation patterns. The subject is concerned to shift the traditional interest of archaeologists away from 'sites' to the wider panorama of their spatial context, and in so far as archaeological techniques are employed these are of a 'non-invasive' nature – earthwork surveys, or fieldwalking – that is, the systematic collection of artefacts lying in the ploughsoil, indicating the location of settlement or past activities. Landscape history also has close links with historical ecology, engaging in what might be called 'habitat history' – with the study of the past systems of management which have created the natural or semi-natural habitats so important for wildlife and biodiversity today. Few landscape historians are period specialists – this is not 'two wet weekends in 1642' style history. Most are 'jacks of all trades', who often range widely across the chronological spectrum, from prehistory to the modern period. Many are concerned with the long term, with grand narrative, at a time when these things have, perhaps, fallen out of favour with most historians. Above all, landscape historians are interested in place and space as much as in time. One might almost say, not entirely flippantly, that they do what historical geographers used to do, before they embraced postmodernism and tore up their maps.[6]

The uses of landscape history

It will be apparent from what has already been said that those who study what Hoskins described as 'the richest historical document' have forged many links with those working in related academic fields. Yet it remains true that many of the key insights provided by landscape history have not been fully absorbed into the mainstream of historical thought, and some historians probably harbour a suspicion that the subject does little more than illustrate other kinds of historical narrative. It might therefore be useful to give some examples of the contributions which the discipline can make, and has made; and, more importantly, the wide range of forms which such contributions have taken.

At the very simplest level, landscape history provides some basic yet immensely important factual information about the past. Systematic field-walking surveys have, for example, demonstrated that population levels in late prehistoric and Roman Britain were much higher than once believed, perhaps comparable with those at the time of Domesday, before falling away again in the fifth and sixth centuries and then rising once more in middle and later Saxon times.[7] Fieldwork, combined with detailed analysis of maps and early documents, has also cast much new light on the origins of the medieval landscape, and in particular on that of nucleated villages and open fields which dominated a broad swathe of England from the north-east, through the Midlands, to the south coast. Landscape historians have shown that rather than being the creation of the earliest Saxon settlers, as was once thought, villages and communal agriculture only developed in the period between the ninth and the twelfth centuries, out of a more scattered settlement pattern, and more individualistic farming practices.[8] They have, moreover, repeatedly emphasised that such agrarian arrangements were only ever found in a relatively limited area of England, and that either side of this broad band – in the south-east, and in the west – dispersed patterns of settlement, and more irregular field systems, were the norm, although debate continues to rage about the meaning and origins of such regional differences. [9]

The careful mapping of structures and forms often allows us to see broad spatial patterns more clearly than we could through the systematic examination of a host of local documents. One example concerns the enclosure of the Midland open fields in the course of the seventeenth and eighteenth centuries. This process is often associated with the adoption of improved farming practices: removal of land from communal systems of rotation made it easier to adopt new crops and rotations. Across much of Midland England, however, documentary sources (such as the 1801 Crop Returns[10]) suggest that much enclosure was associated with changes in regional farming patterns, with the Midlands coming to specialise, in the course of the seventeenth, eighteenth and early nineteenth centuries, in sheep and cattle grazing. Painstaking analysis of estate maps, accounts and other documentary sources could, in theory, allow us to see whether patterns of land use really did change significantly in the region in this period. But the landscape itself provides simpler and more direct evidence. This is because open-field farmers in the Midlands generally ploughed their strips in low ridges; and these were preserved, by conversion to pasture, as the distinctive corrugations known to archaeologists as 'ridge and furrow', a form of earthwork which was widespread in the Midlands before agricultural intensification between the 1950s and the 1970s. The vertical photographs produced in 1946, however, allow its distribution at that date to be mapped (Figure 9.1). At that time, ridge and furrow still covered vast swathes of ground, in spite of the fact that much had already been levelled by wartime ploughing, vividly indicating – more clearly than piecemeal documentary research – the extent to which, in the course of the late medieval and post-medieval periods, the English Midlands moved out of arable agriculture and into pasture farming.[11]

These are some rather simple examples of the way that the landscape can inform us about practical but nevertheless immensely important aspects of social, economic and agrarian history. Landscape history is very good at this kind of thing. But it is equally good at opening up entirely new areas of research, hitherto unnoticed by those already working in other disciplines. One important example relates to the study of designed landscapes – parks and gardens. Landscape

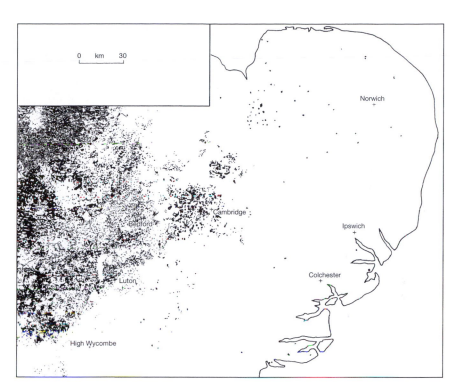

Figure 9.1 The distribution of ridge and furrow in the south-east Midlands, plotted from the 1946 RAF aerial photographs. Large areas of these earthworks had been levelled by conversion to arable during World War II, but the extent to which the medieval open fields of the Midlands were laid to grass, and the ridged 'lands' thus preserved in earthwork form, is nevertheless clear.[12]

historians have been much involved in this since Taylor published his seminal *Archaeology of Gardens* in 1983. Important light has been cast not only on the history of individual sites, but also on the broader development of styles and their social and ideological determinants, through the systematic study of surviving remains (planting, earthworks, standing structures and 'hard landscaping'). But such research has also served to challenge conventional accounts, primarily based on documentary sources and visual representations. In 1990 Taylor and colleagues published an article which argued persuasively that the fourteenth-century castle at Bodiam in Sussex had been provided with an elaborately designed setting, featuring sheets of water, ornamental planting and a carefully contrived approach route.[13] Subsequent studies have argued that 'medieval designed landscapes', considerably more extensive than the *hortus conclusus* normally considered to be typical of the period, were a common feature, and that they resembled in many respects the landscape parks of the eighteenth century – in Michael Leslie's words, there was an 'English landscape garden before the English Landscape Garden'.[14]

Landscape history and historical ecology

Landscape history has thus made significant contributions not only to questions of interest to mainstream social and economic historians, but also – in this and other ways – in areas of study usually considered the preserve of the art historian. Its relations with historical ecology have perhaps been more problematic. The links between the two disciplines are strong but practitioners come from different intellectual traditions and remain conceptually divided by the 'two cultures'. Landscape historians and archaeologists, it must be said, have often treated biological theory and data in a naïve way. Conversely, natural historians often take a simplistic view of social and economic history: while fully aware of the complexity of the *natural* processes shaping the character of landscapes, they often seem to view the past influence of human societies in terms of 'rational' economic activity following straightforward, 'common-sense' strategies of survival. Above all, historians and natural scientists perhaps differ in the emphasis they each place on the respective influences of 'natural' and 'social' processes in the formation of habitats and landscape features.

The strange story of 'hedge dating' perhaps exemplifies this divide. Research into hedges by ecologists Max Hooper and Ernest Pollard in the 1960s and 1970s culminated in Hooper's suggestion that they tended to acquire new species at a relatively standard rate and could, in consequence, be roughly dated by counting the number of different shrubs which they presently contained.[15] Hooper was cautious in this suggestion, emphasising the importance of local variations and stressing that the method only provided a very approximate guide to a hedge's antiquity. But when the theory was embraced by landscape and local historians such caution was often thrown to the winds, and hedges were confidently dated to specific periods, even to particular centuries.[16] Pollard's research was less eagerly embraced by students of landscape. He reached conclusions which, although aired in the same volume as those of Hooper, differed from his in a number of important respects. In particular, he drew attention to a type of very mixed hedge, characterised by large amounts of hazel, dogwood and other woodland shrubs, and containing a range of woodland plants in their herb layer.[17] Pollard believed that these 'woodland relict hedges' had been created by managing lines of vegetation around assarts cut from woodland early in the medieval period.[18] Such very mixed hedges had been thus species-rich from the start, unlike Hooper's species-rich hedges, which had acquired their character through colonisation over time.[19]

A substantial body of research has cast doubt on the validity of 'Hooper's rule'. He evidently underestimated the full extent to which variations in seed supply and soil character could, in practice, affect colonisation. More importantly, he failed to appreciate the fact that whereas eighteenth- and nineteenth-century hedges were normally planted with hawthorn, blackthorn, or a mixture of these species, earlier hedges were often established using a range of different shrubs: in part, that is, older hedges contain more species simply because they started life with more.[20] Generally planted by small farmers in a peasant economy, they were intended to supply a range of resources – fuel mainly, but also perhaps fodder and fruit – as well as serving as stock-proof barriers. Eighteenth- and nineteenth-century hedges, in contrast, were mainly planted by large landowners, who obtained their firewood from coppiced woodland or plantations or used coal on their fires, and who had little use for the other resources which hedges might provide. They saw boundaries as markers of property and barriers to stock and were hostile to 'peasanty' mixed hedges. The early planting of multi-species hedges was also, of course, encouraged by the difficulty of obtaining large quantities of hedging thorn before the development of large commercial nurseries in the middle decades of the eighteenth century. All this makes obvious nonsense of Hooper's 'rule'. Nevertheless, this shift in planting patterns, scarcely noted in written sources, does tell us something important about changing *mentalities* in post-medieval rural England. And much can still be learnt from the study of particular hedges. Pollard's 'woodland relict' hedges, although probably planted rather than created by the management of residual woodland vegetation, do seem in many districts to represent the oldest systems of land division; and a number of other idiosyncrasies and patterns in hedge vegetation have proved to be historically significant. But Hooper's simple 'rule' is incorrect and misleading, not only because it oversimplifies the complex ecology of hedges, but also because it interprets variations in their botany almost entirely in terms of natural factors, rather than as the outcome of the complex interplay of natural and human influences. Similar problems and debates are associated with the study of other 'semi-natural' environments, such as ancient woodland.

Approaches to landscape

In a subject formed from the overlapping interests of people originating in a wide range of intellectual historical traditions it is not surprising to find significant differences of emphasis. Today, one major intellectual divide, among others, concerns what are generally described as 'phenomenological' approaches to past landscapes, approaches which originated in the study of prehistoric landscapes but are now being more widely applied. Landscape historians and landscape archaeologists usually look on the physical structures, spaces and distributions left by past societies as reflections, traces and by-products of social and economic activities. Those adopting phenomenological approaches, in contrast, start from a different range of premises.[21] People inhabiting a particular landscape invested features, both natural and man made, with a range of symbolic associations and significances. Drawing on anthropological studies of non-Western peoples from around the world, such archaeologists argue that the prehistoric landscape was alive with stories, myths and memories, through which individuals and societies constructed their identity and self-image, and through which they related to the cosmos. The location, as much as the design, of early monuments was the outcome of such ideas and beliefs, rather than a simple consequence of the social and economic patterns supposedly reconstructed by archaeologists. Indeed, much of the two-dimensional mapping carried out by archaeologists, of monuments and their distributions, tends to hinder rather than help our attempts to understand their meaning. They tell us next to nothing about how monuments and places were perceived in the past, because their creators never saw them from the air, only from ground level. In short, we need to try to get inside the heads of the people of the past, for only then can we understand their landscapes, and the ways in which they changed them. We need, in Bradley's words, to consider 'the superstructure of meanings and values through which particular landscapes were experienced'.[22]

Such perspectives have not been entirely restricted to prehistorians. Some historians and historical geographers, especially those studying the early modern period, have developed similar approaches. Denis Cosgrove, for example, has emphasised the way in which the concept of 'landscape' itself arose as part of a complex nexus of ideological change in the sixteenth and seventeenth centuries. It was associated with a way of viewing the physical environment which developed, alongside cartography, in association with new concepts of ownership, capitalist forms of production and novel forms of political power.[23] Indeed, to some scholars, the very tools employed by modern students of the past – plans, maps, aerial photographs – are themselves 'Cartesian devices' standing in direct lineal decent to the modes of representation which accompanied the emergence of capitalism, and represent forms of control and surveillance which are of little use in understanding the attitudes to, and experience of, landscapes associated with pre-Cartesian societies. To cultural geographers Daniels and Cosgrove, moreover, the landscape has an 'iconography' which needs to be read and interpreted like a painting or a text.[24] Features such as trees or woodlands, or certain kinds of land use, had symbolic meanings.[25] The historian Dave Rollison, meanwhile, has argued that people in early modern England used the landscape as a 'memory palace'. Meanings attached to the physical environment, through such things as folk stories and popular sayings, were one of the ways in which social knowledge was passed from one generation to the next.[26] Similar ideas have been developed by Nicola Whyte in her studies of the early modern landscape in East Anglia.[27]

In the more remote past, the construction of monuments, their maintenance and their subsequent use and interpretation by later societies – and how these things relate to concepts of time – have been matters of concern to many landscape archaeologists. Monuments were integrated into patterns of ritual, and often of seasonal, movement:

> While places and movement between them are intimately related to the formation of personal biographies, places themselves may be said to acquire a history, sedimented layers of meaning by virtue of the actions and events that take place in them. Personal biographies, social identities and a biography of place are intimately connected.[28]

Monuments and landscapes thus need to be understood not only in terms of the beliefs, memories and stories attached to them, but also in terms of the structured activities which took place at and around them, activities which in turn shaped the way in which these places were experienced. Once constructed, moreover, monuments such as henges or barrows had, as it were, a life of their own: they continued to be powerful presences in the landscape, invested often with new meanings.[29] Such ideas have, once again, begun to be adopted by landscape historians concerned with much more recent periods of time.

Not every historian or archaeologist concerned with the study of landscape has welcomed the 'phenomenological' agenda.[30] Some, in particular, reject the idea that the experience of individuals should be the primary focus of our research. People in the past, as much as people in the present, did not know – could not know – about the complex, multifarious influences on their lives and landscapes. We often know far more about their world than they ever could. They were unaware, for example, of long-term patterns of climate change; of the webs of trade and exchange which connected them with people living very different lives, perhaps half a continent away; or about the ways in which the changing interests or demands of such distant peoples, or events in their worlds, impacted upon their own. To concentrate *only* on what they knew of the world, or thought they knew, seems to many to be a rather limited way of understanding how and why early people lived the lives they did. Reconstructing past experiences of landscape might be important, but it should not necessarily be *the* most important concern. Some scholars, more importantly, simply doubt whether it is possible to know how people in the past, or in the remote past at least, experienced or thought about their environment. Anthropological studies, as archaeologists such as Christopher Tilley are keen to point out, reveal the richly textured character of the associations placed upon the landscape by non-Western cultures, in the form of legends, songs, rituals, customs, stories, social and individual memories. The very extent of this complexity makes it unlikely that we can ever really recover the experience of landscape in the remote past.

Nevertheless, for documented periods we can more easily explore how landscapes and structures were experienced, perceived and manipulated by contemporaries, and this has been a longer tradition in landscape history than some phenomenologists perhaps recognise. Vernacular buildings have, since the time of Hoskins, been studied in terms of regional variations in economic history and class relations, but also as fossilised social spaces: the layout of rooms and spaces within them both reflected, and reinforced, patterns of social interaction between classes and genders, and more widely affected human experience.[31] And a concern for the experience of landscape has, not surprisingly, informed a number of studies of elite-designed landscapes.

Houghton: the making of landscape

I will take as an example of the landscape historian's work the examination of a particular designed landscape – not because landscape historians spend all their time studying such things but rather because it demonstrates well some of the methods and approaches briefly noted above. Houghton is an extensive deer park in west Norfolk, occupying an area of around 4,500 hectares on largely light, freely draining soil, but with small patches of impervious boulder clay. Like most designed landscapes, it is complex and multi-period in character.[32] The Walpole family had held land in the area since the fourteenth century but the present hall was built for Robert Walpole, first prime minister of England, largely with proceeds from government office. It is an important early exercise in Neo-Palladianism, designed by Colen Campbell and James Gibbs (perhaps with some input from William Kent), and was built between 1721 and *c.*1730. A deer park had been laid out around the previous houses, probably in the late seventeenth century, and this is shown on a number of maps and plans, including an engraving published in Campbell's *Vitruvius Britannicus* of 1725 (Figure 9.2). It was filled, in the fashion of the day, with a dense mesh of avenues, some focused on the hall, others continuing the alignments of the allees in a geometric wilderness which – again, typically for the period – occupied much of the garden area.[33]

This landscape was transformed in the 1720s, as the hall was being rebuilt, to designs by Charles Bridgeman; evidently, the existing park was considered insufficiently grand and fashionable for the new house. A version of Bridgeman's design was published as an engraving in Isaac Ware's *Plans, Elevations and Sections of Houghton* in 1735 (Figure 9.3). The lake, and the vast outer perimeter ride with its distinctive 'bastions', were never in fact created, but the other features shown were executed, and form the basis of the landscape as it survives today. The complex mesh of avenues shown on Campbell's plan was removed and in its place a much simpler, monumental arrangement was created, of the kind usually associated with Bridgeman, who was in many ways a transitional designer, mid-way between the formal and geometric layouts of the seventeenth century and the 'naturalistic' landscape parks of the period after *c.*1760. Four great vistas were

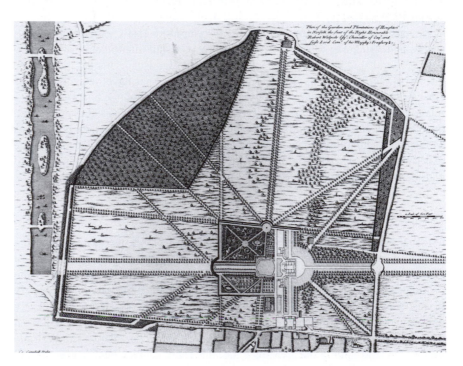

Figure 9.2 Houghton Park, Norfolk, as depicted in Colen Campbell, *Vitruvius Britannicus*, 1725.

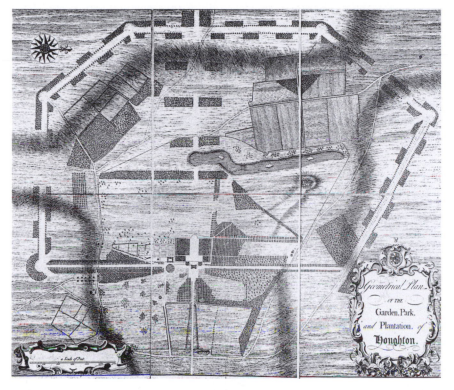

Figure 9.3 Houghton Park, from Isaac Ware, *The Plans, Elevations . . . of Houghton in Norfolk*, 1764 edition.

now focused on the facades of the house, some defined by avenues, others implied by blocks of plantations. The village of Houghton, which in 1722 had stood relatively close to the hall, had been removed, although the parish church remained where it was, now quite isolated. It was not the only building in the park. The 'Water House', a temple-like structure which served as viewpoint, eye catcher and water supply tower, was erected (to designs by Lord Pembroke) to the north of the gardens in *c.*1730. Ware's engraving shows the village's replacement – referred to as 'Houghton New Town' in estate documents – to the south-east of the newly expanded park. It still survives today as two rows of neat, white-washed and pantiled semi-detached houses ranged either side of a road.

Houghton Hall was, to begin with, used only sporadically by Walpole, mainly for his 'congresses' – lengthy house parties at which political allies and local clients would meet to plot, hunt and eat. It was used more regularly following his fall from office in 1733, a period which saw further additions and alterations to the landscape. These came to an abrupt end with Walpole's death in 1745. He left debts of more than £40,000: his successors were ineffectual, ill or old and, while the park was not entirely neglected, no major works were undertaken. Only in 1797, with the

accession of the 4th Earl Cholmondeley, did further changes take place, which
continued under his successors through much of the nineteenth century, although
there is no space to discuss them here.

   The landscape historian begins with maps and documents. But he or she then
turns to the physical evidence. Houghton Park, like almost all such landscapes,
contains a range of earthworks (Figure 9.4). Some of these relate to the designed
landscape itself. Among several such features, attention should be drawn to the
substantial cutting made through the hill to the east of the house, in order to open
up the view towards Raynham, seat of the Townshends – political allies of the

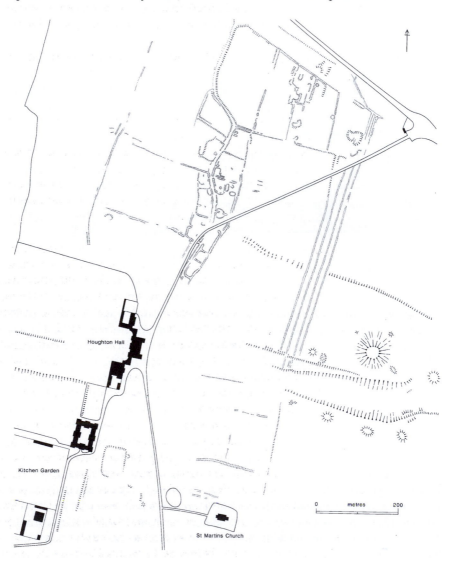

Figure 9.4 The earthworks in Houghton Park.

Walpoles. Its construction, which began in 1742, is only briefly alluded to in the rather incomplete archives for the period. A single memorandum simply states 'item – the matter of removing the hill to be decided'. The excavated earth was used to create tree-planting mounds, and a huge mound covering a large ice house. The entire scheme was vast – but close examination of the remains shows that it was never finished. It was abandoned immediately after Walpole died.

Other earthworks relate to the working landscape which the park replaced. First, there are two main areas of settlement remains. One, close to the parish church, represents part of the village shown on Campbell's plan of 1722, removed over the following years. Typically for settlements cleared to make way for parks, however, its traces are meagre. The site was evidently levelled, following demolition of the houses, with peculiar thoroughness. Far more impressive, and a surprising discovery, is the huge area of village earthworks which extends, on either side of a prominent 'hollow way' (a former roadway), to the north of the hall. At first glance this appears to represent a settlement quite separate from Houghton village but almost certainly it was not. At their southern end the earthworks end abruptly as the hall itself is approached. They have here been very thoroughly obliterated. Originally the hall (or rather its predecessor) would seem to have fronted on to the same north–south road along which the lost settlement is itself ranged, and which presumably continued southwards – accompanied by further house sites – to join the east–west road and associated houses removed in the 1720s. Evidently, Houghton was originally a very large village, shaped like an inverted 'T'. But when did the northern extension disappear? It is possible that it was cleared away when the first park was laid out, probably in the late seventeenth century, but on balance this is unlikely. The population of the parish, as recorded in a tithe list of 1578, was only slightly larger than that of the village cleared in the 1720s, suggesting that it had already contracted in size, and was to do so further over the following century (variations in the character of the earthworks marking property boundaries also seem to suggest gradual decline rather than sudden clearance). The very fact that most of the earthworks here have never been subject to deliberate levelling, unlike those of the village cleared in the 1720s, likewise suggests gradual and organic decline rather than deliberate and catastrophic removal.

These settlement remains are a good example of a wider phenomenon. The clearance of villages to make way for parklands almost always came at the end of an extended period of decline. Emparked settlements had normally once been larger or, to put it another way, the connections between lordship and settlement deser-tion were complex. As population fell in late medieval times, villages in relatively marginal locations often haemorrhaged population: Houghton is on a high, dry interfluve, without good supplies of running water. Demographic and economic decline allowed manorial lords to acquire complete control and ownership of such places. They might then limit or further reduce their population. In part this was because, from the late sixteenth century, each parish was responsible for looking after its own poor. In 'closed' parishes wealthy landowners attempted to limit the number of people who might come to claim poor relief through age or infirmity: seasonal shortfalls in labour could be dealt with by importing workers from neighbouring 'open' settlements, generally larger in character because ownership (and thus the burden of the poor rates) was more divided.[34] But aesthetic ideas, and above all an increasing desire for privacy and social distancing, were also important forces encouraging settlement shrinkage and could culminate, as here, in the actual removal of all dwellings from the immediate vicinity of a great house.

In addition to settlement earthworks the park also contains numerous low banks representing former field boundaries. These indicate that, in contrast to the situation in most of the surrounding parishes, the open fields of Houghton had been entirely enclosed some time before the park was laid out, a minor but nevertheless useful part of the historical jigsaw. In typical fashion, these banks are associated with large oak trees, most of which were once managed by pollarding – a traditional practice, involving the repeated removal of all the branches, at a height of around two metres, at intervals of ten to fifteen years, in order to obtain a regular crop of wood suitable for fuel, tools, fencing and building repairs. Pollarding was, by the eighteenth century, regarded as a peasant practice and in this case appears to have ceased, and the trees allowed to grow on, when the park was created. The trees were retained, when their associated hedges were removed, in order to create an instant 'sylvan' appearance – to make the park appear an ancient one, and thus a badge of long-established status. This was common practice in the eighteenth century but in the case of Houghton at least not everybody was fooled: some were already adept at reading the history of a landscape. William Gilpin, visiting in the 1760s, perceptively noted how it was 'easy to trace, from the growth of the woods, and the vestiges of hedge-rows, where the ambition of the minister made his ornamental inroads into the acres of his inheritance'.[35] Some of the hedgerow trees were evidently quite young when incorporated into the park – less than fifty years old – but others were ancient. One, a massive veteran with a girth of more than nine metres, was probably planted in the fourteenth century (Figure 9.5). Looked at one way, parks destroyed existing landscapes. Yet within them the archaeological traces of early landscapes, in the form of earthworks or planting, are usually better preserved than they are in the surrounding countryside.

Careful survey of the trees planted as parts of successive design phases can also tell us much about a landscape's history. In the case of Houghton, for example, an avenue of massive sweet chestnuts (and isolated trees surviving from others) indicate both the species used for the avenues planted in the seventeenth-century park and demonstrate that, contrary to the evidence of Ware's engraving and a number of other maps, at least one of these was retained through the changes of the 1720s and 1730s. Systematic survey can thus show which elements of design proposals were accepted by landowners, and which ignored, and more generally demonstrate how visual representations such as maps always need to be treated with extreme caution.

Houghton: the meaning of a landscape

Reconstructing the physical appearance of a landscape at a certain point in time, and charting the ways in which it has developed subsequently, are important and

Figure 9.5 Ancient oak pollard growing on an old hedge bank in Houghton Park.

enjoyable tasks, but such activities are only a beginning. How landscapes were experienced in the past, what they meant to contemporaries, is an equally important concern, although understanding such matters is perhaps more difficult than some prehistorians, in particular, seem to assume. Observers brought to a particular place a different set of experiences, preconceptions and associations from ours, and understood references and saw significances in structures and spaces which we can only recover with a conscious effort. Moreover, they compared and contrasted specific landscapes with a range of other contemporary environments, so that it is impossible to understand the meaning of one place without an appreciation of others, local or distant, similar or different.

Three main features of the landscape depicted on Campbell's plan of 1722 are worthy of note. Stylistically, it was more geometric in character than that which succeeded it. The mansion, while already segregated by parkland to some extent from the neighbouring village, nevertheless lay close to and intervisible with it. Lastly, the area of gardens near the house was not entirely aesthetic in character. It included orchards, nut grounds and kitchen gardens. All these features were typical of the greatest residences of the seventeenth century: at lesser mansions, those of the local gentry, practical and productive features would have been even more prominent in the grounds, and the degree of isolation from other homes would have been less. Such places generally lacked deer parks, which were expensive to create, stock and maintain, and thus tended to be the prerogative of the greatest landowners. Parks had long been important markers of status, and since the later Middle Ages had been placed beside or around mansions – rather than, as in early medieval times, usually being located at some distance from them. They had an immense social significance, and so too did the trees growing within them, especially where – as here – surrounding areas mainly consisted of unenclosed open fields and commons, devoid of hedges, hedgerow trees and woodland. The particular kinds of tree planted at Houghton emphasised the contrast with the working landscape, for – judging from surviving specimens – they included species such as sweet chestnut not normally found in the locality.

The transformation of the Houghton landscape under Charles Bridgeman served to increase both the size and the visual prominence of the park, for removing the mesh of avenues created a more open, less minutely subdivided space, although it is important to remember that the uprooted avenues did not then look much like their sole survivor today – their constituent trees were probably only just mature. The new arrangement of vistas was much more tightly focused on the house, and extended out (as we can now appreciate today, on the ground) to the far horizon. The four-square arrangement also mirrored the rigid internal symmetry of the house, thus integrating the geometry of domestic space, and of the wider landscape, in a single scheme, creating a potent symbol of ownership and control. Two other features of the new ensemble are worth noting. The first is that the house was constructed of stone, brought from Lincolnshire at considerable expense. Visitors hardly notice this fact today but in the early eighteenth century nobody could have failed to: Norfolk lacks good building stone, and no edifice this size had ever been constructed of freestone in the county before. This fact, more than the building's innovative style, would have served to overawe and impress visitors, whatever their social standing. The second is that productive facilities – kitchen garden and the like – had now been removed from the vicinity of the house and relocated to a walled enclosure lying to the south of the stables. This was part of a more general pattern. Elite residences were increasingly segregated from practical and productive features in the course of the eighteenth century, a practice which, in the period after *c.*1760, spread down to the level of the local gentry. Great landowners such as Walpole were keen to proclaim their separation not only from local communities, but also from the kinds of practical, productive, agricultural activities in which their members were, of necessity, involved: they were eager, as it were, to make their homes look like mansions, rather than farms.[36]

In physical terms those living in the settlement of 'New Houghton' were not entirely excluded from the new landscape, for all were employed on the estate and many worked in the hall itself. But they were excluded in more subtle ways. What had once been familiar fields had now become an arena for status display, for intellectual aesthetics: the 'Water House' was a foreign temple, the hall itself mimicked an Italianate villa, and even the parish church, left marooned in the parkland, was given a new role, like the former hedgerow trees. Bizarrely, it was comprehensively rebuilt, to give it a more acceptably 'gothick' appearance. It was thus rendered more a garden ornament, and less of a communal place of worship. The park was also an area for elite recreation, especially for riding fast, unhindered by hedges and other obstacles. Blocks of plantation served to divide it, clearly, from the new village, preventing views in and views out.

The neat, rather functional appearance of 'New Houghton' stands in sharp contrast to the whimsical design of the church. Yet to some extent we might be missing something here, as in their proportions the houses have a distinct air of stripped-down Palladianism. Moreover, most have their principal entrances to the side, rather than at the front, perhaps suggesting that the place would on occasion be visited by Walpole and guests: early in the following century the architect P.F. Robinson was to advise against providing cottages with adjacent front doors, facing the street, on the grounds that it would encourage idle gossiping, as well as allowing genteel visitors a glimpse of the 'uncleanly habits' of the inhabitants within. Nevertheless, it is important to note that Ware's engraving, and other maps, make it clear that, when originally built, the village did not stand on a main access road, at the gates to the park, but on a minor side road which, having passed through the village, meandered across the adjacent fields. The present arrangement, with the cottages clustering deferentially at the main entrance, is the result of changes made soon after 1797, which involved the creation of an entirely new approach to the hall. 'The rich man at his castle/the poor man at his gate': from the last decade of the eighteenth century landowners began to manipulate their landscapes to express a paternalistic concern for their tenant and workers. That is another story, which cannot be told here, but this particular example of a much wider phenomenon does serve to show how quite minor alterations in the landscape, channelling movement in new and different directions, can have a profound impact on the meaning of existing structures and spaces.

Conclusion

As I have already emphasised, landscape historians do not always, or even usually, study *designed* landscapes. The example of Houghton does, nevertheless, serve to demonstrate the kinds of activities involved in this kind of history. In some ways the subject is, perhaps, something of an intellectual ragbag. To me at least this is part of its appeal. The diverse range of sources it employs can inform us about aspects of the past which remain poorly or unevenly documented in written sources. But even in contexts in which the latter are abundant, the evidence of the landscape can often cast new light on past experience, exposing to view the unwritten and often unconscious assumptions underlying everyday life.

Notes

1 W.G. Hoskins, *The Making of the English Landscape*, London: Hodder and Stoughton, 1955.
2 T. Rowley, *The Shropshire Landscape*, London: Hodder and Stoughton, 1972; L.M. Munby, *The Hertfordshire Landscape*, London: Hodder and Stoughton, 1977; M. Reed, *The Buckinghamshire Landscape*, London: Hodder and Stoughton, 1979.
3 C. Taylor, *Fields in the English Landscape*, London: Dent, 1975; Taylor, *Village and Farmstead*, London: George Philips, 1983; Taylor, *The Archaeology of Gardens*, Princes Risborough: Shire, 1983.
4 M.D. Hooper, 'Dating hedges', *Area* 4, 1970, pp. 63–5; O. Rackham, Trees and

Woodland in the British Landscape, London: Dent, 1976, Rackham, *The History of the Countryside*, London: Dent, 1986.

5   As the foregoing makes clear, this style of history through the prism of landscape change was born out of and fostered within English history. The majority of Masters' courses and degree schemes which reflect this tend to follow suit. Universities teaching landscape history include the University of Cambridge, Institute of Continuing Education; University of Sussex, Landscape History and Culture MA; and University of Leicester, MA in Archaeology and Landscape History.

6   This chapter will concentrate on the English landscape school, but in recent years landscape studies have expanded to embrace a global perspective, and readers could be directed to the following: Europe – Dagfinn Moe, 'Landscape history and heathland development over the last 4000 years in the Bodø area, northern Norway', *Norwegian Journal of Geography* 57.4, 2003, pp. 194–204; M. Cleary and C. Delano-Smith, 'Transhumance reviewed: past and present practices in France and Italy', *Rivista di Studi Liguri* A LVI, 1–4, pp. 21–38; G.M. Cruise, 'Environmental change and human impact in the upper mountain zone of the Ligurian Apennines: the last 5000 years', *Rivista di Studi Liguri* LVI, 1992, pp. 169–88; Meelis Pärtel, Riina Mändla and Martin Zobel, 'Landscape history of a calcareous (alvar) grassland in Hanila, western Estonia, during the last three hundred years', *Landscape Ecology*, 14.2, 1999, pp. 187–96; North America – Bonj Szczygiel, Josephine Carubia and Lorraine Dowler (eds), *Proceedings of Gendered Landscape*: *Interdisciplinary Exploration of Past Place and Space*, London: Routledge, 2000; Cecilia Rusnak, Thomas Yahner and Daniel Nadenicek, *Perspectives in Landscape History*, University Park, PA, Proceedings from OnSite/InSight and The Clearing Institute, 1999; Daniel Nadenicek, Grace Wang, Christina Marts, Mary Beth Carlin and Thomas Yahner, *Report of the Historic Forest Planning*, Charrette: for the Marsh-Billings-Rockefeller National Historic Park, 2000; The Center for Studies in Landscape History, Penn State University; The Library of American Landscape History, Inc., founded in 1992; India – Sanghamitra Mahanty, 'Insights from a cultural landscape: lessons from landscape history for the management of Rajiv Gandhi (Nagarahole) National Park', *Conservation and Society* 1.1, 2003, pp. 23–47; Kathleen D. Morrison, *Daroji Valley: Landscape History, Place, and the Making of a Dryland Reservoir System*, Delhi: Manohar Press, Vijayanagara Research Project Monograph Series 18, 2008.

7   Taylor, *Village and Farmstead*, pp. 10–54.

8   T. Brown and G. Foard, 'The Saxon landscape: a regional perspective', in P. Everson and T. Williamson (eds), *The Archaeology of Landscape*: *Studies Presented to Christopher Taylor*, Manchester: Manchester University Press, 1978, pp. 67–94.

9   B.B. Roberts and S. Wrathmell, *An Atlas of Rural Settlement in England*, London: English Heritage, 2000; T. Williamson, *Shaping Medieval Landscapes: Settlement, Society, Environment*, Manchester: Manchester University Press, 2003.

10   P.A. Churley, 'The Yorkshire crop returns of 1801', *Yorkshire Bulletin of Economic and Social Research*, vol. v, 1953; The National Archives, Kew, HO 67, Parish Acreage Returns, 1801.

11   Williamson, *Shaping*, pp. 150–3.

12   For Buckinghamshire, Oxfordshire, Warwickshire and Bedfordshire: M.J. Harrison, W.R. Mead and D.J. Pannett, 'A Midland ridge and furrow map', *Geographical Journal* 131, 1965, pp. 366–9. For Northamptonshire: the Royal Commission on Historical Monuments (English). Other counties plotted by the author.

13   P. Everson, C. Taylor and R. Wilson-North, 'Bodiam Castle, Sussex', *Medieval Archaeology* 34, 1990, pp. 155–7; P. Everson, 'Bodiam Castle, East Sussex: a castle and its designed landscape', *Chateau Gaillard* 17, 1996, pp. 66–72.

14   For a summary of research on medieval designed landscapes, see C. Taylor, 'Medieval ornamental landscapes', *Landscapes* 1, 2000, pp. 38–55; and P. Everson, '"Delightfully surrounded with woods and ponds": field evidence for medieval gardens in England', in P. Patterson (ed.), *There By Design*, Oxford: British Archaeological Reports 267,

1998, pp. 32–38. M. Leslie, 'An English landscape garden before *the* "English Landscape Garden"?', *Journal of Garden History* 13, 1993, pp. 3–15, 13.

15 E. Pollard, M. Hooper and N.W. Moore, *Hedges*, London: Collins, 1974, pp. 78–84.

16 See, for example, G. Hewlett, 'Reconstructing a historical landscape from field and documentary evidence: Otford in Kent', *Agricultural History Review* 21, 1974, pp. 94–110.

17 Pollard *et al.*, *Hedges*, pp. 86–90.

18 An assart is a clearing; fields cut out of particularly woodland or heathland.

19 R.A.D. Cameron, 'The biology and history of hedges: exploring the connections', *Biologist* 31, 1984, pp. 203–9.

20 G. Barnes and T. Williamson, *Hedgerow History: Ecology, History and Landscape Character*, Macclesfield: Windgather Press, 2006, p. 74; J. Hall, 'Hedgerows in West Yorkshire: the Hooper method examined', *Yorkshire Archeological Journal* 54, 1982, pp. 103–9; A. Willmott, 'The woody species of hedges with special reference to age in Church Broughton parish, Derbyshire', *Journal of Ecology* 68, 1980, pp. 269–86. W. Johnson, 'Hedges: a review of some early literature', *Local Historian* 13, 1978, pp. 195–204.

21 J. Barrett, *Fragments from Antiquity*, Oxford: Blackwell, 1994; B. Bender, *Stonehenge: Making Space*, Oxford: Berg, 1998; R. Bradley, 'Mental and material landscapes in prehistoric Britain', in D. Hooke (ed.), *Landscape: the Richest Historical Record*, Society for Landscape Studies, Supplementary Series 1, 2000, pp. 1–11; M. Edmonds, *Ancestral Geographies of the Neolithic: Landscape, Monuments and Memory*, London: Routledge, 1999; C. Tilly, *A Phenomenology of Landscape: Places, Paths and Monuments*, Oxford: Berg, 1994; Tilly, *The Materiality of Stone: Explorations in Landscape Phenomenology*, Oxford: Berg, 2004.

22 Bradley, 'Mental and material landscapes', p. 2.

23 D. Cosgrove, *Social Formation and Symbolic Landscape*, London: Croom Helm, 1984.

24 D. Cosgrove and S. Daniels, *The Iconography of Landscape: Essays on the Symbolic Representation, Design and Use of Past Environments*, Cambridge: Cambridge University Press, 1988.

25 S. Daniels, 'The political iconography of woodland in later eighteenth-century England', in Cosgrove and Daniels, *Iconography of Landscape*, pp. 51–72.

26 D. Rollison, *The Local Origins of Modern Society: Gloucestershire 1500–1800*, London: Routledge, 1992.

27 N.Whyte, 'Perceptions of the Norfolk landscape *c.*1500–1750', unpublished Ph.D. thesis, University of East Anglia, 2005.

28 Tilley, *Phenomenology of Landscape*, p. 94.

29 R. Bradley, *The Past in Prehistoric Societies*, London: Routledge, 2002.

30 The best critique is A. Fleming, 'Post-processual landscape archaeology: a critique', *Cambridge Archaeological Journal* 16.3, 2006, pp. 267–80.

31 E. Mercer, *English Vernacular Houses*, London: Royal Commission on Historical Monuments, 1975; M. Johnson, *Housing Culture: Traditional Architecture in an English Landscape*, London: UCL Press, 1993.

32 I have discussed the Houghton landscape on two previous occasions, and readers are advised to consult these works for full references to the documents in the Houghton archive: T. Williamson, *The Archaeology of the Landscape Park: Garden Design in Norfolk, England 1680–1840*, Oxford: British Archaeological Reports British Series 268, 1998; and Williamson, 'The planting of the park', in A. Moore (ed.), *Houghton Hall: The Prime Minister, the Empress and the Heritage*, Norwich: Norfolk Museums Service, 1996, pp. 41–8.

33 An allee is a walkway lined with trees or shrubs.

34 B.A. Holderness, '"Open" and "close" parishes in England in the eighteenth and nineteenth centuries', *Agricultural History Review* 20, 1972, pp. 126–39; see also S.J.

Banks, 'Nineteenth-century scandal or twentieth-century model? A new look at open and close parishes', *Economic History Review* 41, 1988, pp. 51–73.

35   W. Gilpin, *Observations On Several Parts of the Counties of Cambridge, Norfolk, Suffolk and Essex. Also on Several Parts of North Wales; relative chiefly to picturesque beauty, in two tours, the former made in the year 1769. The latter in the year 1773*, London, 1809, p. 41.

36   T. Williamson, *Polite Landscapes: Gardens and Society in Eighteenth-century England*, Stroud: Alan Sutton, 1995.

10 Architecture: the built object

Christopher Long

As an intellectual discipline, architectural history is descended from art history. Many of the concerns of architectural historians – issues of style, aesthetics, connoisseurship, iconography, and social and cultural meaning – parallel those of historians of art.[1] For much of the past century and a half, art historians have also played a leading role in the study of architecture, and many academic architectural historians have worked and continue to work within art history departments.

But the study of architecture engages a number of subjects that fall outside the normal discourse of art history. Buildings are inherently objects of practical use: one must consider not only the 'artistic' features of a church, for instance, but also such factors as its construction, materiality, functionality, and the social and economic conditions necessary for its creation. Architectural historians are further concerned with how space is developed within buildings and with the ways in which structure is both revealed and concealed – with what is known as tectonics, or the poetics of construction.[2]

At the same time, architectural history is part of a web of interrelated disciplines and professions whose purpose is to fashion an understanding of the past – to allow us both to preserve our knowledge of historical events and to aid us in establishing some meaning for the present. In this sense, architectural history properly belongs to the wider discipline of history; it shares many of the same analytic methods, theoretical perspectives, and discursive and rhetorical tactics.

Yet, to a much greater extent than is usually the case with historical inquiry, the study of architecture's past encompasses a practical dimension. The making of architecture has always been a dialogue with itself, with the ways in which architects have solved problems over time. The history of architecture continues to be taught within architecture schools around the world not only to appreciate and conserve our building heritage, but also because architects generally believe that the lessons of former times can contribute to our understanding of the possibilities of generating new architecture. Thus, the study of architectural history extends beyond its intellectual and aesthetic basis: it is bound up with the current formation of our built environment.[3] The history of architecture operates both in and upon the present.

Like the study of art, the history of architecture is a relatively new discipline. Although the earliest architectural histories date back to the first half of the eighteenth century, the formal incorporation of the history of architecture into the universities did not begin until the early nineteenth century.[4] The advent of the new discipline grew out of the contemporary problem of style and its meanings. With the beginnings of the Industrial Revolution, a series of rapid changes were felt within the architectural field. New materials and new building technologies forced architects to rethink how buildings were to be made, and new building types and lifestyles led to widespread questioning about what contemporary structures should look like. Initially, architects sought to address these problems by resorting to past styles – neo-Gothic, neo-Renaissance, and so on. Each new building was erected in the historical style thought to be appropriate to its function. The difficulty for architects lay in adapting these styles to buildings, such as the new governmental edifices, which were often much larger than the originals, or, in the case of structures such as railway stations, which served very different purposes. The study of architectural history was thus driven in large part by the quest to understand what the concept of style meant and how it operated.[5] Indeed, academic chairs in many European universities were tied to particular stylistic directions, usually Gothic, Renaissance, or Graeco-Roman classicism, implying that the holder possessed a consummate knowledge of that style and its possible applications.

Over time, this preoccupation with style gave way to other issues. Art historians who wrote about buildings in the first half of the twentieth century explored questions of meaning – either through iconography (the study of subject matter in art) and iconology (the study of images and their deeper meanings) or through an examination of cultural context. The rise of social history after World War II brought new concerns to the fore: architectural historians over the past several decades have sought to comprehend not only how buildings reflect social conditions, but also how their forms can reveal the intentions of their builders or those who inhabit them. These changes in focus have brought the history of architecture closer to the practice of the wider historical profession, especially the growing field of visual studies.[6]

But significant differences between the disciplines remain. To understand the practice of architectural history and its possible uses for historians, an example can aid us – the story of one of the icons of early modernism in architecture: the Looshaus in Vienna.

The facts of the building's genesis and design are relatively straightforward. In 1909, the architect Adolf Loos received a commission to construct a commercial and residential building on the Michaelerplatz in the heart of Vienna's inner city. The clients, Leopold Goldman and Emanuel Aufricht, were the owners of one of the most exclusive tailor's and men's accessories firms in the city, Goldman & Salatsch. They had acquired an eighteenth-century building, the Dreilauferhaus, a block from their existing shop on the fashionable Graben, with the aim of tearing it down and replacing it with a modern structure that could serve as their new store and workshop. The remaining ground-floor space of the five-storey building they planned to rent out to several retail firms; the additional areas on upper floors they would offer as residential units.[7]

Loos was thirty-eight years old at the time. He had already made a name for himself with a series of writings on architecture and design, but no major commissions had come his way and he had to content himself with designing interiors and occasional remodelling projects of existing buildings. The Goldman & Salatsch project was thus his first opportunity to design an entire building.

Around the end of July 1909, Loos began work on the design. The old Dreilauferhaus was razed, and a building permit was granted in March of the following year. By September 1910, the main part of the construction was complete. The upper façades had been plastered and the scaffolding had been taken down (Figure 10.1).[8]

But almost immediately, there were problems. The simple smooth finish, without any traditional applied ornament, differed from the plans Loos and the clients had submitted initially, and the municipal building authorities ordered an immediate halt to the construction. The newspapers soon gained wind of the dispute and a public controversy erupted.

Most of the press coverage was negative. One newspaper compared the building to a grain elevator; and the same newspaper subsequently published a cartoon suggesting that Loos had found his inspiration for the rectilinear façades from a sewer grate (Figure 10.2).[9] It was not only that the stark upper storeys marked a departure from the customary architectural taste, even for modern edifices in Vienna: the new building – soon dubbed simply the 'Looshaus' – was located on

Figure 10.1 Adolf Loos, Goldman & Salatsch Building (Looshaus), Vienna, 1909–11, shortly after the scaffolding had been removed. Published in *Illustriertes Wiener Extrablatt*, 26 April 1911.

„Los von der Architektur."
(Aus der Silvesterzeitschrift des Oesterreichischen Ingenieur- und Architektenvereines.)

— Kunstbrütend ging der Modernste durch die Straßen. Plötzlich blieb er erstarrt stehen; er hatte gefunden, was er solange vergeblich gesucht

Figure 10.2 'Los von der Architektur' (Away from architecture), cartoon published in *Illustriertes Wiener Extrablatt*, 1 January 1911.

the opposite side of the square from the Hofburg, the imperial palace. Many critics considered the design ill-suited for such an important location and, even, an affront to the emperor.

Loos defended his design in several articles, contending that the building's elemental cast was an attempt to find an expression appropriate to its intended use. Because the purpose of the lower two floors was to house an upscale commercial establishment, this part of the building, Loos claimed, had to be 'dressed' in formal garb, and he selected a blue-green Cipollino marble to clad the shop level (the stone veneer had not yet been installed when the controversy first broke); the upper floors, like older eighteenth-century Viennese townhouses, he argued, should be plain and functional, in keeping with traditional middle-class values. This fundamental division, Loos insisted, reflected the building's meaning and purpose. The straightforward design would also highlight – rather than detract from – the grandeur of the Hofburg and pose a clear separation between the aristocracy and the rising bourgeoisie.[10]

At a meeting of the city council in late October 1910, one of the representatives, a prominent conservative architect, assailed Loos's design and proposed adding ornament to the upper storeys to make the façade more 'acceptable'. Another councillor characterised the building as 'a monstrosity' (*ein Scheusal*) and urged that it undergo fundamental changes before it could be completed and occupied.[11]

The controversy simmered for another year. Finally, in late 1911, Loos proposed adding a small number of bronze window boxes to the façade and installed five boxes to demonstrate the effect. After a speech in December before nearly 3,000 people defending his design (and, in the process, belittling his opponents), public opinion began to swing to Loos's side.[12] The building authorities, in an effort to save face, accepted the compromise; in March 1912, they approved the design and issued an occupancy permit.[13]

The tale of the Looshaus has usually been presented as the triumph of modernism over the forces of reaction; the blank, planar surfaces have been widely viewed as an early announcement of the so-called International Style – the dominant modernist idiom of the 1920s and beyond. The real story is far more complex, however, and it illustrates well the nature of architectural history methods and their potential for enhancing our understanding of urban culture and the built environment.

To understand what happened, it is necessary first to discuss briefly the methods of architectural history.

When researching a particular building, the first requirement is to inspect and document it. What do its façades look like? How is the interior of the building arranged? What is the building's physical context? The most common form of documentation is photography, but in some cases measured drawings or studies of a building's materials may be necessary.[14]

The second set of questions has to do with how the building has changed over time. Has it been altered in some fashion? Are there significant additions or removals? Sometimes, one can readily observe these changes because of the use of disparate materials. It is also often possible to recognise what has been added because such additions are in a different style. And one may at times be able to deduce that some feature, which was standard at a particular time but is no longer extant, must have been removed. Stylistic elements may allow one to date a building and chart the changes made over time. But it is easy to be misled: the history of architecture is replete with stylistic revivals and there can be marked variations in architectural style even during the same period. One has to be aware therefore of very small differences.

The application of materials may also aid one in understanding how the fabric of a building might have been changed over time.[15] Modern materials, such as rolled plate glass or manufactured nails, do not appear before the first half of the nineteenth century; and plastics do not appear much before 1930 and were not in common use until after World War II. Certain technologies, such as plumbing, radiator heat, or air conditioning, might offer additional clues to a building's history.

The next step is to look for documentary evidence. Building permits, tax and property records may aid in uncovering a building's past, as can address books, social histories, insurance records, historical photographs, diaries, newspaper accounts and local histories.

The most useful documents can often be found in the archives of a particular architect or in architectural journals. The surviving architectural drawings of a building may reveal something not only about the original disposition of a building but also the architect's intentions. It is possible in many cases to observe how the design evolved, from the architect's initial sketches to the finished result. Architectural drawings may reveal something not only about its original disposition but also about the architects intentions.

Professional architectural journals, which began to appear around the middle of the nineteenth century, feature articles about notable buildings and portfolios of illustrations. Not only can they supply clues about a building's genesis, but they may also provide information concerning its historical context. Was the architect, for example, part of a larger movement? What were his or her intentions? Were these ideas common at the time?

Architectural historians, however, are not merely concerned with individual buildings. They explore an array of related issues: how did materials or construction technologies evolve over time? How do people perceive the buildings they inhabit? What mark did the clients or users make on these buildings? How were the buildings financed? What do they represent – and what social meaning might we discern? Can architectural objects tell us anything about the power structure of a given society? Do they conform to the normal practice of architecture at a given time?

Historians of architecture also look at specific features of buildings. What is the arrangement of an interior staircase? How does the movement sequence function within a given building? How are the divisions between public and private spaces established? What sort of proportional system is employed in the design of the façade? What larger meaning might one discern from the study of such details? There is an almost infinite number of such questions.

To return to the Looshaus. A simple visual inspection reveals some interesting and important facts. The building is divided into three distinct parts: the lower two floors, which are sheathed in marble; the middle four floors, which have a simple plastered surface; and the large copper mansard roof, which is set off with a protruding cornice sharply angled at the two corners (Figure 10.3). The lower two floors sport classical columns – in this case, of the Doric order – which designate the entry and frame the bay windows along the two sides. The building has an irregular, trapezoidal form (something easier to observe in the plan), with a small

Figure 10.3 Adolf Loos, Looshaus, *c*. 1930. Private collection.

courtyard at the rear. But there are also arresting features: the ground floor windows on either side of the building do not line up with the mezzanine windows, and when one compares the front and sides of the lower two storeys, it is evident that the windows and other features in the bottom portion also do not align horizontally.

Loos's intentions for dividing the building into two distinct zones – one for the shop, the other for the apartments – are clearly manifested in the design. It is also apparent that the front façade operates something like a billboard. The large 'Goldman & Salatsch' sign, which is repeated in the lintel over the entrance, announces the main commercial establishment within. Loos further confirms the importance of the tailor shop by 'dressing up' the building. The Cipollino marble cladding indicates that this is an upscale store; and the brass coats of arms and governmental seals arrayed around the entry certify that the firm is an official court tailor.

In many respects, the building is otherwise unremarkable. The upper storeys are treated matter-of-factly; only the window boxes and the lettering in any way ornament the surfaces. In fact, it was Loos's seemingly artless and frank presentation of this part of the building that gave rise to the controversy. The Viennese expected that the surfaces would follow the conventional use of window surrounds, mouldings and stringcourses. Had Loos handled the entire façade in the same fashion as the lower portion and roof cornice (which though reduced still evince vestigial elements of traditional compositional methods), the building would likely have elicited little public comment.

Although almost nothing was written about the Looshaus's interiors when it was first completed, they, too, harbour surprises. Like the exterior, they are treated simply: Loos's application of expensive materials – marble, mahogany and brass – provides much of the 'ornamental' effect. His treatment of the interior fittings was not new: all of his previous designs for shops and other commercial establishments over the previous decade had followed a similar aesthetic strategy. What stands out is the arrangement of the spaces. Rather than ordering the floors in regular horizontal layers – rather like a wedding cake – Loos varied the heights of the different rooms within. The large foyer is nearly a storey and a half high, whereas the workspaces, fitting areas, and other service rooms in the mezzanine floor are much lower. Loos explained that he employed this idea to ensure that each space would have the height appropriate to its purpose. The variations in height would allow him to reclaim space from areas where it was not needed, providing greater economy of space. All this is possible because Loos made use of what was then still a new construction technique: the reinforced concrete frame. Because the building does not rely on exterior load-bearing walls, it was relatively easy to vary the floor heights; he could simply place the concrete beams higher or lower in relation to the vertical columns to create rooms at various levels.

It is now understood that the Goldman & Salatsch building was the first of Loos's *Raumplan*, or space-plan buildings, an important notion in modern architecture. This emphasis on three-dimensional planning would become a common idea in the new building, and, for that reason, Loos's work is much studied by architects and theorists.[16]

In most accounts, then, the discussion of the Looshaus's stark façades and its complex interlocking interior spaces take centrestage. These are questions that are engaged primarily with the inner dialogue of architectural history – ones that have only limited application to a broader historical understanding. But there are other issues that disclose important aspects of Viennese culture and society just after the turn of the last century.

One of these has to do with social meaning. Loos explicitly rejected the idea that the building should assume an 'aristocratic' guise. As the son of a traditional artisan (his father had been a master stonemason in nearby Brno) and a man with strong Socialist sympathies, Loos, like the majority of the city's young modernists, viewed the Austrian nobility and clergy as impediments to economic progress and social justice. To imitate the forms of the aristocracy – in Vienna, this generally meant the elaborate classical language of the neo-Baroque – was to support, tacitly at least, the existing social order. Loos instead selected elements of an architectonic language associated with the bourgeoisie: the unaffected, purified neoclassicism of the Biedermeier era.

By Loos's time, the Biedermeier style had become a visual emblem of the rising middle class from the period between the end of the Napoleonic wars and the revolutions of 1848. Buildings in the style dot Vienna's inner city and its outer residential districts. It was the antithesis of the noble styles: sensible, frugal and functional – values of a new and autonomous lifestyle. It thus constituted the very symbol of the new middle class's challenge to the old order.

But the Biedermeier style appealed to Loos not only because of its implied social message: the young modernists in Vienna regarded Biedermeier as the last genuine and unaffected style before the advent of Historicism (which they believed was imitative, debased and inauthentic). The recourse to the Biedermeier was not only an avowal of social mission; it was also an essay on the possibilities of generating a new form-language based upon the past. For Loos, unlike many of his modernist contemporaries, the search for a style was not a matter of invention. Indeed, Loos explicitly rejected the notion that a new modern style would have to be created *ex nihilo*. Rather, he insisted that the modern style already existed: in the still 'living' elements of the past; in the pure works of consummate craftsmen; and in the simple forms of quotidian appliances (such as the latest plumbing fixtures).[17]

Still, Loos's vision of a composite and pre-existing modernism was never solely a matter of aesthetics. His rejection of a contrived modernism, whether the ascetic look of Viennese Secessionism or any of the other modern 'isms' after the turn of the century, had at its core a social declaration: that the new style would arise from the efforts of those who made things – from skilled artisans and manufacturers, not from 'effete' decorative artists. Loos's plea for the continuation of a handcraft system that was already threatened with extinction ran counter to prevailing trends. His rejection of the idea of the new industrial design reversed the standard modernist belief about how the new style should be created. The Looshaus, thus, might be read not as a modern gesture, but as a reactionary one. In spite of its stark appearance, it was born of Loos's embrace of the past – at least a part of it – not of his headlong flight into the new.

But one could also offer a somewhat different reading: that the building was socially progressive because it restated the aspirations of the bourgeoisie. In a famous essay, the cultural historian Carl Schorske argued that the nearby Ringstrasse, the great avenue that encircles Vienna's old city, 'embodied in stone and space' the social values of the capital's *Großbürgertum* – its upper middle class.[18] The nobility and the new industrial elite also made up Goldman & Salatsch's clientele. Loos's building provided for them: the sumptuous interiors mimic the finest tailor shops of London's Savile Row and exalt the possibilities of luxury. Yet the Looshaus's exteriors – and its English-inspired interiors – offered a divergent version of bourgeois ambition: rather than appropriating the taste of the nobility by recasting the historical style canon as the architects of the Ringstrasse had done, Loos substituted elements of the staid and sober language of the English middle class. The Looshaus was a lesson in concrete, plaster and glass about how modern man should live. The new middle class, as Loos declared repeatedly in his writings, had a duty to elevate Austria, to bring the country out of the Middle Ages. Casting off the repressive hand of church and crown was a crucial first step. Learning to live unfettered by the old strictures was another. The dignified and quiet look of the Looshaus presented an object moral lesson in this pursuit.

The Looshaus might also be understood as a harbinger of the modern world in quite a different way. Its construction (the concrete frame) and its materials (concrete, industrially manufactured bricks, glass and steel) were all elements of a revolution then sweeping the building industry. The introduction of new construction methods and materials in the period after 1850 transformed the world's cities in profound ways. Cheaper and stronger materials and the rationalisation of the building industry itself resulted in much larger structures and a rapid expansion of the urban environment. Fin-de-siècle Vienna was not in the vanguard of this movement: cities such as Chicago, New York and Berlin felt these changes earlier and with far greater force. But the Looshaus and a handful of related modern buildings constructed just before World War I suggested a new formula for making modern architecture: the possibility of joining fully the ideas of the new construction with an architectonic language of purity and simplicity. The final step would not come until after the war, when Ludwig Mies van der Rohe, Le Corbusier and others developed the form of the modern glass and steel skyscraper. The Looshaus, in that sense, can be understood as an early experiment in the shaping of a radically new architectural order.

Indeed, in the 1920s, Loos was celebrated throughout European avant-garde circles as having almost single-handedly eradicated ornament and thereby introduced the new International Style.[19] (Loos would reject this notion, explaining that he had not called for the complete eradication of all ornament, only that which no longer fulfilled a meaningful role.[20] Little notice was taken of his corrective, however, and, ever after, he became closely identified with the movement towards architectural asceticism.) Here we encounter another possible reading of the Looshaus, one having to do with its broader cultural meanings. In the literature on turn-of-the-century Vienna, Loos and the Looshaus have become symbols of the move away from the modernist experiment with Art Nouveau (specifically, the

Jugendstil, as the style was known in Austria) and towards a radical new conception.[21] This shift towards a new simplicity of expression, which began around 1908, was registered not only in architecture, but also in painting, music, philosophy and literature. Many of the leaders of this new direction were associated with Loos or members of his circle: Arnold Schönberg, Oskar Kokoschka, Ludwig Wittgenstein and Georg Trakl. Loos assumed a prominent role in fostering this movement: he actively supported and promoted Schönberg's concerts; he became the young Kokoschka's most important patron; and a short time after he completed the Looshaus, he started his own private school to train young architects.

Loos's quest for a new purism, as a number of commentators have argued, formed the leading edge of a critique of the sham pretensions of the Viennese artistic establishment. Like the writer Karl Kraus, his close friend and ally, Loos regarded the corruption of beauty and truth as an ethical failing; his writings and built work were a plea for renewal of moral and aesthetic values. The Looshaus, viewed in this light, may be understood as a statement of a new honesty based on simplicity, modesty and unobtrusiveness.

But is the building honest? Loos's supporters wrote at length about how it reflected the practical tenor of the age; it was a functional building (*Zweckbau*), they argued, in decided contrast to the neighbouring neo-Baroque Palais Herberstein. Yet some commentators at the time recognised that a number of the building's features ran counter to the spirit of modern architecture. This was especially true of its construction, which is entirely concealed behind its outer cladding. The Viennese critic Hans Berger charged that Loos had used 'an illusory construction' which made 'the actual construction disappear behind the decoration'.[22] And another writer, Felix Speidel, accused Loos of having designed 'a completely unmodern building' and called him a 'falsifier of our time'.[23]

The building's façade is indeed a lie. Almost all of the apparent structural elements – the four columns framing the entrance and the large I-beam above them, as well as the smaller columns on the sides – are not load bearing. They are instead decorative and therefore not much different from the plaster pilasters and entablatures of the 'false' buildings along the Ringstrasse. Loos contended that the columns did in fact 'help to support the structure' – that they were, in essence, a redundant structural system. But the building's concrete frame, as early construction photos clearly demonstrate, was fully self-supporting; it required no further structural elements.

Many of the later analyses of the Looshaus have focused on the ways in which the rules of form and function are violated in the building's design.[24] Hermann Czech and Wolfgang Mistelbauer wrote, for example, that Loos's design arose 'less from function and construction than from intellectual will'.[25] Leslie Topp, however, has posed a counter argument: she suggests that one might instead regard the building as an 'honest mask' – that Loos, while concealing the truth about its construction, nevertheless revealed other truths about modern life and the cultural situation in Vienna.[26]

Buildings, like other works of art, always admit multiple readings. Architecture differs from literature, painting, or film, however, because its signs and symbols are limited. Most buildings 'say' very little. They possess few conveyors of meaning – at least in comparison with a poem or movie. The language of architecture is partly stylistic. (A style, like a language, is essentially a recognisable system of forms and motifs that operate by the rules of a conventional syntax.) A building in a specific style 'communicates' through the disposition of its details: they reveal meanings about its time and place, and about its purpose and import. The language of architecture is also wrapped up with form and context.[27] Traditional architecture is sometimes replete with rich iconography that may tell a story or stories (one might think here of the stained glass and sculptures in a Gothic church). Sometimes these narratives are intrinsically related to the building itself (for example, the hieroglyphs of an ancient Egyptian tomb); sometimes they are quite separate (such as modern advertising in a nineteenth-century railway station). In the end, though, a given building as an isolated object can only reveal a small amount about itself. Even in its most refined form, iconography, the 'reading' of these signs, does not usually offer a direct and complete interpretation; at its most basic level, it almost always relies on pre-existing knowledge. One must be versed in the symbol system before interpretation is possible. And one must also be aware that what the building is 'saying' may be difficult to communicate in linguistic terms.

Iconography, then, is neither self-contained nor fully logocentric. To understand more, one must examine a particular building within its historical framework. Understanding the tenets of Christianity and the particular preoccupations of the Counter-Reformation in Europe, for example, would greatly aid one in interpreting the paintings and sculpture in a Baroque church.

But this type of analysis may also work in the reverse. A very different reading of the Looshaus would focus not on the building itself but on what it might tell us about its economic and political context. The mere fact that such a building was constructed in central Vienna in the years just before World War I was a consequence of the rebuilding of the city that began in the 1850s, during the so-called *Gründerzeit*, Austria's period of economic takeoff and industrialisation. As the city developed a modern governmental bureaucracy and a corresponding white-collar workforce, new building types – especially large office buildings – were required to house them. The sudden expansion of the middle class, a direct outcome of governmental and capitalist expansion, also necessitated a new urban apparatus: educational and cultural institutions, shops, restaurants and improved living quarters. Though densely built, Vienna, like most European cities, could not readily accommodate these demands. Many old buildings were torn down and replaced with larger and more appropriate structures. The myriad new buildings erected in the inner city form a barometer of Vienna's vigorous economic health at the time.

That Loos's clients for the building, Leopold Goldman and Emanuel Aufricht, were both Jewish tells another story: the rising presence of Jews in the city's economy and culture and their role as makers of modernism. By the turn of the century, the Jewish population of Vienna was around 147,000 – 9 per cent of the city's inhabitants. Other cities, including Warsaw and Budapest, had larger Jewish populations, but Jews attained a prominence in Vienna that was unmatched elsewhere. By the time Loos was at work on his building on the Michaelerplatz,

Jews made up nearly a third of all university students, and Jews dominated the legal and medical professions, as well as banking, journalism and the textile industry. Jewish families also owned most of the city's department stores.

Although there is no mention of Goldman's or Aufricht's Jewish backgrounds in the press during the months of controversy about the Looshaus, anti-Semitism undoubtedly occupied some place in the debate. The city's small shopkeepers bitterly resented the competition of the large department stores; the emergence of these stores after 1860 fuelled anti-Jewish feelings in the city. Because so many of the clients of Vienna's modern architects and designers were Jewish, some also came to believe that the new style was linked with Jewish culture; they regarded it as alien and incompatible with the city's traditions. Such views would have disastrous results in the 1930s, but in 1910 anti-Semitism played out in a less overt but still important way.

By the autumn of that year, when the dispute about the building became public, the matter came before city council. The attacks on Loos's design that followed all came from Christian Socialist representatives, who dominated the city government. Founded by Karl Lueger in 1893, the Austrian Christian Socialist Party drew on the urban lower middle class and the rural population for support. The party was staunchly Catholic (a number of its leading members were priests) and conservative. After the party's victories in the 1895 and 1896 municipal elections, Lueger, who became mayor, embarked on an ambitious programme of municipal socialism.[28]

Though progressive in many ways, Lueger was also anti-Semitic, at least in public. (In private, he was quite genial with his Jewish friends.) To challenge the Jewish-owned banks, he created a city-owned mortgage bank in 1906, and over the course of his fifteen-year administration, he pursued various 'anti-capitalist' initiatives. He seized control of the street railways and electrical works and established a city-owned gas company.

Lueger's death, in March 1910, and the Christian Socialists' stunning losses to the Socialists in the 1911 elections, left the party in disarray. The controversy over the Looshaus offered the Christian Socialists members of the city council a *cause célèbre,* which they hoped might bring them back into favour with voters, especially with their conservative and lower middle-class base. The Looshaus was an easy and logical target: it not only flew in the face of convention but also the tastes of most *petit bourgeois* Viennese. Yet the reaction on the part of the Christian Socialist representatives was about more than stylistic taste or electoral advantage. One of the most vocal critics, Karl Rykl, who had been elected from the heavily lower middle-class seventh district, was a sculptor and manufacturer of cast stone products. He understood clearly that a modernism *à la* Loos, which rejected traditional architectural ornament, was a threat to his livelihood and that of many workers in the construction industry. Another of Loos's critics on the council, Hans Schneider, also had a vested interest in the controversy. Schneider was an architect who had made his reputation with a series of neo-Baroque buildings, including the city-financed Technical Museum, which had been completed just a year before. He volunteered to redesign the Looshaus's façades (by adding the 'appropriate' ornament to the plans Loos had previously submitted to the city building authorities). Schneider's motive, of course, was to de-legitimise a competing design vision and to add to his own notoriety. The ploy almost worked. For a time, it appeared that his changes might be implemented. Loos's design was saved at the last minute when the vice mayor, Josef Porzer, interceded, calling for time to study the question.[29]

The controversy around the Looshaus thus grew out of the intersection of a constellation of factors. And Loos's ultimate triumph in 1912 came not because he had appealed to the force of reason or a sound aesthetic vision, but because he managed to rally the students and young intellectuals to his cause, and because most of city's leading architects, though they disliked the building's design, eventually took his side, fearing apparently that they, too, might lose their artistic freedom.

Interpreting a building or an urban complex with regard to such social, political and economic issues probably has the greatest utility for historians. Architecture, in this way, forms part of a larger story; it is a material manifestation of broader historical forces and may serve as a tool for comprehending these trends.

But, in recent years, historians of architecture, like other historians, have begun to explore the built environment in other ways. One of these new approaches arose from gender studies. Architectural historians have become increasingly aware that in many instances buildings, or portions of buildings, are gendered; the ways in which men and women use space is sometimes markedly different. Space can be manipulated to offer freedom (one might think of the open, flowing spaces of the American ranch houses of the 1950s, which merged kitchen and family room) or exert control (the formation of Jewish ghettos in medieval Europe).[30] We have come to understand that women, though historically not involved in the building professions, have often had a part – frequently as clients or patrons – in determining the look and specific features of built edifices.[31] Through their domestic roles, women have also fashioned interiors, forging through their efforts individual and distinctive environments.

Again, the Looshaus is revealing in this regard. The store was intended to be a male domain, and Loos's treatment of the leather furnishings and dark and robust finishes emphasises its 'masculinity'. Almost all of those who worked within were male: the tailors, fitters and accountants. But, as a photograph from an early company brochure shows, Goldman & Salatsch also had a shirt workshop staffed entirely by women (Figure 10.4). Their treatment seems to underscore the decidedly male-dominated character of the establishment. Not only were these women segregated from their male co-workers, they occupied one of the least appealing spaces in the building – a cramped room with low ceilings (the space 'won' by dropping the ceiling was accorded to the gentlemen clients) and without attractive finishes. The workshops occupied by the men, by contrast, were all larger and better lit, with more direct access to the main store.

The 'gendering' of space in the Looshaus, at least with regard to the women who worked there, is about exclusion. But in other buildings Loos designed, this process worked in a rather different way. In 1927, Loos drew up plans to rebuild two

Figure 10.4 Shirt workshop in the Goldman & Salatsch shop. From a Goldman & Salatsch company brochure, *c.* 1911.

existing corner buildings in Paris into a residence for the American dancer Josephine Baker. The centrepiece of the house was to be a large indoor swimming pool on the second floor, lit from above by a skylight. Below this space were to be two long corridors on either side of the pool, which would have thick glass windows, allowing one to view the activity in the pool.

In recent years, scholars have interpreted Loos's intentions for his startling design in various ways: as Loos's celebration of Baker and her beauty; as his chauvinistic desire to see Baker naked or dressed only in a swimsuit; as his attempt to display Baker's 'otherness' as a black woman; or as an expression of Loos's belief in the distinction between 'modern' and 'primitive'. Most of these writers also argue either that Loos wanted to 'control' Baker, or be dominated by her – or perhaps, in some fashion, both.[32]

Beatriz Colomina has taken another approach. Her work is focused on how we interact with architecture; she is particularly interested in examining how we perceive it and how it is represented. 'Architecture', she writes, 'is not simply a platform that accommodates the viewing subject. It precedes and frames its occupant.'[33] Drawing on this idea, she contrasts the windows in the swimming pool in Loos's Baker House (which corresponds, she tells us, to 'a peephole') with another of Loos's houses designed around the same time, the Moller House. 'In the Moller House,' she observes,

> there is a raised sitting area off the living room with a sofa set against the window. Although one cannot see out the window, its presence is strongly

felt. The bookshelves surrounding the sofa and the light coming from behind suggest a comfortable nook for reading. But comfort in this space is more than just sensual, for there is a psychological dimension. A sense of security is produced by the position of the couch, the placement of its occupants against the light. Anyone who, ascending the stairs from the entrance (itself a rather dark passage), enters the living room, would take a few moments to recognize a person sitting on the couch. Conversely, any intrusion would soon be detected by a person occupying this area, just as an actor entering the stage is immediately seen by a spectator in a theater box.[34]

Colomina here is after more than how a subject might perceive this space: 'This spatial-psychological device', she argues, 'can also be read in terms of power, regimes of control inside the house. The raised sitting area of the Moller house provides the occupant with a vantage point overlooking the interior. Comfort in this space is related to both intimacy and control.'[35]

This sort of analysis is derived from post-structuralism, especially the writings of Roland Barthes, Jacques Derrida, Michel Foucault and Jacques Lacan.[36] It is concerned not so much with the composition of a system of visual signs, but how such a system might be created and how it is used, for instance, to establish patterns of authority or dependence. When applied to architecture, post-structuralism functions as a critical process, demonstrating, on the one hand, the ambiguity of visual systems of meaning, and, on the other, the position and attitudes of the observer. In architectural history, post-structuralist analysis has tended to shift the focus away from particular buildings or designers towards questions about how we make judgements about them. The result has been a re-examination of long-held beliefs of issues such as quality and meaning.

A post-structuralist reading of the Looshaus might question how the building has been represented over time or how we have viewed Loos's place in history. The visual presentation of the Looshaus is particularly interesting in this regard. Almost all of the photographs of the building published during the period of the controversy show only its front façade. These images highlight the manifest differences with the adjacent structures, underscoring the building's 'otherness'. There are few published photographs that capture Looshaus's sumptuous exterior detailing – aside from those in a small number of books intended for architects that focused on new storefront design (Figure 10.5). In the professional architectural world, the Looshaus's portal was shown because it was perceived to be analogous with other new designs.[37] In the popular press, however, the building received the opposite treatment: it was either subjected to attack or ignored. In one picture book sold to tourists around the time is a photograph of the Michaelerplatz that seems deliberately to exclude the Looshaus (Figure 10.6). Only a small sliver of the building is visible, greatly diminishing its modern cast and thus its impact. (The editor of this book was the architect Karl Mayreder, who had been Loos's first employer in Vienna!)

What is striking about the media treatment, too, is that the Looshaus's interiors, with their very modern finishes and innovative spatial arrangement, were never

Figure 10.5 Adolf Loos, Looshaus, entry. From *Moderne Wiener Geschäftsportale*, Vienna: Schrool, 1914, plate 17.

shown during the controversy. The reason may have had to do with Loos's belief that photographs could not capture the unique qualities of his designs. Indeed, he discouraged the photographing of his works, preferring that people visit his buildings and experience them first-hand. Loos may have been among the first architects to consider carefully the differences between modern representation and object. One of his criticisms of the Viennese Secessionists is that they relied too much on graphic presentation; the drawing, Loos argued, was only a description of a built work, not its equivalent, and a drawing, no matter how impressive, was not the same thing as architecture.

The manipulation of images, as we are now all too aware, may impact our judgements. The more interesting question for scholars, though, may revolve around the issue of intentionality: who is determining how we see something – and why? Some scholars have gone even further, probing our abilities to direct or even understand our own actions. Colomina, for example, has called into question Loos's relationship to his own buildings:

Even Loos, supposedly the very figure of mastery as the architect of space, is also a troubled spectator of his own work. The illusion of Loos as an authority, a man in control, in charge of his own work, an undivided subject, is suspect. In fact, he is constructed, controlled, and fractured by the work. The idea of

Figure 10.6 View of the Michaelerplatz, with the Looshaus just visible on the left, from
         Karl Mayreder, *Wien und Umgebung: Eine Auswahl von Stadt- und
         Landschaftsbildern*, Vienna: Gerlach & Wiedling, n.d. [*c.*1912], p. 21.

the *Raumplan*, for example: Loos constructs a space (without having completed the working drawings), then allows himself to be manipulated by this
construction. Like the occupants of his houses, he is both inside and outside
the object. The object has as much authority over him as he over it. He is not
simply an author.[38]

Such profound doubts about authorship and meaning are extreme. Most
architectural historians continue to believe that the intentions of architects and their
works can be interpreted more or less reliably, even if these interpretations are
fraught with ambiguities and difficulties. Still, post-structuralism has operated to
force architectural historians to become much more aware of their biases and
subjective impact, and the many pitfalls we face in comprehending the past.

Though it began as an inward-looking scholarly discipline, architectural history
has gradually moved much closer to other historical fields. Over the past two or
three decades, historians of the built world have drawn increasingly on the methods
of other historians, and it seems likely that this trend will continue. At the same
time, the recent growth of interest in visual and cultural studies on the part of
historians has brought them closer to the problems and methods of architectural
history. In coming years, we will no doubt see more studies that integrate the built
object into a larger and more fully cultivated historical landscape.

Notes

I am indebted to Timothy Parker, Francesco Passanti and Monica Penick, who read a draft of this chapter and made valuable suggestions. I am also grateful to my research assistants, Laura McGuire and Elana Shapira, and to Janine Henri and Daniel Orozco of the Architecture and Planning Library, University of Texas at Austin, for aiding me in assembling the material for this chapter.

1 On the development of architectural history as a discipline and its methods, see Bruce Allsopp, *The Study of Architectural History*, New York: Praeger, 1970; Dana Arnold, *Reading Architectural History*, London and New York: Routledge, 2002; Dana Arnold, Elvan Altan Ergut and Belgin Turan Ozkaya (eds), *Rethinking Architectural Historiography*, London and New York: Routledge, 2006; John Gloag, *The Architectural Interpretation of History*, London: Adam and Charles Black, 1975; Gabriella Orefice and Giuseppina Carla Romby, *La Storia dell'architettura: problemi di metodo e di didattica*, Florence: Istituto di storia dell'architettura, Universita degli studi, 1976; and David Watkin, *The Rise of Architectural History*, London: The Architectural Press, 1980. There is a large literature on art historical methods. Among the most useful texts are Eric Fernie (ed.), *Art History and its Methods: A Critical Anthology*, London: Phaidon, 1995; and Donald Preziosi (ed.), *The Art of Art History: A Critical Methodology*, Oxford and New York: Oxford University Press, 1998.

2 For an excellent discussion of the problem of tectonics in architecture, see Kenneth Frampton, *Studies in Tectonic Culture: The Poetics of Construction in Nineteenth and Twentieth Century Architecture*, Cambridge, MA, and London: MIT Press, 2001.

3 This is true also for the history of architectural theory, which continues to have an important place in architectural curricula. For a good general survey of the history of architectural theory, see Hanno-Walter Kruft, *A History of Architectural Theory: From Vitruvius to the Present*, New York: Princeton Architectural Press, 1997.

4 Watkin, *The Rise of Architectural History*, pp. 1–33.

5 The most famous and important of these texts is Gottfried Semper, *Der Stil in den technischen und tektonischen Künsten; oder, Praktische Aesthetik: Ein Handbuch für Techniker, Künstler und Kunstfreunde*, Frankfurt am Main: Verlag für Kunst und Wissenschaft, 1860–63 (English edn: Gottfried Semper, *Style in the Technical and Tectonic Arts; or Practical Aesthetics*, eds and trans. Harry Francis Mallgrave and Michael Robinson, Los Angeles: Getty Research Institute, 2004).

6 See the series 'Teaching the History of Architecture: A Global Inquiry', in the *Journal of the Society of Architectural Historians* 61.3 and 4, September and December 2002, and 62.1, March 2003; 'Learning from interdisciplinarity', *Journal of the Society of Architectural Historians* 64.4, December 2005, and 'Learning from architectural history', *Journal of the Society of Architectural Historians* 65.1, March 2006.

7 On the Looshaus and its history, see Hermann Czech and Wolfgang Mistelbauer, *Das Looshaus* (3rd edn), Vienna: Löcker Verlag, 1984; Ludwig Münz and Gustav Künstler, *Der Architekt Adolf Loos*, Vienna and Munich: Verlag Anton Schroll, 1964, pp. 92–103; Raiffeisenbank Wien, *Das Looshaus: Eine Chronik 1909–1989*, Vienna: Raiffeisenbank, 1989; Burkhardt Rukschcio and Roland Schachel, *Adolf Loos: Leben und Werk*, Salzburg and Vienna: Residenz Verlag, 1982, pp. 141–68, pp. 460–9.

8 Czech and Mistelbauer, *Das Looshaus*, pp. 24ff.

9 'Der Getreidespeicher gegenüber der Hofburg', *Illustriertes Wiener Extrablatt*, 26 October 1910; 'Los von der Architektur', *Illustriertes Wiener Extrablatt*, 1 January 1911. See also 'Der "Kornspeicher" am Michaelerplatz', *Neuigkeits-Welt-Blatt*, 1 October 1910.

10 Adolf Loos, 'Wiener Architekturfragen', *Reichspost*, 1 October 1910, pp. 1–2; and Adolf Loos, 'Mein erstes Haus!', *Der Morgen*, 3 October 1910, p. 1.

11 'Stenographischer Bericht über die öffentliche Sitzung der Gemeinderates vom 21. Oktober 1910', in *Amtsblatt der k.k. Reichshaupt- und Residenzstadt Wien* 19, 1910, p. 2558.
12 The text of Loos's talk has survived. See Adolf Loos, 'Mein Haus am Michaelerplatz', lecture delivered 11 December 1911, in *Parnass*, special issue, 'Der Künstlerkreis um Adolf Loos: Aufbruch zur Jahrhundertwende' ,1985, pp. ii–xv.
13 Czech and Mistelbauer, *Das Looshaus*, pp. 38–43.
14 Measurements, however, are usually not part of the standard references for buildings. Most sources include only the names of the building and the architect, if known, the date (or dates) of construction, and its location.
15 See, for example, Cecil D. Elliot, *Technics and Architecture: The Development of Materials and Systems for Buildings*, Cambridge, MA, and London: MIT Press, 1992; and Robert Mark (ed.), *Architectural Technology up to the Scientific Revolution: The Art and Structure of Large-scale Buildings*, Cambridge, MA, and London: MIT Press, 1993.
16 For a discussion of Loos's ideas of the *Raumplan* and its larger meanings for development of modern architecture, see Max Risselada (ed.), *Raumplan versus Plan libre: Adolf Loos and Le Corbusier, 1919–1930*, New York: Rizzoli, 1987. There is also a large body of architectural historical writing dealing with the problem of space and its evolution. See, for example, Paul Frankl, *Principles of Architectural History; the Four Phases of Architectural Style, 1420–1900* (ed. and trans. James F. O'Gorman, with a foreword by James S. Ackerman), Cambridge, MA: MIT Press, 1968; and Bruno Zevi, *Architecture as Space: How to Look at Architecture*, New York: Horizon Press, 1957.
17 Cf. Loos's famed essays in Adolf Loos, *Ins Leere gesprochen 1897–1900*, Paris and Zurich: Éditions Georges Crès et Cie, 1921.
18 Carl E. Schorske, 'The Ringstrasse, its critics, and the birth of urban modernism', in Carl E. Schorske, *Fin-de-siècle Vienna: Politics and Culture*, New York: Alfred A. Knopf, 1980, p. 62. For an analogous analysis of the country house, see Mark Girouard, *Life in the English Country House*, New Haven, CT, and London: Yale University Press, 1978.
19 The British historian Kenneth Frampton, for example, has written that Loos prefigured the International Style by least eight years. Kenneth Frampton, *Modern Architecture: A Critical History*, London and New York: Thames and Hudson, 1980, pp. 90–5.
20 Adolf Loos, 'Ornament und Erziehung', in Adolf Loos, *Trotzdem 1900–1930*, Innsbruck: Brenner Verlag, 1931, pp. 198–205.
21 See, for example, Carl E. Schorske, 'Revolt in Vienna', *New York Review of Books*, 29 May 1986, pp. 24–9.
22 Hans Berger, 'Architektonische Auslese Wien 1910', *Neue Freie Presse*, 26 August 1911 (morning edition), p. 21.
23 Felix Speidel, 'Vom modernen Haus', *Neues Wiener Tagblatt*, 31 December 1910, p. 3.
24 Cf. Benedetto Gravagnuolo, *Adolf Loos: Theory and Works*, New York: Rizzoli, 1988, pp. 128, 130.
25 Czech and Mistelbauer, *Das Looshaus*, p. 115.
26 Leslie Topp, *Architecture and Truth in Fin-de-siècle Vienna*, Cambridge and New York: Cambridge University Press, 2004, pp. 132–73.
27 For an interesting discussion of architecture as language, see Anthony Alofsin, *When Buildings Speak: Architecture as Language in the Habsburg Monarchy and Its Aftermath, 1867–1933*, Chicago and London: University of Chicago Press, 2006, esp. pp. 9–15.
28 On the rise of the Christian Socialist Party, see John W. Boyer, *Political Radicalism in Late Imperial Vienna: Origins of the Christian Social Movement, 1848–1897*, Chicago and London: University of Chicago Press, 1995.

29 Porzer's mother was Jewish, but it is unclear whether his background played any role in his decision. John W. Boyer, *Culture and Political Crisis in Vienna: Christian Socialism in Power, 1897–1918*, Chicago and London: University of Chicago Press, 1995, pp. 259–60.

30 Diane Ghirardo, for example, has examined the brothels of Renaissance Ferrara, focusing on how the city was structured to restrict such 'unruly women'. Diane Ghirardo, 'The topography of prostitution in Renaissance Ferrara', *Journal of the Society of Architectural Historians* 60.4, December 2001, pp. 402–31.

31 See Alice T. Friedman, 'Architecture, authority and the female gaze: planning and representation in the early modern country house', *Assemblage* 18, 1992, pp. 41–61.

32 Cf. Farès el-Dahdah, 'The Josephine Baker house: for Loos's pleasure', *Assemblage* 26, 1996, pp. 72–87; Elana Shapira, 'Dressing a celebrity: Adolf Loos's house for Josephine Baker', *Studies in the Decorative Arts* 11.2, Spring–Summer 2004, pp. 2–24; and Kim Tanzer, 'Baker's Loos and Loos's loss: architecting the body', *Center* 9, 1995, pp. 76–89.

33 Beatriz Colomina, *Privacy and Publicity: Modern Architecture as Mass Media*, Cambridge, MA: MIT Press, 1994, p. 250.

34 Colomina, *Privacy and Publicity*, pp. 234–8, p. 260.

35 Colomina, *Privacy and Publicity*, p. 238. For a similar argument, see Colomina's article, 'Intimacy and spectacle: the interiors of Adolf Loos', *AA Files* 20, Autumn 1990, pp. 5–15.

36 See, for example, Roland Barthes, 'What is an author?', in Preziosi (ed.), *The Art of Art History*, pp. 299–313; Jacques Derrida, 'Restitutions of the Truth in Pointing', in Preziosi (ed.), *The Art of Art History'*, pp. 432–49; and Josue V. Harari (ed.), *Textual Strategies: Perspectives in Post-Structuralist Criticism*, New York: Cornell University Press, 1979.

37 Cf. the image of the lower portion of the Looshaus with others in the portfolio *Moderne Wiener Geschäftsportale*, Vienna: Schroll, 1914. For a similar images, see Hugo Licht (ed.), *Charakteristische Details von ausgeführten Bauwerken mit besonderer Berücksichtigung der in der Architektur des XX. Jahrhunderts*, Berlin: Verlag von Ernst Wasmuth, 1914.

38 Colomina, *Privacy and Publicity*, p. 279.

11 Material Culture: the object

Adrienne D. Hood

Objects, artefacts, things. They are three-dimensional, visual, tactile and sometimes odorous and auditory manifestations of the past, yet for the historian this category of evidence possesses some challenging problems. According to Thomas Schlereth 'objects made or modified by humans, consciously or unconsciously, directly or indirectly, reflect the belief patterns of individuals who made, commissioned, purchased, or used them, and by extension, the belief patterns of the larger society of which they are a part'.[1] While the validity of material evidence is no longer suspect, how to unlock its secrets in a meaningful way remains a challenge. Historians learn effective ways to interpret written evidence, but what about its material counterpart? How can we extract meaning from things such as clothing, furniture, utensils, tools and machines and transparently present it to support and shape the arguments we make?

Many academic disciplines have objects at the core of their research but history does not. With access to rich documentary sources, historians have left the study of things to scholars who are largely denied access to text or for whom artefacts are paramount: archaeologists, who rely on material evidence excavated from (often) prehistoric sites; anthropologists, who until recently concentrated their research on non-literate cultures, devising theoretical constructs with which to make sense of them; and art historians, whose focus on works of art necessitated the development of formal and stylistic modes of analysis. Historians have not entirely overlooked material culture, but tend to use it to illustrate arguments derived from documents or to examine textual evidence such as household inventories, diaries, letters or novels, for example, that contain information *about* things. Rarely do we *begin* our research with objects or use them as an integral form of evidence. Moreover, some argue that the absence of objects makes little difference to our ability to study the past since we can more comfortably learn most of what we need from written material. But this is mistaken. By dismissing or ignoring 'stuff' we overlook a major category of evidence. Perhaps even more important, we neglect a source that can lead to unique, often inspired, questions about the past.

My experience as a museum curator working closely with artefacts (textiles), followed by over a decade teaching a graduate course in material culture method and theory, has demonstrated beyond doubt the power of objects to open up new avenues of historical thinking and to provide insights into the past not possible with documents alone. What my students find so daunting when confronted with the task of beginning a research project with objects rather than questions, however, or trying to extract information from material evidence to support their documentary research, is, first, how to unlock the layers of meaning embedded in the items and, second, how to integrate that into their written work.[2] A chronological overview of the evolution of material culture studies over the past half century indicates they are not alone. Simply put, unlike archaeologists or anthropologists, most historians are not equipped to do object-centred research. Moreover, even after learning some of the skills needed to analyse objects, their reliance on traditional written evidence still tends to take over. One of the problems, as my colleague Sarah Amato recently observed of her undergraduate class in material culture, is that 'the research into the history of the objects sometimes overwhelmed the process. Students didn't use information derived from the methodology [a systematic analysis of the objects] to illuminate or complicate this history. Sometimes it is as if they never examined the object at all.'[3] In an attempt to overcome this chronic difficulty, and directly confront history students with objects, I have chosen to begin with a discussion of the evidence, laying out and demonstrating some of the methodologies that can help obtain information from objects. The historiographical discussion that follows illuminates various reasons why historians have been slow to embrace physical evidence, the increasingly sophisticated approaches with which to tackle it, and some of the complex historical issues it can elucidate.

I tend to agree with material culture scholar and advocate Thomas Schlereth, who argues that material culture cannot be considered a discipline in its own right nor is it a field of study. Rather, he says, it is

> a mode of inquiry primarily (but not exclusively) focused upon a type of evidence. Material culture thus becomes an investigation that uses artifacts (along with relevant documentary, statistical, and oral data) to explore cultural questions both in certain established disciplines (such as history or anthropology) and in certain research fields (such as the history of technology or the applied arts).[4]

Nevertheless, it is also an interdisciplinary mode of inquiry, or as Victor Buchli has recently noted, 'it is effectively an intervention within and between disciplines; translations from one realm into another'.[5] The challenge for historians is to learn how to think with the object, and how to understand the 'thingness of the thing' – an exercise that is far more difficult than it sounds, in part because it seems so obvious.[6]

Most graduate students arrive in my class, 'Topics in Material Culture', with a research interest in mind: North American immigration, early-modern transatlantic trade, music in Europe, American slavery, medical history, twentieth-century Asian popular culture, or North American urban history, for example. Others take it because they have an item that resonates for them: silk scarves, music boxes, coffee cups, banks (both piggy and institutional), ballet costumes, watercolours, or a Korean public square, come to mind. Early on everyone must select an object associated with their research (an artefact, a tool, an artwork, a building, a landscape) around which they will build a research project. The premise of this exercise is that a systematic and detailed consideration of the chosen thing(s) leads to a series of questions that would not arise in any other way. As a result, what begins with a deliberation of the singular or exceptional leads to a consideration of a complex, multifaceted historical question.[7]

Unfortunately, one of the greatest obstacles to seeking relevant material evidence is that museums, the largest repositories of historical objects, are relatively inaccessible these days because of lack of staff, time and money. With persistence and sometimes creativity, however, it is usually possible to come up with some thing to study: objects on public exhibit can be seen if not touched; smaller museums are more accessible than larger ones. It is useful to note that graduate students doing a sustained research project may be given more access than an undergraduate with a tight time frame, and professional intervention might help. If a relevant museum object proves elusive, what are the options? Is a representation an acceptable stand-in for the real thing? I would argue that it can be a reasonable alternative provided one addresses and recognises the shortcomings, most notably the lack of detail, three-dimensionality and the sensory/tactile elements. Very often, however, my students begin with a contemporary object, or one to which they have ready access: a contemporary wedding cake led to a study of marriage rituals from the Renaissance to the present and a perfume bottle initiated a study of gender and scent. Whatever the source of the material evidence, the task is to devise a method with which to analyse it.

It is useful to try to set aside the literature on which historians are so reliant and to extract as much information as possible from the chosen thing(s). For those who have already learned a lot about a subject, however, it can be problematic to disengage from the textual evidence and allow the object to suggest new ways to think about it, whilst something familiar can be difficult to regard from a fresh perspective. Nevertheless, these are the two distinct ways in which historians do object-centred research: one's interest is so piqued by an item – a museum artefact, a family heirloom, a personal collection or just a quirky object – that it becomes the basis of a research project; or one seeks out things related to one's scholarly interest, in my case, eighteenth- and nineteenth-century textiles.

Consider, for example, the simple white textiles in Figures 11.1 and 11.2. As a textile curator at the Royal Ontario Museum, my attention was drawn to this pair of bed coverings that seemed remarkably similar except that the accompanying information suggested that one (on the left) was made in England in the first half of the nineteenth century, while the other one (on the right) was made in Quebec about the same time.[8] What could these two artefacts, now out of their historical context, tell us? Convinced there was an important story to be told through these items, they became the catalyst for a major research project that has turned up similar examples in the United States and England and led me to reflect on their production, dissemination and use in the nineteenth-century Atlantic world; in addition I am interested in investigating why they have been collected and preserved by so many museums.[9]

Figures 11.1 and 11.2 A pair of bed coverings: on the left, English early nineteenth century; on the right, Quebec, early nineteenth century. With permission of the Royal Ontario Museum.

To go beyond speculation, it is critical to develop an analytical system for the purposes of extracting as much data as possible and presenting them in a way that others can evaluate. Sarah Amato suggests to her students that before anything else they should

> use the object (*or imaginatively go through the process of using it* [useful if the object is not physically accessible]) to consider its function and context of use – where was it used? when was it used? how was it used? how does it feel to use it? what conditions were necessary for (contribute to and condition) its use?

She then asks them to consider 'what surprising fact(s) did I learn through contact with the object . . . and how do these surprises enhance my understanding of the project I'm working on?' A more formal way of accomplishing this is to design and apply some kind of model, one of the best known and useful of which continues to be Jules Prown's, 'Mind in matter: an introduction to material culture theory and method' (1982).[10] Prown, an art historian by training, advocates a three-stage approach that begins with a deep description of the object, taking care to be as objective as possible. Description leads to deduction based on sensory and intellectual engagement and here an emotional response is permitted. The final stage is speculation, a process that points the way to a hypothesis and research plan. What is particularly important about Prown's model is that one step leads to another, which in turn highlights the relationship among things, emotions and texts.

While Prown provides a solid basis with which to engage and analyse objects, many scholars feel the need to devise their own models to capture the full potential of different types of material evidence. For example, ethnographer Jean Claude Dupont borrowed concepts from folklore and linguistics to explore the ritual and magic surrounding a simple French-Canadian poker.[11] Textile and gender historian Beverly Gordon investigated how a proxemic analysis that defines perception based on zones of contact – intimate, personal, social and public – could illuminate women's relationship to things such as quilts.[12] Interested in researching Victorian churches, historian Gregg Finley used Prown as a starting-point but spelled out more systematically the importance of integrating verbal and non-verbal sources.[13] Scientist David Kingery demonstrated how materials science can help to date an artefact and ascertain its provenance and internal structure, while Robert Friedel highlighted the practical, economic, social and aesthetic considerations that determine the materials that constitute an object.[14] Steven Lubar, a historian of technology, developed a tripartite means to explore the relationship of machines to society, culture and politics.[15] A semiotic analysis allowed social scientists Betsy Cullum-Swan and Peter K. Manning to interrogate everyday contemporary objects such as T-shirts.[16] And anthropologist Grant McCracken came up with a theory to evaluate the cultural meaning of consumer goods.[17] Whether or not one draws on an existing model or creates a specialised one, the important point is to articulate it clearly and apply it rigorously. Prown recently elaborated on the importance of such a sequential analysis, arguing that

> [t]he requirement of following a particular analytical sequence should not be construed as arbitrarily rigid – it is rigid but not arbitrary. I would argue that the *process* of investigation – the sequence – is critical for the accuracy of material culture analysis, for making it hew as closely to the culture as possible, even if the explication is of culture's fictions. Each step, each observation, each idea, affects what follows. Premature speculation colors thought, premature conclusions foreclose it. By pursuing different investigative sequences, a scholar may well arrive at other conclusions. The particular sequence of steps I prescribe prolongs the information gathering process and defers the judgmental process as much as possible.[18]

Whatever the desired outcome, it is useful to begin with a close description of the object.

There are many levels on which one can analyse an artefact: the micro, which includes a detailed material(s) analysis and the macro which helps recover its context and cultural meaning. One of the most useful preliminary exercises (if at all possible), however, is to engage with the physicality of the object by touching, handling, smelling and listening to it.[19] In the case of the coverlets, they are very heavy with a design created by raised loops of thread on the surface, giving them a bumpy texture. If it is not feasible to physically handle the object, however, it is possible to gain some insight from images: a close-up suggests texture, materials and structure, if not weight (Figure 11.3). If these textiles are for beds, what would

Figure 11.3
Bed covering:
close-up image
suggestive of
texture, materials
and structure, but
not weight.
Image with
permission of the
Royal Ontario
Museum.

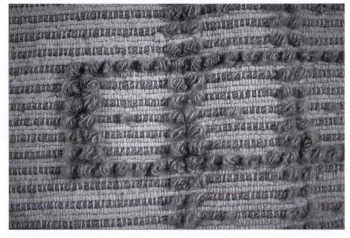

it be like to sleep under such heavy, rough things? Or were they meant to be only decorative? Lift them and feel their weight. The heaviness of both these artefacts causes one to consider the act of making the bed with them or laundering them – difficult onerous work. Turn them over (an image of the back would be useful if you are not dealing with the actual item). Only one side of these textiles is patterned, the other is plain, so there is clearly a front and back or top and bottom. Look at or imagine them with different levels of light. How would they appear in the low glow of a bedroom at night or bright morning daylight? View them on varying planes. Bed coverings were used and seen in a horizontal position on a bed, but today many museums display them vertically on the wall. Does that affect the original design decisions or how we perceive the pattern now? These actions may seem obvious, but they help us to 'touch' the past, to think about original context, to consider changing environments, and to question how they were made and how they were used. The next step would be to describe them in more detail and for this a comparative table can be helpful (Figure 11.4). Again, in the absence of the actual object, such a table is still useful to describe what can be discerned from a representation.

These textiles are part of a larger museum collection, so there is information relating to their provenance, though this too must be evaluated.[20] If the researcher has no direct knowledge of the object, it is important to uncover its collecting and documentation history in order to assess the accuracy of the information related to it: museums usually retain these data in some kind of registration file; collectors or owners may have supplementary data. These particular coverlets were acquired by the Royal Ontario Museum in the 1970s and described and analysed by curators Harold Burnham and Dorothy Burnham, who had been collecting and identifying textiles for several decades. As a result, one can be reasonably confident of the authority of their catalogue descriptions that include the approximate dates of manufacture and origin of each.

Several observations are immediately apparent: the two coverlets look very similar and the design elements, while not identical, resonate strongly with each

Artefact Bed coverings in the collection of the Royal Ontario Museum, Toronto	 970.284	 970.90.6
Provenance	Bolton, Lancashire, England 1825–50	Kamouraska, Quebec, Canada 1863; made by Alida Thiboutat, who won first prize for it at the first Quebec Provincial Exhibition
Raw materials	Cotton	Linen that was grown, processed and spun by the weaver
Dimensions (width)	203cm (single width – no seam)	195cm (2 widths of 97.5cm seamed in centre)
Dimensions (length)	243cm	252cm
Weave structure	Tabby weave with pattern made with loops of weft Burnham, *Comfortable Arts* p. 68	Tabby weave with pattern made with loops of weft Burnham, *Comfortable Arts* p. 68
Design elements	• Large eight-pointed star with a framed flower head in the centre • Each of the eight angles of the star contains a stylised flowering tree • Square, fretted border surrounds the large star • Inner border of flowers and stylised crossed pine trees • Outer border of chain links with stylised flowers at regular intervals • Small eight-pointed star inside corners of outer border • Lower left corner are the initials OFXII	• Large eight-pointed start with a smaller star in the centre • Four of the eight angles of the star contain a stylised flowering tree and four contain two flower heads and two diamonds • Square border of flower heads surrounds the large star • Inner border of meandering bands and flower heads • Outer side borders of stylised flowers alternating with small eight-pointed stars at regular intervals connected by rings; end borders connected by lines • Small triangles inside corners of outer border • No initials

Figure 11.4 A descriptive table of the coverings in Figures 11.1 and 1.2.

other; the weave structure is also similar. But the dimensions and materials analysis indicate that the British piece is made of cotton on a wide loom; the French-Canadian one is woven with homespun linen on a narrow loom that necessitated a seam. The British coverlet has initials that suggest some kind of identifying feature – a weaver's name, an owner, or perhaps a fact about the object itself – absent in the French-Canadian example. While space does not permit a full exploration of everything yielded by this comparison, even a partial consideration of one or two components reveals some of the possibilities of this type of analysis for historians. What can be learned from the materials of which these bed coverings are made?

Robert Friedel suggests numerous reasons for selecting the raw material from which something is made, first and foremost being that it must be *functional*.[21] The cotton and linen used in the coverlets makes them drape well so they will fit a bed. But these fibres are not as warm as wool, or as light and lustrous as silk. Both the cotton and linen are undyed but bleached, making washing easier as there are no colours to fade, nor are they as likely to shrink as wool. Next, says Friedel, the raw material must be *available and affordable*. Cotton is not indigenous to either England or Quebec: its cultivation requires a warm climate. Therefore this raw material was imported to England but not used in the Quebec piece, suggesting that either linen or cotton might be equally suited for use in items such as these bed coverings, but if so, what would be the advantage of one over the other? Linen grew in both countries, but was labour-intensive to produce. Does that mean it was more cost-effective for the Quebec weaver to expend the effort to process linen and perhaps that imported cotton was more affordable to the British manufacturers than locally grown linen? Or maybe it was not about cost, but fit better into a tradition of using linen for coverlets in French Canada or a fashion for cotton goods in Britain. Function, availability and tradition are not the only factors to take into account, and it is also important to consider geography, technology, science, fashion, or socio-economic competition. Cotton was grown in India, Egypt and America, all a substantial distance from England, so how could it be affordable? Is it a very special luxury good imported at great expense, or was it relatively inexpensive to ship raw materials over such long distances?[22] What about technology? Why is one textile woven without a seam, which requires a very wide loom, while the other – seamed – on a narrower device? We must account for science, with the realisation that both the cotton and the linen have been bleached – in their natural state they are much greyer. What is the chemical process involved and why was it important to have a white textile? This leads to a consideration of fashion. Why would the coverlets look so similar given their different ethnic and geographic origins? It is clear from this simple descriptive analysis how many potential avenues of research open up. But is it possible to go further and develop a research strategy that might build on this to help uncover more of the cultural meaning of these artefacts?

One way to accomplish this would use Beverly Gordon's adaptation of anthropologist Edward T. Hall's concept of proxemics to examine the four distance zones in which Westerners operate.[23] These begin with the *intimate zone* (6–18 inches) where visual and tactile senses are heightened, as are emotions. Thinking about the coverlets in these terms leads to a consideration of the bed and its functions (sleep, sex, procreation, death, illness, rest); the body lies under or on it, or lifts it to cover or uncover the bed. The person who made the counterpane also interacts with it at the intimate level as he or she must handle each thread as the textile is being created. Is the work pleasurable, onerous, creative or boring? Next is the *personal zone* (1.5–4 feet), which is still tactile and personal, though physical contact is limited, and the visual qualities are most important. Who would have access to the personal space in which beds are usually situated? Why are the design and texture important? Perhaps a family member or close friend coming into the bedroom would see the counterpane and admire it on the bed. What does this particular item communicate to the viewer or owner about status, class, ethnicity or gender? The *social zone* (4–12 feet), where visual detail and intimacy are lost, becomes the zone of impersonal business or casual gatherings. Is the bed placed in such a way as to be gazed at impersonally? What does this say about notions of privacy? Or is the coverlet to be admired by neighbours as it is hung outside to dry after being washed? Here we also begin to think about these objects in a commercial context. How are such things acquired? Are they costly? And finally the *public zone* (12 feet to 'end of visual range') 'where communication becomes more formal, detail is lost, and one is outside the "circle of involvement"'.[24] This causes us to reflect on the movement of material goods. How did the British-made piece get to Canada where it was used? Why was it treasured and given to a museum? And how does the public react to it when it is put on display there? These are just some of the questions that arise when a different layer of investigation is added to the description; one might also use a semiotic or art historical analysis of the designs, for example. Any of the questions and observations suggested above, alone or combined, could lead to a major research project.

It is clear from the preceding examples that working from the object outward can generate many exciting lines of inquiry, but what if we turned the situation around and began with a research question based on documentary research? Without a curatorial background or easy access to historical artefacts, this is how most historians are likely to approach material culture. How would objects like these coverlets even come to the attention of students of history? Drawing again on my own experience, the documentary sources most useful for exploring textile history and the expansion of late eighteenth- and early nineteenth-century consumer culture in the Atlantic world are household inventories that record the belongings of a deceased, newspaper advertisements that might list imported dry goods recently arrived in port, shipping and merchants' records that keep track of imports and exports, artisans' account books that show what they made and for whom, or storekeepers' ledgers that document what people actually purchased. Sources such as these reveal the importance of textiles at the time and further demonstrate that bedding (mattress covers, sheets, blankets, coverlets and counterpanes) made up a large percentage of cloth goods.[25] With textual sources that bring to light the importance of fabric as a consumer commodity during this period, I could easily base my subsequent analysis solely on the information contained in these documents by doing things such as categorising the goods, then quantifying the results and looking for more descriptive information that might be contained in diaries and letters.[26] But this type of evidence discusses and describes actual *things* that people made, bought and used. We have seen that even without a lot of documentary research, objects can reveal and suggest a lot, so it stands to reason that if it were possible to see some of the surviving material it would enhance the understanding of our reading. So the question becomes: how would a history student go about finding related objects?

Museum collections are the obvious starting point for locating artefacts, so it is important to recognise that these institutions have a variety of purposes that determine the nature of their collections. Most historical objects are exceptional, based solely on the fact that they survive. But so are documents. It is imperative, therefore, for researchers to interrogate the representativeness of the artefacts they use just as they would with texts and a growing museological literature can help. Susan Pearce's books *Museum Studies in Material Culture* (1989) and *Museums, Objects and Collections* (1992) are excellent sources with which to begin to think about why, how and what museums collect.[27] A large museum such as the Victoria and Albert in London, for example, is interested in the decorative arts and tends to collect the finest examples of objects categorised by media (textiles, metals, glass, etc.). As a result, it has a specialised textile collection that covers the world, but given its mandate it is unlikely to have a wide variety of mundane objects such as plain blankets or sheets. On the other side of the Atlantic, another major museum, the Smithsonian Institution, also has an extensive textile collection but because it is housed at the National Museum of American History, it has been collected differently; everything will be related to American history in some way and is likely to be more representative of items made and used everyday. Smaller local museums and historical societies everywhere tend to hold material related to their own regions, but the collections may not be as large or specialised as in the major museums. These days with internet access it is far easier to determine where one might find objects of relevance, including private and corporate collections. Online images, too, are increasingly available and, as mentioned, there is a lot that can be done with images alone. But at a certain point it may become clear that it is crucial to encounter the real thing and to this end polite letters of introduction and persistence very often will gain entrée to a relevant collection for the serious scholar.

Once the researcher locates objects of interest (or images of them), the systematic analysis outlined above begins. Here it could be useful to collaborate with an expert, a curator or collector for example, who can assist in opening up the details of the things (often called *connoisseurship*) that might be inaccessible to a neophyte.[28] My area of historical expertise is colonial British America, in particular Pennsylvania, and not French Canada or Quebec. As I pursued my interest in the counterpanes discussed earlier, I began to collaborate with Quebec historian David-Thiery Ruddel.[29] Together we combined my curatorial connoisseurship skills and his knowledge of French-Canadian history to explore how these textiles fit into the Quebec context. Historians tend to work alone, but as we demonstrate in the article we wrote together, 'Artifacts and documents in the history of Quebec textiles',

Ruddel and I were able to gain much more insight through collaboration than would have been possible for either of us on our own.[30]

If, however, such collaboration is not feasible, what my students find is that while they may not know a lot about the material evidence at the outset, their knowledge expands cumulatively as they work with it. The best way to begin is with a simple visual comparison either with the overall artefact or with an interesting component of it. It does not take a great deal of expertise to recognise the differences in the central medallion of the four coverlets in Figure 11.5: all have an eight-pointed star and a border, but two are all white and two are coloured; one is very regular, the two coloured pieces are less so; the one on the bottom left looks like the product of skill, the other three do not. A simple mention of a coverlet or counterpane in a household or merchant's inventory could not convey this information. Moreover, even such basic observations lead to historical

Figure 11.5 Visual comparison among four similar but not identical bed coverings. Images with permission of the Royal Ontario Museum.

understanding not possible with words alone. If it proves necessary or desirable to move beyond this level and acquire the skills to delve deeper into materials and weave structure, then one must seek out the available expertise to assist in the same way one might learn a computer programme to help analyse data, for example. Whether working collaboratively or on an individual basis, it is clear that a systematic analysis of objects at any level of intensity can yield many interesting observations and questions, but can they answer them?[31]

Historical objects are usually far removed from their original context. A single item can be especially intractable in providing information, making it useful to seek out as large a database of material evidence as possible. One counterpane, however interesting or attractive it might be on its own, is only able to generate limited information. The presence of two of them made comparison possible and four were even better. Over the years, I discovered many more of these bed coverings in collections in Canada, the United States and England, such that I now consider the entire North Atlantic world. While I have learned a great deal from the objects themselves, it has only been by combining that knowledge with my historian's ability to locate and interpret the relevant documentary evidence that I am able to probe more deeply into the issues they raised. Beyond the collaborative Quebec component, my research has turned up city directories, newspaper accounts, and guild records that shed light on the counterpane weaving industry in Bolton, Lancashire. In addition, nineteenth-century English port records demonstrate that these bed coverings were shipped in huge quantities to North America and over time to many other parts of the world. In North America local records indicate that women learned to weave them, sometimes from immigrants from Lancashire. I am presently in the process of trying to find out why these simple, domestic items resonated so strongly for so many people that they learned how to make imitations of them and valued and treasured them so much that they preserved them for many years before donating them to museums. The point is that whether objects are the catalyst for research or simply a component of it, there must be a symbiotic relationship between traditional textual evidence and its material counterpart as each informs and improves the interpretation of the other. Keeping the process of object-centred research in mind, it is useful to reflect on how the study of material culture has evolved and played out over the past half century, especially from a historian's perspective.

For so long an academic orphan, material culture seems to be turning into a star pupil. While it may now seem obvious that objects are an important resource for understanding the past, one of the reasons historians neglected them is because, as demonstrated above, they are not easy to access or decode. Moreover, written records provide a wealth of historical data with the result that unlike archaeologists or anthropologists, historians have not acquired comparable skills with which to analyse material evidence. Beginning in the 1960s, however, with the development of social history, and its focus on the mundane and non-literate, scholars began to look for new sources with which to learn about people who were not part of the traditional written record, in the process generating innovative practices with which to do history from below. Micro-histories, demographic studies and quantitative analysis borrowed from social scientists occupied the energies of this generation of historians who sought a better understanding of issues of gender, race, ethnicity and class. One would think that the things people made and used would stand at the top of the list in this endeavour. Surprisingly, in North America at least, this was not the case until quite recently, a fact that has been wondered at by those scholars who work closely with material evidence and understand its unique power to create a more nuanced and holistic interpretation of the past.

For the first half of the twentieth century in the United States, the study of artefacts was largely relegated to folklorists, early anthropologists, connoisseurs and antiquarians; when everyday objects started to enter the realm of historical research the practice was derogatorily nicknamed 'Pots and Pans History'.[32] By the mid-1970s, however, there was increasing scholarly interest among social historians, decorative arts specialists and a new generation of folklorists, in what they began to call 'material culture', a term borrowed from late nineteenth-century anthropologists. The expanding academic awareness of the inherent cultural power of objects initiated a series of conferences and publications that sought to articulate their value for historical research and to establish fruitful interdisciplinary connections among a diverse group of practitioners. One such conference, held in 1975 at a major node of material culture studies in North America, Winterthur Museum in Delaware,[33] represented a watershed of sorts. In his preface to those conference proceedings, *Material Culture and the Study of American Life*, editor Ian Quimby summed up the past:

> The collection, preservation, and interpretation of our material heritage has generally been accomplished by a variety of amateurs and specialists rather than by professional historians. The latter group has traditionally ignored material culture in favor of documentary research. The study of American history proceeded largely without reference to the three-dimensional remains of the American past, while the preservation, restoration, and interpretation of artefacts too often proceeded on the basis of outmoded historical theories or for non-historical reasons.

The future would look different if the papers presented in Quimby's volume by 'eleven noted experts' and collected by Quimby in *Material Culture* were any indication. Indeed, the meeting concluded with sanguinity about the prospect of an interdisciplinary approach to material evidence that would enable scholars to 'achieve a far richer, broader picture of the American past'.[34] Even social historian Cary Carson, a noted cynic about the ability of mainstream scholarship to appreciate and value objects as 'sources of ideas' as opposed to mere illustrations or as 'props' for teaching, expressed confidently that '[a]rtifacts are no longer just evidence; they are part of what the New History is all about'.[35] Where better to begin the process, James Kavanaugh argued, than in university-based programmes in American Studies?[36]

North of the border, however, many felt that rather than the university, museums with their artefact collections and interdisciplinary focus were the natural leaders in material culture research, a fact made abundantly clear at another conference, *Canada's Material History: A Forum*, sponsored by the National Museum of Man in Ottawa in 1979.[37] The Canadian meeting brought together North American and European scholars representing a variety of disciplines to probe how better to integrate object study into Canadian historical research. Interestingly, the goal of both Canadians and Americans at this time was to investigate how material evidence, much of it stored in museums, could be used to explore one's national history. Barbara Riley, editor of the Canadian conference proceedings, echoed the observations of her American counterpart, Ian Quimby, when she discussed the problems facing the practice of 'material history'.[38] According to Riley, 'the material evidence of Canada's historical past has remained largely the domain of antiquarians, genealogists, connoisseurs, and collectors; only rarely did their interests coincide with those of historians. As a result, many of the museum collections and publications reflected that divide, presenting 'historical artifacts for the most part as either antiquarian objects or "collectibles"'. But things were beginning to change, and the goal of that conference was to explore 'the place of material history within the larger context of the discipline of history',[39] because one thing was very clear – that of all disciplines, history was the least interested in the material past.[40] By the late 1970s, however, both Canadians and Americans believed that the dialogue required to modify the situation had begun.

While the North Americans were grappling with how to integrate objects into mainstream historical research, Europeans were doing it differently. According to Joseph Goy, in France at this time there were three branches of history concerned with material evidence whose practitioners were borrowing the tools of historical anthropologists and ethnographers to investigate aspects of everyday life: medieval archaeology, the history of technology and economic history.[41] In Britain, as in Canada, most object-based research activities were driven by museum scholars or those interested in folk-life or rural studies, or vernacular architecture. [42] It would be almost a decade before the term 'material culture' gained significance for British scholars, after which it picked up surprising momentum, led not by historians but by archaeologists and anthropologists.

By the end of the 1970s what was clear to a small but slowly expanding group of historians was that objects were an important source of evidence that could, in new ways, open up the understanding of everyday life. In order to realise that potential, however, the study of material culture had to move out of the realm of antiquarianism and into the scholarly lexicon. In 1982, shortly after the Canadian and American conferences, Thomas Schlereth edited an important anthology, *Material Culture Studies in America*, which went a long way to accomplishing this by summarising the work in American material culture to date and setting an agenda for the future. Indeed, this publication still provides a useful starting-point for history students who are grappling with the value of using objects and provides a worthwhile introduction to some of the basic methodologies with which to interpret them. After surveying the practice of material culture in America from 1876 until 1976, Schlereth draws together and introduces a variety of articles under the headings of Theory, Method, and Practice, and concludes with a bibliographic essay. Although material culture studies have evolved a lot over the ensuing decades, it is useful to review the early debates swirling around the merit of using objects in historical research; to be introduced to several of the first models devised to extract systematically information from such things as handmade furniture, landscapes and contemporary, mass-produced items such as the coke bottle; and to see it all in action in essays that examine, for example, eighteenth-century gravestones, Victorian hall furnishings, kitchen gadgets, McDonald's arches and garbage. But despite the budding optimism of the early material culture conferences and the usefulness of Schlereth's anthology, it seemed that mainstream historians continued to ignore this valuable source of evidence. As a result, the 1980s and early 1990s witnessed a series of North American conferences that brought together material culture practitioners to showcase their applied research, to evaluate how far material culture studies had come and where it was going.

A transitional moment in the evolution of North American material culture scholarship was the 1991 publication of *Living in a Material World: Canadian and American Approaches to Material Culture*. Deriving from a 1986 conference, it showcases the work of Canadian and American scholars and despite the fact that the editor and conference organiser, Gerald Pocius, felt that the 'study of objects continues to be hampered by a focus on disciplinary concerns', the book is organised along disciplinary lines – ethnography, history and art.[43] Taken together, however, several trends useful for historians emerge here, the first of which is methodological. Reading through the essays on pokers, barns, textiles, portraits, teapots, folk art and furniture, it becomes clear that one could combine components of the diverse approaches apparent in each to reach a deeper understanding of the material past through such things as fieldwork, oral interviews, or formal and aesthetic analyses, variously combined with the historian's documentary evidence. Perhaps most important, though, at the core of each is a sustained description of the object, the value of which is clear from the first part of this chapter.[44] What also emerges from this publication is a shift in the nature of the questions scholars were asking of objects. The folklorists, decorative arts scholars and historians who were at the forefront of material culture studies in the 1960s and 1970s, were mostly concerned with the producers and production of handmade objects, but here we begin to see a shift into the industrial period with a growing interest in the user or consumer. In addition, material culture scholars were beginning to transfer their attention from individual objects to collections of them or from artefacts, which according to Henry Glassie are 'what the artisan makes with art', to goods which 'are artifacts used as commodities'. His elaboration on this important shift helps to explain why material culture was beginning to become more attractive to historians: '[t]he student of artifacts studies them as creations, as the blending of nature and will, and slights their use and the economic systems of which they are a part. The student of goods studies them as aspects of commerce, slighting their creators', and he adds warningly, 'avoiding the dreadful moral issues raised in the contemplation of systems of production'.[45] Systems of production are of major interest to historians and collections of objects are in many ways more informative than a single item. Anthropologist Jeanne Cannizzo pointed to a more nuanced understanding of collections by introducing a fundamentally critical concept: that museums, which house so many of the objects and collections available to students of history, are 'negotiated realities'. Not only can they be considered artefacts in their own right, but their collections are also 'the product of certain periods in history, and of certain mentalities, associated with particular kinds of worldviews, social structures, and economies'.[46] Scholars who use these collections, therefore, must be aware of their biases.

These trends were more fully realised at a 1993 Winterthur conference, 'American Material Culture: The Shape of the Field', along with new developments. The published proceedings contained an excellent introductory essay by the editors/conference organisers, Ann Smart Martin and J. Ritchie Garrison, and provides a succinct but comprehensive overview of the multidisciplinary nature of material culture, summarising the development of the three distinct American intellectual traditions that 'created a definable, if varied, field at the heart of material culture analysis by the late 1970s' – anthropological, historical and art historical.[47] We see these traditions in Pocius's book, but Martin and Garrison also draw our attention to a different approach to material culture emerging in the work of British archaeologists and anthropologists. North Americans were focused intently on objects, influenced heavily by decorative arts scholars such as E. McClung Fleming, Jules Prown and Kenneth Ames.[48] They 'researched and recorded the basic time lines of stylistic and technological change, and they forced material culture scholars to consider objects as primary forms of evidence'.[49] On the other hand, British scholars, led by archaeologists and anthropologists such as Ian Hodder and Christopher Tilley, were interested in exploring theoretical frameworks such as structuralism, hermeneutics and post-structuralism that would help them integrate the physical and intellectual and the past and present.[50]

Although the papers presented in the Martin and Garrison volume continued to be object-oriented – axes, dolls, portrait miniatures, Tupperware, hunting shirts and verandahs – they were increasingly theoretical and sought to uncover more complex realities about objects and explore how people assign them meaning, and that meaning changes over time and place, making cultural context highly relevant. In addition, consumer culture was evolving into a major concern and gender, ethnicity and race were becoming more pronounced in material culture scholarship. Finally, there was further consideration of museums, but now as sites of interpretation of material culture rather than as repositories of it.

By the mid-1990s, there were other emerging strands of scholarship that were concerned with material culture as the focus shifted increasingly from objects and their makers to the users and consumers. The influences came from cultural anthropologists and sociologists such as Grant McCracken, Mary Douglas and Baron Isherwood, Mihály Csikszentmihályi and E. Rochberg-Halton, and Daniel Miller, for example, who were interested in understanding consumer culture and examining the meaning of goods or commodities in everyday life.[51] These works influenced museum-based social historians such as Katherine Grier, who combined the object-centred approach of the American tradition with tools of the historian and the cultural anthropologist in her important book, *Culture and Comfort:*

People, Parlors and Upholstery, 1850–1930. Researching Victorian parlour furniture, Grier brought together production and consumption by examining the minute details of furniture upholstery and construction, then placing it in the larger context of the parlour, the home and Victorian society. She argues that through their household furnishings Victorian Americans participated in the construction of a middle-class identity and an expanding world of consumer goods. In the process she demonstrates that a detailed knowledge of these mass-produced goods and how they were made and consumed leads to a better understanding of the economic history of the time, shedding light on the growing industrial and commercial culture with its rapidly expanding networks of distribution, marketing, consumer credit and retailing.[52] Grier's research also resulted in a conference and a major museum exhibition, full of the objects that propelled her study.[53] This was material culture in action, highlighting the value of museum collections for historians.

Other scholars were generating a body of literature to help interpret these collections in a post-modern world. Based in the Museum Studies programme at the University of Leicester, museologists such as Susan Pearce, Eilean Hooper-Greenhill and Gaynor Kavanagh explored how to decode and extract meaning from artefacts, collections and museums themselves.[54] North American anthropologists, among them George Stocking, Ivan Karp and Steven Lavine in the United States and Michael Ames, Jennifer Brown, Elizabeth Vibert, Ruth Phillips and Trudy Nicks in Canada, wrote about the politics of researching, interpreting and exhibiting collections of the material culture of indigenous peoples.[55] As scholars like these, many of them museum based, began to deconstruct collections held by cultural institutions, others realised the importance of coming to terms with collecting in general. Why and what do people collect? How do collections change over time? How useful are amalgamations of objects that have been taken out of context? What is the impact of memory on collecting? Indeed, the history of collecting has become an important strand of historical research, investigating such issues as the origin of Western collecting, the psychology behind it, gender bias and memory.[56] This body of literature is essential reading for history students aspiring to include collected objects in their research.[57]

In the twenty-first century the study of material culture has become so extensive that it is no longer the 'scholarship nobody knows'.[58] Led by British anthropologists, design historians and students of consumer culture, research has focused on non-Western material culture, and the theoretical constructs underpinning our understanding of commodities, beginning with Arjun Appadurai's *The Social Life of Things*, while Christopher Tilley's *Reading Material Culture* brought out the importance of anthropological theory in understanding material culture.[59] Combined interdisciplinarity and theoretical approaches (Marxist, semiotic, psychological) can be seen in Arthur Asa Berger's *Reading Matter*, updated by Victor Buchli in 2002 as *The Material Culture Reader*.[60] Judy Attfield adds an important design perspective in *Wild Things*.[61] Most recently, the trend is towards 'materiality', that is, according to Daniel Miller, more than just a study of artefacts and includes 'the ephemeral, the imaginary, the biological, and the theoretical; all fat which would have been external to the simple definition of an artefact'.[62]

A useful tool with which to navigate this burgeoning literature is the recent text book edited by Christopher Tilley *et al.*, *Handbook of Material Culture*, although it is interesting to note that with one exception, no historians contributed.[63] Tilley's definition of material culture echoes and refines that of Schlereth, articulated more than a quarter of a century ago:

> Material culture studies . . . inevitably have to emphasize the dialectical and recursive relationship between persons and things: that persons make and use things and that the things make persons . . . Material culture is part of human culture in general, and just as the concept of culture in general has hundreds of potential definitions and manifestations and is never just one entity or 'thing' so has the material component of culture.[64]

The historian's need to master a vast historiography and command of the strengths and weaknesses of a gamut of historical texts can make adding objects to that expertise daunting. So how can we recognise and utilise the valuable source of material evidence? We need to return to the object-centred analyses of the early practitioners, work outwards from the object, or from text to object and back to text, as demonstrated at the beginning of this chapter. As Leora Auslander observes, 'expanding the range of our canonical sources will provide better answers to familiar historical questions as well as change the very nature of the questions we are able to pose and the kind of knowledge we are able to acquire about the past'. She continues:

> [t]he use of material culture for the writing of history entails . . . the use of both theoretical or conceptual work that addresses the relation between people and things in the abstract, and that which focuses on those relations under particular forms of economy and polity. It also requires careful reflection on the relation of texts and things, how people have represented their object worlds in writing or used textual invocations of objects.[65]

Moving outward from the objects, or including objects as an integral extension of our textual research, we can draw on whatever interpretative theoretical constructs or documents we need. If objects are our driving force and the questions asked of them interdisciplinary, our research will be nuanced, complex and historically valid.

Notes

1 Thomas J. Schlereth, *Material Culture Studies in America*, Nashville, TN: Rowman Altamira, 1982, p. 3.

2 My graduate History course at the University of Toronto, 'Topics in Material Culture', attracts students from Art History, English, Museum Studies, Geography, History and Philosophy of Science and Technology, Information Studies, etc. Regardless of how far advanced their research is, I ask them to step away from what they already know, select a related object and begin their questioning process again by developing the skills with which to interrogate that object.

3   Email from Sarah Amato to the author, 12 April 2008. Amato was grading papers from a course she taught as an introduction to material culture when she made the observation.

4   Thomas J. Schlereth, 'Material culture or material life: discipline or field? Theory or method?', in Gerald L. Pocius (ed.), *Living in a Material World: Canadian and American Approaches to Material Culture*, St John's, Newfoundland: Institute of Social and Economic Research, 1991, p. 236; Schlereth, *Artefacts and the American Past*, Nashville, TN, 1980; Schlereth, *Material Culture, A Research Guide*, Lawrence, KS: University Press of Kansas, 1985.

5   Victor Buchli (ed.), *The Material Culture Reader*, Oxford: Berg, 2002, p. 13.

6   My thanks to Sarah Amato, a former graduate student, whose recent experiences teaching material culture to undergraduates allowed us to engage in a helpful discussion including this phrase.

7   In 1996/7 Bruce Retallack began with a collection of razors that led him to think first about how they were made, then about how they were marketed, and ultimately to consider how they participated in the construction of modern masculinity: G. Bruce Retallack, 'Razors, shaving and gender construction: an inquiry into the material culture of shaving', *Material History Review* 49, 1999, pp. 4–19. In my 2000/1 class, Heather George chose a toilet as her object and after first considering plumbing, she observed that toilets are rarely shown in bathroom advertisements, which resulted in a project that used a semiotic analysis of these advertisements to consider the twentieth-century evolution of bathrooms from a site of hygiene and cleanliness to one of relaxation, luxury and leisure. A silver hairbrush led Ariel Beaujot to a study of vanity sets in my 2002/3 class that culminated in her recently completed doctorate, 'The Material Culture of Women's Accessories: Middle-Class Performance, Race Formation and Feminine Display, 1830–1920', University of Toronto, 2008.

8   Textile scholar Harold Burnham noted this similarity: Harold B. Burnham, 'Bolton "quilts" or "caddows": a nineteenth century cottage industry', *CIETA Bulletin* 34, 1971, pp. 22–9.

9   Adrienne D. Hood and David-Thiery Ruddel, 'Artifacts and documents in the history of Quebec textiles', in Pocius, *Living in a Material World*. We also have an article in progress, 'Comfort, culture and identity: making beds in the Atlantic world'. In Canada, counterpanes such as these can be found at the Royal Ontario Museum in Toronto, McCord Museum in Montreal, and the New Brunswick and Nova Scotia Museums. Many museums in the USA have them, for example the New Hampshire Historical Society, American Textile History Museum, Winterthur Museum and Valentine Museum in Richmond, Virginia. In England I have seen them at the Bolton Museum and the Victoria and Albert Museum.

10 Jules Prown, 'Mind in matter: an introduction to material culture theory and method', *Winterthur Portfolio* 17, 1982, pp. 1–19; Prown, 'On the "art" in artifacts', in Pocius, *Living in a Material World*; Prown, 'The truth of material culture: history or fiction?', in Steven Lubar and David W. Kingery (eds), *History From Things: Essays on Material Culture*, Washington, DC: Smithsonian Institution Press, 1993; Susan M. Pearce, *Museums, Objects and Collections: A Cultural Study*, Washington DC: Smithsonian Institution Press, 1993, Appendix 'Models for object study', pp. 265–73; Elspeth H. Brown, 'Reading the visual record', in Ardis Cameron (ed.), *Looking for America: The Visual Production of Nation and People*, Malden, MA: Blackwell, 2005.

11 Jean Claude Dupont, 'The meaning of objects: the poker', in Pocius, *Living in a Material World*.

12 Beverly Gordon, 'Intimacy and objects: a proxemic analysis of gender-based response to the material world', in Katharine Martinez and Kenneth L. Ames (eds), *The Material Culture of Gender, the Gender of Material Culture*, Winterthur, DL: The Henry Francis du Pont Winterthur Museum, 1997.

13 Gregg Finley, 'The Gothic revival and the Victorian church in New Brunswick: toward a strategy for material culture research', *Material History Bulletin* 32, 1990, pp. 1–16.

14 W. David Kingery, 'Materials science and material culture', in W. David Kingery (ed.), *Learning From Things: Method and Theory of Material Culture Studies*, Washington DC and London: Smithsonian Institution Press, 1996; Robert Friedel, 'Some Matters of Substance', in Lubar and Kingery, *History From Things*.

15 Steven Lubar, 'Machine politics: the political construction of technological artifacts', in Lubar and Kingery, *History From Things*.

16 B. Cullum-Swan and Peter K. Manning, 'What is a t-shirt? Codes, chrontypes, and everyday objects', in Stephen Harold Riggins (ed., introduction), *The Socialness of Things: Essays on the Socio-Semiotics of Objects*, New York: Mouton de Gruyter, 1994.

17 Grant McCracken, 'Meaning manufacture and movement in the world of goods', in *Culture and Consumption*, Bloomington and Indianapolis: Indiana University Press, 1988.

18 Jules David Prown and Kenneth Haltman (eds), *American Artifacts: Essays in Material Culture*, East Lansing: Michigan State University Press, 2000, p. xii.

19 Museums often have strict rules about handling objects in order to preserve them, so it may not always be possible to execute this useful step.

20 Information from: catalogue records for these two artefacts (970.284 and 970.90.6), Royal Ontario Museum, Toronto, Canada; Harold B. Burnham and Dorothy K. Burnham, *Keep Me Warm One Night: Early Handweaving in Eastern Canada*, Toronto: University of Toronto Press/Royal Ontario Museum, 1972, pp. 145–9; Dorothy K. Burnham, *The Comfortable Arts: Traditional Spinning and Weaving in Canada*, Ottawa: National Gallery of Canada, National Museums of Canada, 1981, pp. 63–75; and my own observations – Hood and Ruddel, 'Artifacts and documents in the history of Quebec textiles'.

21 Friedel, 'Some matters of substance', pp. 43–5.

22 Beverly Lemire, *Fashion's Favourite: The Cotton Trade and the Consumer in Britain, 1660–1800*, Oxford: Oxford University Press, 1991; Chris Aspin, *The Cotton Industry*, Shire Album, 63, Oxford: Shire Publications, 1981; Stanley D. Chapman, *The Cotton Industry in the Industrial Revolution*, Studies in Economic History, London: Macmillan, 1972; Mary B. Rose, *The Lancashire Cotton Industry: A History Since 1700*, Preston: Lancashire County Books, 1996; Brenda Collins and Philip Ollerenshaw (eds), *The European Linen Industry in Historical Perspective*, Pasold Studies in Textile History, 13, Oxford: Oxford University Press, 2003; Sophie-Laurence Lamontagne and Fernand Harvey, *La Production textile domestique au Québec, 1827–1941: Une approche quantitative et régionale*, Ottawa: Musée national des sciences et de la technologie, 1997; Hélène de Carufel, *Le Lin, Traditions du geste et de la parole*, 4, Ottawa: Leméac, 1980; D.-T. Ruddel, 'The domestic textile industry in the region and city of Quebec, 1792–1835', *Material History Bulletin* 17, 1983, pp. 95–125; Kris Inwood and Phyllis Wagg, 'The survival of handloom weaving in rural Canada circa 1870', *The Journal of Economic History* 53.2, 1993, pp. 346–58.

23 Gordon, 'Intimacy and objects', p. 238.

24 Ibid., p. 240.

25 Susan Prendergast Schoelwer, 'Form, function, and meaning in the use of fabric furnishings: a Philadelphia case study, 1700–1775', *Winterthur Portfolio* 14, 1979, pp. 25–40.

26 Adrienne D. Hood, *The Weaver's Craft: Cloth, Commerce, and Industry in Early Pennsylvania*, Philadelphia: University of Pennsylvania Press, 2003; with little material evidence I had to rely on these types of documentary sources.

27 Susan M. Pearce (ed.), *Museum Studies in Material Culture*, Leicester: Leicester University Press, 1989; Pearce, *Museums, Objects and Collections: A Cultural Study*, Leicester: Leicester University Press, 1992.

28 Marjorie Akin, 'Passionate possession: the formation of private collections', in Kingery, *Learning From Things*; Benno Forman, 'Connoisseurship and furniture history',

in *American Seating Furniture 1630–1730, An Interpretive Catalogue*, New York: W.W. Norton, 1988; Patricia J. Keller, 'Methodology and meaning: strategies for quilt study', *The Quilt Journal* 2, 1993, pp. 1–4; Gregory Landrey, 'The Conservator as curator: combining scientific analysis and traditional connoisseurship', *American Furniture*, 1993, pp. 147–59; Edith Mayo, 'Connoisseurship of the future', in F.E.H. Schroeder (ed.), *Twentieth-Century Popular Culture in Museums and Libraries*, Bowling Green: Bowling Green University Popular Press, 1981; Mansfield Kirby Jr Talley, 'Connoisseurship and the methodology of the Rembrandt research project', *The International Journal of Museum Management and Curatorship* 8, 1989.

29   D.-T. Ruddel, 'Consumer trends, clothing, textiles and equipment in the Montreal area, 1792–1835', *Material History Bulletin* 32, 1990, pp. 45–64.

30   Hood and Ruddel, 'Artifacts and documents in the history of Quebec textiles'.

31   Barbara G. Carson and Cary Carson, 'Things unspoken: learning social history from artifacts', in James B. Gardner and George Rollie Adams (eds), *Ordinary People and Everyday Life: Perspectives on the New Social History*, Nashville, TN: American Association of State and Local History, 1983, p. 201; Adrienne D. Hood, 'Toward collaboration? Museums, universities and material culture studies in Canada', *Muse* XV, 1998, pp. 37–40; Adrienne D. Hood, 'The practice of [American] history: a Canadian curator's perspective', *Journal of American History* 81, December 1994, pp. 1011–19; Elizabeth M. Brumfiel, 'It's a material world: history, artifacts, and anthropology', *Annual Review of Anthropology* 32, 2003.

32   Elizabeth B. Wood, 'Pots and Pans History: relating manuscripts and printed sources to the study of domestic art objects', *American Archivist* 30, 1967, pp. 431–42.

33   University of Delaware, the Winterthur Program in American Studies and Center for Material Culture Studies, http://www.materialculture.udel.edu/index.htm, accessed 28 April 2008.

34   Ian Quimby (ed.), *Material Culture and the Study of American Life*, New York: W.W. Norton, 1978, p. xi.

35   Cary Carson, 'Doing history with material culture', in Quimby, *Material Culture*, pp. 43, 63.

36   James V. Kavanaugh, 'The artifact in American culture: the development of an undergraduate program in American studies', in Quimby, *Material Culture*.

37   The National Museum of Man later became the Canadian Museum of Civilization.

38   Canadian museum-based historians preferred the term 'material history' to 'material culture': Robb Watt and Barbara Riley, 'Introduction', *National Museum of Man Mercury Series: Material History Bulletin*, History Division Paper, 15, 1976, pp. 1–6, 2–3.

39   Watt and Riley, 'Introduction', *Material History Bulletin*, pp. 5, 6.

40   John J. Manion, 'Multidisciplinary dimensions in material history', *Material History Bulletin* 8, 1979, pp. 21–5, 23; and F.J. Thorpe, 'Remarks at the opening session of Canada's material history: a forum', *Material History Bulletin* 8, 1979, p. 9.

41   Joseph Goy, 'L'histoire de la culture matérielle en France: Progrès récent et recherches futures', *Material History Bulletin* 8, 1979, pp. 83–8.

42   Alexander Fenton, 'Material History in Great Britain: Present Developments and Future Trends', *Material History Bulletin* 8, 1979, pp. 77–82.

43   Pocius, *Living in a Material World*, p. xv.

44   Clifford Geertz's concept of 'thick description': Clifford Geertz, *The Interpretation of Cultures; Selected Essays*, New York: Basic Books, 1973.

45   Henry Glassie, 'Studying Material Culture Today', in Pocius, *Living in a Material World*, p. 265.

46   Jeanne Cannizzo, 'Negotiated Realities: Towards an Ethnography of Museums', in Pocius, *Living in a Material World*, p. 24.

47   Ann Smart Martin and J. Ritchie Garrison, 'Shaping the Field: The Multidisciplinary Perspectives of Material Culture', in Ann Smart Martin and J. Ritchie Garrison (eds),

American Material Culture: The Shape of the Field, Winterthur, DE: Henry Francis du Pont Winterthur Museum, 1997, p. 4.

48 E. McClung Fleming, 'Artifact study: a proposed model', *Winterthur Portfolio* 9, 1974, pp. 153–73; Kenneth L. Ames, *Death in the Dining Room and Other Tales of Victorian Culture*, Philadelphia, PA: Temple University Press, 1992.

49 Martin and Garrison, 'Shaping the field', p. 12.

50 Ian Hodder, *Reading the Past: Current Approaches to Interpretation in Archaeology*, Cambridge: Cambridge University Press, 1991; Ian Hodder (ed.), *The Meanings of Things: Material Culture and Symbolic Expression*, Boston, MA: Unwin Hyman, 1989; Christopher Tilley, 'Interpreting material culture', in Hodder, *The Meanings of Things*; Christopher Tilley (ed.), *Reading Material Culture: Structuralism, Hermeneutics, and Post-Structuralism*, Cambridge, MA: Blackwell Press, 1991.

51 Grant McCracken, *Culture and Consumption*, Bloomington and Indianapolis: Indiana University Press, 1988; McCracken, '"Homeyness": a cultural account of one constellation of consumer goods and meanings', *Interpretive Consumer Research*, 1989, pp. 168–83; Mary Douglas and Baron Isherwood, *The World of Goods – Towards an Anthropology of Consumption*, London: Allen Lane, 1979; Mary Douglas, 'The idea of a home: a kind of space', in Arien Mack (ed.), *Home: A Place in the World*, New York: New York University Press, 1993; M. Csikszentmihályi and E. Rochberg-Halton, *The Meaning of Things: Domestic Symbols and the Self*, Cambridge: Cambridge University Press, 1981; and M. Csikszentmihályi, 'Why we need things', in Lubar and Kingery, *History From Things*; Daniel Miller, *Material Culture and Mass Consumption*, Oxford: Basil Blackwell, 1987.

52 Katherine C. Grier, *Culture and Comfort: People, Parlors and Upholstery, 1850–1930*, Rochester: Strong Museum, 1988, p. 8.

53 Adrienne D. Hood, 'Exhibit review of "culture and comfort: people, parlors, and upholstery, 1850–1930"', *Journal of American History* 76, 1989, pp. 211–15.

54 Susan M. Pearce (ed.), *Museums and the Appropriation of Culture*, London: Athlone Press, 1994; Eilean Hooper-Greenhill, *Museums and the Shaping of Knowledge*, London: Routledge, 1992; Eilean Hooper-Greenhill (ed.), *Museum, Media, Message*, London: Routledge, 1995; Gaynor Kavanagh, *History Curatorship*, Leicester: Leicester University Press, 1990.

55 George W. Stocking Jr (ed.), *Objects and Others: Essays on Museums and Material Culture*, Madison: University of Wisconsin Press, 1985; Ivan Karp and Steven D. Lavine, *Exhibiting Cultures: The Poetics and Politics of Museum Display*, Washington DC and London: Smithsonian Institution Press, 1991; Michael Ames, *Cannibal Tours and Glass Boxes: The Anthropology of Museums*, Vancouver: UBC Press, 1992; Trudy Nicks, 'Dr. Oronhyatekha's history lessons: reading museum collections as texts', in Jennifer S.H. Brown and Elizabeth Vibert (eds), *Reading Beyond Words: Contexts for Native History*, Peterborough, Ontario: Broadview Press, 2003.

56 Paula Findlen, *Possessing Nature: Museums, Collecting, and Scientific Culture in Early Modern Italy*, Berkeley and Los Angeles: University of California Press, 1994; Maria Zytaruk, '"Occasional specimens, not complete systemes": John Evelyn's culture of collecting', *Bodleian Library Record* 17, 2001, pp. 185–211; Russell W. Belk and Melanie Wallendorf, 'Of mice and men: gender identity and collecting', in Katharine Martinez and Kenneth L. Ames (eds), *The Material Culture of Gender, the Gender of Material Culture*, The Henry Francis du Pont Winterthur Museum, 1997; Russell W. Belk, *Collecting in a Consumer Society*, London: Routledge, 1995; Jean Baudrillard, *The System of Objects*, London: Verso, 2005.

57 Randolph Starn, 'A historian's brief guide to new museum studies', *American Historical Review* 110, 2005, p. 68–98.

58 Cary Carson, 'Material culture history: the scholarship nobody knows', in Smart Martin and Garrison, *American Material Culture*.

59   Arjun Appadurai (ed.), *The Social Life of Things: Commodities in Cultural Perspective*, Cambridge: Cambridge University Press, 1986.
60   Arthur Asa Berger, *Reading Matter: Multidisciplinary Perspectives on Material Culture*, New Brunswick, NJ: Transaction Publishers, 1992.
61   Judy Attfield, *Wild Things: The Material Culture of Everyday Life*, Oxford: Berg, 2000.
62   Daniel Miller, *Materiality*, Durham, NC: Duke University Press, 2005, p. 4.
63   Christopher Y. Tilley *et al.* (eds), *Handbook of Material Culture*, London: Sage, 2006.
64   Tilley *et al.*, Handbook, p. 4.
65   Leora Auslander, 'Beyond words', *The American Historical Review* 110.4, 2005, pp. 1015–45.

Index

Page numebers in *italics* denotes an illustration